Reclaiming Prosperity

Reclaiming Prosperity

A Blueprint for Progressive Economic Reform

Edited by Todd Schafer & Jeff Faux

Preface by Lester Thurow

Eileen Appelbaum · Dean Baker · Peter Berg
Jared Bernstein · Jane D'Arista · Gary Dymski · Robert Eisner
James K. Galbraith · Irwin Garfinkel · Thea Lee · Jerome Levinson
Ann Markusen · Ray Marshall · Lawrence Mishel · Michael Oden
Edith Rasell · Max B. Sawicky · Todd Schafer · Tom Schlesinger
John Schmitt · Elliott Sclar · Robert E. Scott · William Spriggs
Ruy Teixeira · John Veitch · Paula Voos

M.E. Sharpe · Armonk, New York · London, England

Economic Policy Institute

Library of Congress Cataloging-in-Publication Data

Schafer, Todd.
Reclaiming prosperity : a blueprint for progressive economic reform /
Todd Schafer and Jeff Faux, editors.
p. cm.
Includes bibliographical references and index.
ISBN 1-56324-768-2 (hardcover : alk. paper).—ISBN 1-56324-769-0 (pbk. : alk. paper)
1. United States—Economic policy—1993– .
I. Title.
HC106.82.S34 1996
338.973—dc20
95-43828
CIP

Printed in the United States of America

The paper used in this publication meets the minimum requirements of
American National Standard for Information Sciences—
Permanence of Paper for Printed Library Materials,
ANSI Z 39.48-1984.

MV (c) 10 9 8 7 6 5 4 3 2 1
MV (p) 10 9 8 7 6 5 4 3 2 1

® GCIU

To the 75% of the American workforce that economists and politicians dismissively and inaccurately characterize as "unskilled."
May their efforts and talents be both appreciated and compensated.

Table of Contents

Acknowledgments

Every book is the result of an extraordinary collaboration of efforts. Author, editor, and production team must all be in sync. When a book combines the authorship of 29 people from across the country, as this volume does, the number of participants in the process explodes. The names of the myriad research assistants, administrative assistants, proofreaders, and sounding boards involved in the preparation of each chapter are known only to the authors with whom they worked. To their thanks, we add our own.

The opinions expressed are solely those of the authors. However, all were made better by helpful comments received from dozens of experts along the way. Particularly helpful were the research and communications staffs at EPI, especially Dean Baker and Nan Gibson.

Finally, the contributions of three individuals are evident in every chapter of the book. Patrick Watson, senior editor at the Economic Policy Institute, had the overwhelming task of turning 29 soloists into a choir. His magic touch is apparent throughout. His sidekick, EPI publications manager Kim Arbogast, is owed deep thanks for her competence and creativity in tackling every aspect of production. Finally, we are indebted to jack-of-all-trades Miranda Martin, who kept more than her share of the balls in the air. Without the professionalism of these three, the reader would be holding a far less readable stack of words and numbers.

— The Editors

PREFACE

by Lester Thurow

THE SUCCESS OR FAILURE OF AN ECONOMIC SYSTEM IS EASY TO MEASURE. Does the system raise the earnings of most of its participants? If this measure is applied to the American economic system, we see a clear failure in the past two decades.

In 1973 real wages started to fall for males with high school degrees or less, and this decline has spread since then to affect males at all educational levels—including those with Ph.D.'s. A decade ago real wages started to fall among America's least-educated women, and these declines have now moved up the education ladder to affect all women except those with college degrees. One can argue about the exact percentages, but something on the order of 80% of the workforce is now experiencing falling real wages. That is failure on a monumental scale.

At the same time, real per capita gross domestic product has risen by a third. All of this extra income has gone to the top 20% of the population, and most of it to the top 1%. Probably no country has ever had as large a shift in the distribution of earnings without having gone through a revolution or losing a major war.

The economic purpose of democracy is to insure the inclusion of most of its citizens in the fruits of economic progress. For 20 years the American democracy has failed to insure inclusion for a majority of its citizens.

Clearly someone needed to be punished for this disaster. The punishment came in the political revolution of the 1994 election. The mystery is not why it happened but why it didn't happen earlier. Nor is there

---

Lester Thurow is professor of management and economics at the Sloan School of Management at the Massachusetts Institute of Technology.

any mystery as to why the electorate chose to punish the Democrats. Even though the American economic system is sometimes run by Republicans, everyone understands that the system was built by the Democrats during the Great Depression, World War II, and the 1960s. If the system doesn't work, it is they who should be blamed. The Democrats deserved to be punished since they had forgotten to look out for the welfare of those who had historically been their strongest supporters—high-school-educated workers. The Democrats deserted their supporters long before their supporters deserted the Democrats.

At the same time, the Republican winners of the 1994 political revolution have nothing in their "Contract With America" or in their 1995 legislative agenda that is going to reverse the fortunes of those who are now suffering a decline in their real wages. In the short run, one may feel better kicking the welfare mother (no one likes the idea of paying for someone else's children), but however hard she is kicked, that kicking isn't going to raise the wages of high-school-educated workers.

The Republican economic agenda can be summarized in three words—"make government smaller." Whatever one thinks about the virtues of governments that spend less, cutting the size of government is not a recipe for raising wages. Most of the proposed spending cuts are not even direct cuts, just transfers of federal programs to state governments with caps on the amounts the federal government will contribute in the future. Initially this move does not make government smaller—it merely transfers functions to a different level. But the competition between states to persuade business firms to locate in their states will in the long run force expenditure cuts. These cuts will reduce the demand for goods and services and the labor necessary to produce them, and they will force some who are not now working to offer their labor services at wages lower than those now paid to current workers. Cutting the demand for labor while raising its supply is not a route to higher wages in anyone's economic scenario.

In some future election (it remains to be seen whether it is the 1996 election), the frustrated voters with falling real wages who voted Newt Gingrich into power are going to be back, even more frustrated, interested in punishing Newt, and wanting to vote for someone who has something credible to offer that might lead to a reversal in their economic fortunes. This book is an attempt to build something economically "credible to offer" when that political opportunity appears.

Credibility has to begin with policies that will run the economy with tight labor markets. Although the official unemployment rate is now between 5% and 6%, if one adds in those not officially measured as unemployed (i.e., those who are too discouraged to look often enough for work to be considered officially unemployed) and those working part time who would like to work full time, at least 15% of the American workforce is looking for more work. With this "reserve army of the unemployed," even Marx would not have had much difficulty explaining falling wages. In capitalism real wages go up only if the demand for labor exceeds the supply. Unless government is willing to commit to generating tight labor markets, nothing else (training, whatever) will work.

Conservatives will shout "inflation" if anyone proposes to adopt aggressive economic policies, but it is important to understand that the asset crashes of the 1980s and 1990s along with the development of a global economy have altered both psychological expectations and the economy's structural proclivities to generate inflation. As long as wages are falling while productivity is rising, it is not possible to have wage-induced inflation. The time to worry about that is when real wage increases are threatening to exceed productivity gains.

There is an important role for government in future economic success. It has to be the provider of the long-tailed social investments that underlie private economic success in an era of manmade brainpower industries. The Internet (financed for the first 20 years of its life by the Defense Department) and biotechnology (financed for the first 30 years of its life by the National Institutes of Health) are but two recent examples. Both are going to yield enormous private payoffs, but neither initially could have been, or would have been, financed by the private sector—the time to those payoffs was simply too long. In the rest of the industrial world where government did not finance these activities, they simply did not exist.

Twenty-first-century government should focus on infrastructure investment, investment in human skills, and investment in generating the knowledge that creates new industries. The issue is not government, big or small, but investment versus consumption. America needs to become a much higher investment society in both its public and private sectors. Neither is world class when it comes to the level of investment activities they now support.

Getting real wages to grow will take a very different governmental structure more interested in social investment than in social consumption. The Republicans are clearly not going to lead in this transition. It is an open question as to whether the Democrats will, but the pieces of the agenda that have to be implemented are here to be examined.

Reclaiming Prosperity

OVERVIEW
New Eyes on a New Century

by Jeff Faux

AS WE MOVE TOWARD THE MILLENNIUM YEAR 2000, IT IS GENERALLY acknowledged that the United States has entered a different economic era. Our marketplace has become more global and more competitive. Changes in communications technology and deregulation of domestic markets are transforming relationships among workers and managers, businesses, and public institutions. And the Cold War—which was invoked to justify public investments in education, infrastructure, and new technology—is over.

But perhaps more important, for the last 20 years we have also slipped into a different era in terms of the way we *think* about the economy. The evolving debates about taxes, jobs, trade, and financial markets have hidden a remarkable shift in the definition of the fundamental economic problem that the nation faces. A quarter century ago, full employment and rising incomes for all Americans were considered the goals of economic policy, and the measure of successful policy was how close it came to those goals. Largely because of the earlier Keynesian revolution in economics, policy makers assumed that governments had the power to enhance the performance of market economies. The late American economist Arthur Okun remarked in 1970 that recessions were "fundamentally preventable, like airplane crashes and unlike hurricanes."

Today, conventional opinion is that recessions, and most of our other major economic problems, are more like hurricanes. The debate over public policy is currently monopolized by those, on the one hand, who believe that it is solely the individual's responsibility to find safety from

---

Jeff Faux is president of the Economic Policy Institute.

economic storms wherever he or she can and those, on the other, who accept that some limited form of government assistance might be appropriate to help the weak "adjust" to the wild forces of a globalized, deregulated, technology-driven marketplace. Positive public goals such as full employment, economic security, and stable communities have no place in the narrow space between these two political poles. And for the elites who dominate the policy debate, the absence of these goals is of little concern. Thus, an economic columnist for a major "liberal" newspaper admonishes us that governments should not be held responsible for recessions. A recession, he adds, "is not usually a tragedy. It's merely a problem. For a while, there are fewer jobs and more anxiety. That's about it."

Ironically, eliminating government responsibility for economic performance has shifted much of the public policy debate to the so-called "social" issues such as crime, dependency, and teenage sex. This has led policy makers toward endless pontification concerning the state of the human heart, over which the government arguably can do little, and away from the fiscal problems of our cities, interest rates, and the distribution of income, about which the government actually can do something.

The essays contained in this book reflect a fundamentally different point of view. First, the authors are generally more optimistic about the capacity of the public sector to influence and regulate market forces in order to achieve better outcomes for society. Much economic suffering commonly attributed to immutable market forces is rather caused by the way we respond to these forces. Thus, policy makes a difference. Implicit in this view is that there are collective economic interests, for example, that nations—as well as individuals and firms—function as economic units. An extension of this idea is that institutions such as public agencies, labor unions, and nonprofit organizations are integral parts of the economic landscape.

Second, the contributors to this book tend to measure economic success primarily through the lens of those who work for a living—rather than through, for example, the changing values of financial assets. They do not assume that a rising stock market compensates for a falling real wage. In part, this reflects the basic value that meaningful work at fair compensation is essential for a healthy life for the individual and society. And that work is a necessary although not always sufficient condition for social stability. When parents don't work, families don't work. When families don't work, societies don't work. Social progress is, in part, a function of economic advance. Thus, to give one example, the gains in civil rights for African Americans in the 1960s were strongly facilitated by the extraordinary general expansion in jobs and incomes during that decade.

Third, the perspective that informs these essays tends to be skeptical of the claim that unregulated markets can be trusted to turn near-term pain for the majority—through downsizing, unstable jobs, and falling living standards—into prosperity for all in some unspecified future. Policies that shift income from those working for $5 and $10 per hour to those who live on their investments and make six figures cannot be justified by assertions about the duty of one generation to sacrifice for the next. We do have an economic obligation to the future that requires us to forgo some of today's consumption so that we can invest in tomorrow. But the question of how savings is generated and transformed into investment is open to question. Too many economic crimes have been perpetrated in the name of the "long term."

Yet, while the contributors to this volume share these general perspectives, different values and different assumptions about how the world works inevitably lead to different approaches to economic policy. The reader should explore these articles as pieces of a not-yet-completed economic strategy mosaic. The vision of that mosaic is an America that will provide jobs for everyone willing and able to work, a rising standard of living for those who put in their hours and pay their bills, and economically stable communities within which citizens can pursue their private and public lives.

Our Current Condition

In the new economic environment in which we find ourselves, the market is working its will. Individuals, companies, and communities are increasingly left to fend for themselves in a scramble to survive against new competitors who enter the domestic and global markets every day. Some Americans have prospered, but most have not. In 1993, despite an increase in hours worked, real median family income—the level of inflation-adjusted income at which half of families are above and half are below—was roughly at the level it was 20 years before. Over the same period, median real hourly wages had fallen almost 8%. By that same year, American production workers in manufacturing received less overall compensation than workers in both Germany and Japan. The Germans already work shorter hours than Americans. Certainly before the decade is over, blue-collar workers in Japan will also be working fewer hours a year than their American counterparts. In effect, to meet the competition, Americans are, as candidate Bill Clinton observed in his 1992 campaign, "working harder for less."

Still, our trade deficit remains huge, our industrial base continues to shrink, and real family incomes continue to decline. The signal from the market is that Americans haven't suffered nearly enough. Lawrence Mishel and Jared Bernstein tell us that, on our current trajectory, real median wages for men will fall another 10% over the next 10 years.[1] Entry-level wages for high school graduates without any college, who make up half of the workforce, will fall 24% for young men and 13% for young women. If the trend since 1987 continues, earnings for college graduates will also decline.

The consequence of a continued decline in real incomes and wealth for those in the bottom 75% of the income distribution will—as it has in the recent past—ripple beyond the pay envelopes. There is a clear relationship between economic stress and the dissolution of families, increases in crime, and a deterioration in the public health.[2] This, in turn, puts greater demand on the public sector at a time when tax revenues are weak and the resistance to tax increases is high because of falling real incomes. Indeed, the public sector has become the scapegoat for the anxiety and anger over the squeeze in middle-class incomes. On its current course, the fiscal crisis of governments at all levels will worsen. This will jeopardize public investment in education and infrastructure, public health and safety, environmental protection, and the public amenities—parks, museums, libraries—that characterize an advanced society. Thus will the fiscal crisis exacerbate the social strains among class, race, and sex that already underlie much of our country's political stress.

Therefore, the central policy question facing the United States as we approach the end of the 20th century is, how do we Americans prosper (that is, reverse the downward trend in real incomes for the majority of working families) in this new economic era?

The Phony War Over Economic Policy

Competing answers to that question are generally presented to the public as a debate between conservative and liberal or Republican and Democratic views of the world. But the differences between these supposedly competing ideologies are quite narrow. In fact, despite the fierce partisanship with which Republicans and Democrats battle each other rhetorically, they are two sides of the same policy coin.

The standard conservative prescription is: shrink government, lower taxes, and deregulate markets. Although these are sometimes curiously labeled as "new ideas," the conservative story is the same under Newt Gingrich as it was under Ronald Reagan, Calvin Coolidge, and William McKinley: domestic government has grown too large, and it transfers too much money from private-sector investors to the poor who consume. Once that assumption is granted, the conservative prescription automatically follows. It is no different today than it was 50 years ago when a headline in the *Wall Street Journal* proclaimed, "GOP Plan: Cut Taxes, Balance Budget, Remove Controls From Business."

But most of the decline in real wages and incomes has occurred *before* taxes, not after. The share of family income going to federal income taxes that support "big government" has remained roughly constant at least since 1977.[3]

The available evidence does not fit the conservative assumption. Moreover, the United States already has the smallest domestic public sector of any of the world's advanced industrial nations—including Japan and Germany, whose family incomes, currency values, and competitive performance have been outpacing America's for years. Moreover, during the years of declining income from wages, the returns to capital have risen, and the rich have gotten an even larger share of income and wealth. Meanwhile, the poor have suffered. Both the real minimum wage and welfare benefits have dropped substantially over the past two decades.

In 1981, America embarked on an experiment designed by conservatives to test their claim that cutting tax rates would generate more than enough economic growth and therefore tax revenues to compensate for short-term revenue loss. Indeed, we were promised enough for a balanced budget by 1984. The result was a major financial disaster: in 12 years of conservative rule, the national debt rose from $1 trillion to $4 trillion.

Over the same period Republicans and Democrats progressively deregulated the finance industry, resulting in a savings and loan scandal that added another $163 billion to our national debt and encouraged the flow of national savings away from direct investment in plant, equipment, and housing and into volatile short-term speculation.

Speaker of the House Newt Gingrich defines the core conservative perspective: "The price of labor is set in South China, because that is the largest center of workforce on the planet. So if you want to live seven times as well as somebody in Canton, you're going to have to be seven times as productive." Gingrich's numbers are wrong; the gap between labor in South China and the United States is much larger. And so are his economics: the price of labor in South China is set not by a free market but by one controlled by an authoritarian government that represses labor costs and labor rights. But the message is clear: in the world economy, you are on your own.

Thus to the question: what does it mean in economic terms to be an American? The conservative answer is, "not much." If U.S. employers can contract out your job to Indonesia, where wage suppression is official policy, if your company decides to downsize you out of a job after 20 years of loyal service, if you can't afford health insurance premiums, too bad. Other than voluntary acts of personal charity, we have no obligations to each other as Americans. Implicitly, and sometimes explicitly, the conservative view is that if American wages are falling, they were too high to begin with.

The other face of the coin of conventional economic wisdom is the liberal—or more properly, neo-liberal—version. According to neo-liberal doctrine, the central problem is that the majority of workers have not been able to keep up with the new job skills demanded by the global marketplace and therefore have seen their incomes fall. The answer then is to raise the level of education and training for America's workers.

Investment in education and training is certainly beneficial—both for the individual and the economy. But the notion that educational deficiency is the central problem of the U.S. labor force and that remedying that deficiency is the central solution to reversing declining incomes does not stand scrutiny. Education levels are rising while wages are falling. Recent research by Jared Bernstein at the Economic Policy Institute shows that, although the gap between blacks and whites on test scores narrowed in the 1980s, the wage gap widened. College graduates already represent a larger share of the labor force in the United States than in any other advanced nation. But the U.S. Bureau of Labor Statistics shows 20% of college graduates working at jobs that clearly do not require a higher education, and it projects an even larger share of these graduates will be underemployed by the turn of the century. It is true that more-educated people (conventionally defined by economists as the 25% of the labor force with college educations) earn more than those with less, and that the gap between these groups has grown. But the data show a general downward trend for the vast majority of the labor force—including college graduates, whose earnings in 1993 were 2% less than they were in 1987.

But even if one accepted the neo-liberal remedy of more education and training, the practical solution has been undercut by another neo-liberal principle—that deficit reduction must take priority over public investment in human resources. Thus, a large number of Democrats have embraced the Republican principle for balancing the budget by a date certain entirely with cuts in domestic spending. The result is a virtual bipartisan consensus for a decade of austerity that will shrink federal investment in human capital, with no possibility that the gap can be made up by the states.

This commitment to austerity raises the specter of inadequate purchasing power in an economy where incomes are stagnating and where savings are to be favored over consumption. The fundamental Keynesian insight is still correct; consumer demand is the driving force in a modern economy, and the prospect of expanded sales is the primary inspiration for investment. Attempting to increase savings by reducing government deficits in an underemployed economy reduces domestic consumption. Thus, it leads to lower, not higher, investment. The question therefore arises: if we must reduce domestic consumption, to whom will we sell the increased production?

The neo-liberals' answer is that we will sell it to other nations' customers. Without national debate, a major shift in economic policy has occurred: the promotion of exports—rather than the growth of our internal market—is now America's central economic strategy. The Commerce Department, the State Department, the U.S. Trade Representative, the Defense Department—even the Central Intelligence Agency—have been enlisted in the effort. Since the more-developed markets in Europe and Japan are protected against large, chronic trade deficits in America's favor by government policies and restrictive private behavior, this has meant concentrating on Third World "emerging markets." Among many casualties, U.S. concern for human rights has been abandoned whenever authoritarian governments have threatened to deny access to their labor or their markets.

The obsession with foreign markets has led to policies that in effect encourage the transfer of investment and technology out of the United States to other nations on the grounds that this will secure markets for this country. With bipartisan support, the American government bails out speculators in the Mexican stock market, rationalizing that this will bolster the Mexican middle-class market for U.S. goods. The government looks the other way as major aerospace contractors sell technology, paid for by U.S. taxpayers, to countries whose unabashed aim is to create their own industry to capture U.S. aerospace markets—one of the few remaining areas of significant U.S. industrial advantage.

Ultimately, the commitment to foreign markets creates more pressure to lower U.S. labor costs—and therefore wages and incomes. It should have been no surprise when, after supporting the passage of NAFTA, Gingrich argued against increasing the minimum wage (the value of which had dropped 41% in 15 years) because it would make U.S. workers less competitive against Mexican workers. The point is not that we should restrict trade, but that we should recognize that pinning our hopes on export-led growth brings risks and costs. Those who propose such policies have a responsibility to address them. But conservatives tell us that government should not interfere, and neo-liberals tell us we have no money for serious adjustment programs.

Thus, for different reasons, both avoid the problem of erosion of wages and incomes for roughly three-quarters of American working people by leaving the answer solely to a global labor market, where wages are increasingly set in the Third World. The inevitable result is a standard of living that is spiraling downward. Both ideologies avoid this ominous implication of their economics by hiding behind the notion that we are simply in a difficult "transition" to a world of high-technology production that, when completed, will make us all better off than before. Current difficulties are necessary short-term sacrifices for long-term gain. We are told that cutting back on public spending on education, health, and safety now is necessary for us to eliminate the fiscal deficit, so that some time in the future we can spend more. Today's job and income losses stemming from deregulated trade are justified by promises of increased incomes that will eventually be produced by a more efficient global economy years or decades—the time frame is rarely specified—from now. Dismantling environmental protections, we are assured, will generate more income growth out of which consumers will individually pay—in some unspecified way—for their demand for clean air and water.

Although the circumstances are different, the current conventional wisdom is eerily reminiscent of the economic discourse of the 1930s. Economists then justified their stubborn insistence on balancing public budgets in the face of large-scale unemployment on the grounds that the world had to rely on market forces to "restructure" its way out of the Depression. The economist Alvin Hansen—later to defect to the Keynesian position that government could jump-start growth—expressed the consensus in 1932 when he wrote: "We shall come out of it only through hard work and readjustments that are painful. There is no other alternative."

But, of course, the world did not wait for market-driven restructuring. Before the forces of supply and demand could drive incomes and prices low enough to spark a revival of investment (if, indeed, they could have at all), the political reaction to economic pain set in motion the most destructive war in history. As we all know, the unemployment problems of the 1930s were solved not by market forces but by expanded government deficits to finance World War II—the exact opposite of the conservative fiscal strategy advocated by the economic policy intellectuals of the time.

A Better Way

The policy discussions between advocates of the parallel versions of the conventional wisdom have been unimaginative and enervating. If one looks at the world with a fresh eye, it is not hard to see another possibility. A fresh eye is the key. By raising common-sense questions about the economic world—by asking "why not?" as well as "why?"—and following the answers to their common-sense conclusion, the citizen-reader can often see what "experts," whose view is often limited by ideology, cannot.

A sense of economic community. Let's start with a fundamental question: who are we? Secretary of Labor Robert Reich has made an important distinction between the fortunes of multinational American companies and the fortunes of American working families. The distinction reminds us that America is itself an economic unit. Many economists maintain that nations do not compete, only people and companies do. But so do nations. Lester Thurow illustrates the point when he asks why an American economics professor makes two or three times as much as British professors and 20% to 30% less than their German counterparts. His answer is that, although the individual professors may be equally productive, the Americans play on a more productive "team" than the British but a less productive one than the Germans. As we have seen, higher productivity is not a sufficient condition for high wages, but it is a necessary one. Thus, we will all prosper or not depending on the larger team—the national community of which we are all a part.

Thus, being an American involves a set of mutual responsibilities to each other, now and in the future. This is an economic point as well as a principle of politics and social morality. It means that when Americans are in poverty, are uneducated, are prevented from developing their talents and making their contribution, then all of us who work in America will suffer.

A strong public sector. At the level of the workplace and the business enterprise, the power of teamwork and collective action is almost universally recognized. But in recent years, a great deal of conscious political activity has been devoted to denying the usefulness of collective—that is, public—action in generating national income and wealth.

Yet a reading of our history indicates that a strong, healthy public sector has been crucial to our development. Throughout the 19th century, the growth of U.S. industrial power was nurtured and protected via government intervention and targeted subsidies. In the 20th century, the economic importance of the public sector should be obvious to all but the hopelessly ideological. Eleven years after World War I, we sank into the Great Depression, but 50 years after World War II we have still managed to avoid a collapse. It is no accident. The better performance the second time around has to do with our willingness to have government intervene in the marketplace. Unemployment compensation, welfare, the progressive income tax, and other automatic stabilizers maintained purchasing power during the downside of the business cycles. Targeted government spending built up public infrastructure and pulled reluctant private financiers into areas of national priority. The postwar boom was studded with public initiatives such as the GI Bill, the National Defense Education Act, the national highway program, airport and housing construction, NASA, and Medicare that sustained growth, increased economic opportunities, and installed a compassionate safety net. Government also organized and regulated the international market with the Bretton Woods agreement, the Marshall Plan, the General Agreement on Tariffs and Trade, and the World Bank. One can legitimately quarrel with the policies and programs of these particular institutions, but it is absurd to think that, without them, we would have seen the economic progress of the last half century. During this time, *precisely because of the enlarged size and increased responsibility of the public sector,* the personal freedom of the overwhelming majority of the American people expanded. Taming the excesses of unregulated markets created opportunities for upward career mobility, for education, and for personal development that would have been impossible at earlier times in our history.

Today, these hard-earned lessons of the past are being pushed out of our collective memory, ironically in the name of conservatism. The public sector has been vilified, and the false notion that America was built on laissez-faire has become the assumed truth. But reality cannot be denied: the proposition that prosperity in a modern economy must rest on a mix of public and private economic activity remains essential to a sensible answer to the question of how we reverse the decline in U.S. incomes and living standards.

A progressive economic nationalism. To the premises of America as an economic community and the public sector as a tool of development, we add a third strategic element—the importance of internal development. The United States is still an evolving society, and an evolving economy as well. The United States remains the largest national market for traditional consumer goods, the most rapidly growing market for sophisticated consumer goods, and the only significant market for a wide range of face-to-face services. The notion that our markets are "saturated" and therefore that our prosperity depends on our competing for Third

World customers is mistaken. It is already leading to bizarre policies in which we subsidize the creation of wealthy elites abroad in order to create consumer demand for our products, while we encourage the reduction in wages and domestic purchasing power at home on the grounds that we must reduce labor costs. This policy can lead only to moral as well as economic bankruptcy; the goal should be rising incomes for working people at home and abroad.

Large parts of our own American society are impoverished and crying for investment. This is strikingly obvious in our cities, where deficient investment in people and infrastructure is taking a tragic human toll. But it is also true of other sectors of our economy as well. Our public facilities are decaying, our environment is assaulted, and our lives are more stressful as the work week relentlessly expands into time once reserved for family life and personal enjoyment.

It is a mistake therefore for American economic policy to turn away from the challenge of generating economic growth out of the revitalization of our own people and environment. This is not a case for crude protectionism or jingoism. It is the proposition that, in order to play a leadership role in creating a peaceful and prosperous world order, we must get the American house in order. Just as America could not survive half slave and half free in the 1860s, its democratic institutions cannot survive the 21st century under an economic regime that promotes the prosperity of a smaller and smaller mobile elite while diminishing the living standards and opportunities for the vast majority.

THE STRATEGY

Out of a framework of a progressive economic nationalism flows a common-sense answer to the question of reversing wage decline in this new economic environment. It involves four major steps: (1) expanding the demand for labor—particularly in areas of high underemployment and poverty; (2) improving labor skills and the way work is organized; (3) reforming our financial institutions; and (4) regulating the global marketplace.

Expanding the demand for labor. A tight labor market is a necessary condition for reversing the long-term decline in wages. Moreover, it is essential for reestablishing the mutual obligation of the individual and society. A society can rightly expect that those who are able to work do so, but it cannot demand a work ethic of its people if public policy insures that there will always be many fewer jobs than there are people wanting to work.

Even at the peak of our business cycles—a few months of high production every five to eight years—we have not had full employment for decades. Indeed, the term is often dismissed as old-fashioned and naive, which tells us how far from the needs of ordinary people the national policy discussion has drifted.

The dramatic upward redistribution of income and wealth is in part a result of policies that give priority to the protection of financial assets over the creation of jobs. Interest rates are kept high to appease the financial markets' hypersensitivity to any threat of inflation, no matter how remote. This, we are told, is part of the price that must be paid for the expansion of the national debt in the 1980s. But as Robert Eisner and James Galbraith suggest in their essays, the conventional views are bound up in myth. As both authors show, neither of these conditions need prevail, and more expansive monetary and fiscal policies to gradually push the economy to lower levels of unemployment are well within our grasp.

But generating a paying job for everyone who is willing and able to work is not simply a matter of macroeconomic policy. America remains a place of large pockets of joblessness that will not be absorbed back into the labor force simply with lower interest rates. The nation's cities have especially been plagued by a vicious cycle of lowering income, disinvestment, and shrinking job markets. By now it is obvious that they will not be renewed without substantial new, targeted public investment.

As Todd Schafer shows, no matter how it is measured, we have fallen behind our major economic rivals in our investment in education, training, physical infrastructure, and civilian research and development. Economists may argue about the precise estimates, but we know that the relationship between public investment and long-term growth is positive and strong. Under different guises, public investment has historically been a major factor in the development of what Robert Heilbroner has called economic "klondikes," new technologies that create clusters of wealth-producing industries. Our current obsession with achieving a balanced federal budget is perverse: in the name of relieving the debt burden on our children, we are cutting the investment in the future that will make them more productive. Particularly important, as Elliott Sclar points out, is investment in our cities—the hubs of our nation's economic activity.

The essays herein suggest that there are two parts to a more sensible budget policy. One is to recognize that the structural deficit—that part of the deficit that is independent of the business cycle—is solely a function of a dysfunctional health care system. As Edith Rasell has shown, if the United States kept the growth of health care costs to the level of the average of other advanced industrial countries, the structural deficit would continue to decline as a share of our national income as far into the future as we can see. And as Robert Eisner shows, so long as annual deficits do not exceed the annual growth in income there is no crisis—and therefore no need for us to sacrifice the public investments necessary for the next generation's economic success. Comprehensive health care reform, not the futile effort to balance the budget by this or that date, is the real answer to our fiscal problem.

The second answer, as Schafer suggests, is to develop a federal budget that distinguishes between capital and operating expenses. The goal should be to allow borrowing for the former and to permanently balance the latter. Countercyclical spending would be therefore concentrated in investments that make the nation more productive.

Creating such a budget and developing the public understanding of its uses and limitations is a long-term project. But an interim step that would immediately help reverse the dangerous decline in public investment would be the creation of a capital investment trust fund to finance new investments separate from the current budget accounts.

Third, we need a shift of national technology priorities. One important example is offered by Michael Oden and Ann Markusen. The Department of Defense has been the prime source of such investment in much of the 20th century. With the end of the Cold War, the military budget is shrinking. But as Oden and Markusen show, there is little prospect that the private economy by itself will play the role that the Defense Department has played as a major source of support for cutting-edge industrial technologies. Indeed, it is apparent to everyone that the continued support for a bloated military budget is today generated almost entirely by fear of the economic impact of true demobilization. A serious program of converting military resources to civilian use must be led by the government.

Once we are free to pursue an investment-led strategy, other parts of the so-called deficit crisis can also be resolved. Dean Baker shows us that the Social Security trust fund is not in fact endangered, as the accepted wisdom would have it. And Robert Eisner offers a simple and progressive solution to the perennial crisis of the tax code.

Reorganizing the labor market. The second element in a high-wage strategy concerns the supply of skilled labor and how it is put to use.

Lawrence Mishel shows that raising productivity and increasing the demand for labor are not sufficient conditions for reversing the decline in wages. Labor-market institutions such as trade unions must be strengthened to assure that the fruits of progress are evenly shared.

In this regard, Peter Berg makes the compelling case that we need to expand our vision of training from one that simply helps displaced workers adjust to market forces to one that allows all workers to participate in productivity growth and generates higher incomes. Our ability to integrate training into the development of high-performance workplaces will ultimately determine whether we can reach a higher path to productivity growth.

William Spriggs and John Schmitt make the case for strengthening one labor-market institution in particular—the minimum wage. In addition, they suggest that raising the price of labor—particularly at the bottom reaches of the income distribution—will provide incentives for employers to improve efficiency.

Of all industrial nations, the United States has the system of labor law and practice that is most tilted against unions. Both Ray Marshall and Paula Voos address the role of the labor union in both assuring a just distribution of the benefits of productivity and expanding opportunities for workers to participate in the management of the workplace. They show that the encouragement and strengthening of collective bargaining through independent labor unions is absolutely necessary to construct a framework for a true partnership between labor and capital.

Finally, Jared Bernstein and Irwin Garfinkel examine the importance of full employment for solving the problem of those at the bottom of the labor market. They show that, without creating more jobs at the lower end of the job market, welfare reform cannot work, and it will at best simply shuffle unemployment and poverty from some individuals to others.

Financial markets. The high-wage path to the future cannot be pursued without dealing with the impact of the deregulated financial system. The development of high-performance workplaces requires front-loaded investments in training and the building of trust between labor and management. At present, these requirements are constantly undercut by the demand emanating from highly mobile capital markets that companies maximize short-term profits. Jane D'Arista and Tom Schlesinger make the case for a modern re-regulation of the financial markets that would once more put them at the service of productive investment. By making regulations uniform across activities, we can eliminate the distortions that make credit markets incapable of promoting sustainable growth.

Gary Dymski and John Veitch describe how American financial markets do not make capital accessible to the places where the economy most desperately needs it. And they suggest ways in which to channel more resources to the country's No. 1 development problem—our inner cities.

At the top of the banking system, of course, sits the Federal Reserve. Today it is the most powerful government influence on the economy, yet it is unaccountable to the democratic process and inaccessible to almost everyone. James Galbraith argues for a major overhaul of the central bank as an essential step in economic reform.

The global economy. One of the most damaging of the myths about our present economic circumstances is the notion that the growing importance of the international sector of the U.S. economy denies us the ability to control our own destiny. Yet the fact remains that Americans still buy about 90% of what we produce. The threat of globalization is often used as a convenient weapon in strictly domestic struggles—such as when a company threatens to move to Mexico if its workers organize. And contradictions on this subject pervade the business media. For example, we are told by the same people that the Federal Reserve has no control over long-term interest rates because they are set in a global marketplace *and* that it is essential to expand the U.S. savings rate in order to generate a greater supply of saving for U.S. investment. If we are in a global market, savings can flow anywhere. So why should we sacrifice current consumption to provide savings for other economies?

Robert Scott shows us that there is much that the United States can do to address its trade deficit. Our problems are centered on China and

Japan. In the short term, temporary import protection is needed to restore balance. In the longer term, we need industrial policies that maintain balanced trade and rising wages.

Jerome Levinson makes the important political as well as economic point that, as the economy becomes more global, rising wages and living standards in America will increasingly depend on rising living standards elsewhere. This requires us to face the need for global regulation of the world's labor markets.

Finally, there is the question of political feasibility. In the midst of a supposedly conservative trend in American politics, can a broadened progressive agenda have an appeal? Ruy Teixeira demonstrates that in electoral terms there is less to this conservative trend than meets the eye. In fact, underneath much of the widespread discontent with government is not so much an ideological disagreement about the role of government but rather a frustration that government has not been effective in dealing with the decline in living standards. If, as seems evident, neither the Republicans' "Contract With America" nor the strategy of selling to "emerging markets" will reverse that decline, the electorate will eventually look to a different path—in all likelihood by the time we reach the new century.

Notes

1. Mishel and Bernstein 1994.
2. Merva and Fowles 1992.
3. Mishel and Bernstein 1994.

References

Merva, Mary, and Richard Fowles. 1992. "Effects of Diminished Economic Opportunities on Social Stress: Heart Attacks, Strokes, and Crime." Briefing Paper. Washington, D.C.: Economic Policy Institute.

Mishel, Lawrence and Jared Bernstein. 1994. *The State of Working America 1994-95.* Economic Policy Institute Series. Armonk, N.Y.: M.E. Sharpe.

Bernstein, Jared. 1995. *Where's the Payoff? The Gap Between Black Academic Progress and Economic Gains.* Washington, D.C.: Economic Policy Institute.

SECTION I

The National Economy

Overview
The National Economy

by Max B. Sawicky

FISCAL POLICY IS ABOUT MAKING PLANS FOR FEDERAL SPENDING. SUCH plans enable commitments to various missions in public policy. Taxing or borrowing to finance such commitments are mere means to an end, but these days the elimination of borrowing per se has been miscast as the foremost mission of the national government.

It was discovered long ago that government need not and often should not attempt to finance all of its spending with current revenues: some amount of borrowing is often recommended. This insight has been pushed aside by the prevailing obsession with budget deficits, with tragic consequences for the nation.

Rapid elimination of current and projected deficits is now held to be the highest goal of economic policy. Zero deficits or even budget surpluses, along with a fixed rate of growth of the money supply, are touted as the best medicine for long-term economic growth. Moreover, there is said to be a rate of unemployment—the "non-accelerating inflation rate of unemployment," or NAIRU—below which the economy cannot be moved without provoking an inflationary spiral.

In the first chapter, Robert Eisner rebuts the prevailing hysteria about federal budget deficits, debunks the concept of the NAIRU, and reminds us of the constructive uses of deficit spending. Eisner first elaborates on the tolerable limits for borrowing, which are much more flexible than commonly assumed, and on how deficits are best managed within such limits. An important finding is that deficits and increases in the rate of growth of the money supply can raise employment, private investment, and long-term growth without undue risk of inflation.

Max B. Sawicky is an economist specializing in public finance at the Economic Policy Institute.

The standard response to this approach has been to invoke the danger of hyperinflation by reference to the NAIRU theory. By presenting empirical evidence to assuage such fears, Eisner tells us that greater efforts can safely be exerted toward reducing unemployment below 5%, with obvious economic and social benefits for the nation.

The deficit issue is often understood by flawed analogies to household or business budgets. "I balance my checkbook. Why can't the government?" But as Todd Schafer points out, households allow themselves many "off-checkbook" purchases, such as those for homes, education, or cars, that are paid for by borrowing. Is this financial profligacy? Clearly not. Schafer points out that borrowing to finance household and business—or public—investments makes perfect economic sense. The assets purchased have extended lives of usefulness, and the future benefits defray the costs of borrowing and free up cash to meet debt obligations.

But our insistence on moving to a zero deficit has hamstrung our ability to make long-term national investments. Recent research has shown expenditures for such purposes to be a crucial missing ingredient in a policy mix that has failed to encourage economic growth and high employment. Schafer explains that the proper way to accommodate such interests is through the inauguration of a capital budget for the federal government. Under this plan, operating expenditures would be paid for with current revenues, and investments would be financed by borrowing.

The nation's Social Security system is commonly held to be a chief culprit in our deficit woes. Much popular comment has it that Social Security "won't be there" when the Baby Boom retires, that reductions in benefits are necessary to "save the program," and that payment of such benefits is an affront to future generations of workers because our children and their children will face gigantic tax rates to pay for them.

Dean Baker addresses these charges first by underlining the obvious: currently the program is running a cash surplus that is reducing the need for federal borrowing and deficits. By the Social Security Administration's own pessimistic projections, the trust fund is not scheduled to go into the red until 2030, and Baker calculates that relatively small tax increases can keep the trust fund in the black indefinitely. He also notes that the projections of the Social Security administrators may be overly pessimistic, which means that future shortfalls will come later, if at all, and further tax increases may never be needed.

As many have acknowledged, the U.S. health care system will roll off a cliff unless comprehensive, structural reform is achieved. This is not a fiscal problem but rather a more fundamental question of how the nation as a whole will produce and pay for health care. Edith Rasell writes that thoughtless reductions in Medicare and Medicaid will threaten access to services and quality of care for beneficiaries. Such reductions do not reduce the costs of health care so much as change the way services are paid for. As payment obligations are shifted out of the public programs and into family budgets, the pressure will cause people to receive poorer care or defer care.

Rasell criticizes the leading proposals for cost cutting, including the reduction of fees paid to health care providers, the contraction of covered services, the rush to managed care, the institution of vouchers, "medical savings accounts," and incremental, market-oriented reforms in general. She argues instead for a single-payer approach that would simultaneously control costs and provide universal coverage.

National health care reform is currently off the radar screen of American politics, but as Baker and Rasell point out, fiscal realities will surely drive it back to center stage. A single-payer solution may be politically impossible, but it is less impossible than any other resolution of the U.S. health care crisis.

How should we pay for health care, much less government in general? As Robert Eisner says in the final chapter of this section, "our tax system is a mess." It supports an unproductive industry in accountants, attorneys, tax preparers, lobbyists, and, dare we say it, economists, but it also provides numerous incentives for economic decisions that would otherwise make no sense.

Eisner takes up one of the leading proposals for comprehensive tax reform: the flat tax. As currently proposed, the major flat tax plans are fundamentally consumption taxes. Any tax-rate reductions would be borne by consumers in the form of a higher price level throughout the economy. As such, the plans would shift a great part of the tax burden from the wealthy to everyone else. Eisner suggests an alternative approach: a new comprehensive tax on personal income that would reduce rates across the board by broadening the tax base through the elimination of most deductions and the inclusion of all capital gains income. In the process, the corporate income tax would be abolished, and payroll taxes would be eliminated, with the revenues replaced by proceeds from the income tax. The Eisner plan manages to be as flat as current flat tax proposals but more progressive—flat because it charges only one rate on income above the generous standard deduction, and progressive because it expands the earned-income tax credit, eliminates regressive deductions, and taxes all capital gains income as it accrues.

The chapters in this section show how fiscal policy can prudently manage deficits without sacrificing employment, economic growth, and essential public programs upon which Americans depend. They reveal the real problem of fiscal policy to be not fiscal at all, but one of the organization of the nation's health care system. They show how revenues can be raised to support the nation's essential public missions, consistent with concerns for economic efficiency, tax simplicity, and basic fairness. In short, they provide a foundation for the enterprise of government, whose principal, affirmative purposes continue to command the support of the vast majority of the American people.

CHAPTER 1

Deficits and Unemployment
Dogmas Blocking Economic Policy

by Robert Eisner

MUCH OF THE ECONOMICS PROFESSION AND BODY POLITIC HAVE BEEN infected by a virus spreading the belief, if not the reality, of policy impotence. Monetary policy—changing the quantity of money or its rate of growth—will generally, except possibly for brief "surprises," have no real effect. Monetary expansion will only raise prices or the rate of inflation, in the latter case raising nominal rates of interest but leaving real rates ultimately unchanged. Fiscal expansion by means of deficits will not be stimulatory because the public will understand that lower taxes now will have to be paid for in higher taxes later; people will hence save for that grim future rather than spend more now.

Further, we are doomed, we are told, to a "natural" rate of unemployment with which we cannot tamper without wreaking economic havoc. According to this dogma, permitting unemployment to get "too low," let alone actively trying to reduce it, will set off not just higher inflation but inflation getting higher and higher and higher. Simply returning to the natural level of unemployment will still leave inflation at the higher rates it reached in our period of delinquency. Reasonable price stability can only be restored then by excess unemployment.

As if all this is not enough, those who might see some merit in using fiscal policy for good see the "huge" deficits left from the Reagan years as making impossible any "costly" new initiatives. We cannot, we are told, interfere with deficit reduction and add even more to the debt. And raising taxes is a political no-no, and perhaps particularly bad for the economy as well.

Robert Eisner is the William R. Kenan professor emeritus of economics at Northwestern University and a past president of the American Economic Association.

It is time to reject these counsels of doom and do-nothing. Government and its fiscal policy can help the economy and improve our lives. To open the path we must expose the humbug of the current discussion of the public debt and deficits. And we must dispel the notion that we are bound by a natural rate of unemployment short of full employment.

Debt and Deficits Can Be Good for You

A first step is to eliminate the deficit paranoia that infects political discourse. *There is nothing wrong with prudent, responsible deficits.* By the methods of federal accounting we all run them—households, businesses, and state and local governments. Families borrow to buy homes, automobiles, and other durable goods and to send their children to college. Corporations borrow to finance the capital investment so widely viewed as a key to growth. And state and local governments borrow, unconstrained by "balanced budget" requirements in their constitutions, to finance their capital outlays. All such spending financed by borrowing, considered prudent financial planning when anyone else initiates it, constitutes what we call a deficit in the federal budget.

What is important for government, as for individuals and business, is not that there be no deficit but that the deficit be such that the resulting debt does not get out of line with income. Current and prospective federal deficits for the rest of this century meet that test. With a debt held by the public of $3.5 trillion and a growth of national income of 6%—and a greater growth is quite possible—an increase in the debt of $210 billion would leave the ratio of debt to income unchanged. The 1994 deficit was $203 billion, the 1995 deficit is projected at $160 billion, and for the year 2000 the Office of Management and Budget forecast a deficit of $208 billion.[1] That would constitute a growth in the debt significantly *less* than the growth in income.

There is in fact nothing sacrosanct about the current ratio of debt to income. That ratio, in terms of gross domestic product, was 51.7% at the end of the 1994 fiscal year.[2] The ratio was only 26.1% in 1981 before the big Reagan-era deficits, but it was as high as 114% in 1946, a year that ushered in a quarter century of unparalleled growth and prosperity. But even maintaining the current ratio over the long run would permit large increases in deficits to combat recessions or to undertake major public investment. These would be balanced by the decreases in deficits in booms or when the investment paid off in higher incomes.

The one meaningful argument against deficits is that they absorb private saving that would otherwise go to private investment. And by thus permitting excessive consumption, they are presumed to sacrifice the future for the benefit of the present.

The argument seems unassailable to many as they repeat the mistake of economists of more than six decades ago. Simply enough, the argument assumes full employment or full utilization of our resources. In the words of John Maynard Keynes, they apply the rules of plane geometry to a world of more than two dimensions, particularly to a world where the level of employment is an additional dimension whose variability cannot be ignored.

Of course, if employment is full and income and output are therefore fixed at what can be produced at full employment, more output going to consumption must mean less going to investment. If a deficit finances increased consumption there must be less investment. And since reducing the deficit, whether by cutting government spending or raising taxes, must reduce after-tax income, it must reduce consumption. Again, with given output, less consumption must mean more investment.

But in the real United States economy of this century we have rarely had full employment, except in times of war.[3] Higher employment has coincided with greater output—and more saving and investment. And lower employment has coincided with lesser output—and less saving and investment. What can be said of the role of deficits in such a world?

To accurately assess the effect of the deficit on the economy we must make two adjustments to the deficit as it is ordinarily measured. First, we must adjust for the impact of the business cycle. Even if there are no changes whatsoever in tax and spending policy, the deficit will fluctuate as the economy goes through the high and low points of the business cycle. At the low point, large numbers of workers are unemployed and incomes are low. The deficit then becomes larger mostly for two reasons: there are more unemployed or underemployed workers collecting unemployment, food stamps, or other government benefits, and there is less money collected in taxes, since people are earning less. The opposite effect occurs at the high point of the business cycle: government spending on benefits falls because fewer people are out of work, and tax collections increase because incomes are high.

Removing the effect on the deficit of these cyclical fluctuations allows us to construct a structural or cyclically adjusted measure of the deficit.[4] This is a measure of what the deficit would be year by year holding the level of unemployment constant, at, say, 6%.[5] Changes in this measure of the deficit are entirely attributable to changes in tax or spending policy, not fluctuations in the economy.

Second, we must adjust the deficit by the extent to which inflation reduces the real value of the government's debt. A large amount of government spending each year (currently about $200 billion) goes to pay interest on the government debt. A portion of this interest is not real interest but is actually an inflation premium that compensates for the loss of purchasing power due to inflation.

This point can be illustrated with a simple example. Suppose the government's debt is $3 trillion and that it must pay 7% interest on the debt this year, or $210 billion. Let's also assume that inflation over the course of the year is 3%. What this means is that the $3 trillion in debt that the government owes bondholders will be worth 3%, or $90 billion, less at the end of the year because of the impact of inflation. The bondholders receive $210 billion in interest payments, but the first $90 billion just compensates them for their losses due to inflation. After adjusting for the loss of purchasing power of their bonds, the amount of real interest they received was just $120 billion.

This inflation premium rises whenever inflation goes up, meaning that the actual deficit rises even though the amount of real interest paid out remains the same. By removing this effect of the inflation premium, we get a better idea of the real value of the deficit.

I have constructed a measure of the deficit, which I call the price-adjusted, high-employment[6] deficit (PAHED), that adjusts for these two factors. It removes the effects of both the business cycle and inflation on the deficit. In widely reported work over a number of years,[7] I have found that PAHED has exactly the sort of effects that would be expected if the economy were operating below its full employment levels of output. Specifically, larger deficits in one year are associated with higher real GDP growth and decreases in unemployment the next. They are also associated with higher levels of investment and national saving, even though the effect on the trade deficit and foreign investment flows is somewhat negative.

Monetary policy and real exchange rates also play a role. Easier money, as measured by the rate of increase in the money supply, has also been associated with higher GDP and saving and investment and lower unemployment a year later. Similarly, but after a lag of two or three years, lower real exchange rates have proved stimulatory. Neither of these factors, however, obscures the clear role of real, inflation-adjusted budget deficits, in themselves, as stimulants to the economy and contributors to real economic growth.

If these results of analysis of data over a period of almost 40 years are to be accepted—and I have seen no persuasive rejection of the fundamental findings—some clear conclusions must follow for policy makers. Fiscal policy, as measured by budget deficits, has had a significant impact on the economy. Larger structural deficits should be accepted and indeed pursued when the economy is sluggish. They have proved potent—whether consciously applied or stumbled into without acknowledgment, as was the case with the supposedly "supply side" tax cuts and increases in military expenditures of the 1980s. And rather than blindly striving to reduce the deficit regardless of the shape of the economy, let alone reduce it to zero with a "balanced budget," we should aim at a deficit sufficiently large to provide the effective demand for all of the goods and services our economy can produce.

There is more to the issue, though, than merely the size of the deficit. What the government and the private sector do with the money is also important. Just as the amount of private investment matters for the future, so does the amount of public investment or private investment financed by the government. One of the ironies of the deficit reduction rhetoric that says we must reduce the burden on our children and grandchildren is that deficit reduction is likely to take a heavy toll on public investment of all kinds—crucial infrastructure of roads, bridges, harbors, and airports; protection of the environment; support of basic research; food for children and pregnant women and their infants; and the basic education at all levels that is most vital to our future.

These needs suggest a policy rule of thumb: we should aim, on the average, at a high-employment deficit such that the debt-to-GDP ratio remains constant. What this would mean now, with a ratio of about 50%

and a rate of growth of GDP of (at least) 6%, is a deficit that would grow year by year but that would generally remain at 3% of GDP. (As indicated above, that would mean a current deficit of about $210 billion, significantly more than we have.) This deficit, however, should be used to finance net public investment, broadly defined to include human and intangible capital of education and research as well as the tangible capital of public infrastructure. The growth and improved supply of labor that such investment would bring would help the economy attain and maintain the high employment that would correspond to the employment rate for which the deficit was set. And high employment would also be brought about by a monetary policy aimed at low interest rates, which would promote private investment, and the lower real exchange rates that they would bring.

The Bugaboo of the "Natural" Level of Unemployment[8]

A major force blocking the path to sane macroeconomic policy is the continuing hold, in the face of increasing contrary evidence, of the doctrine of a natural or "non-accelerating inflation rate of unemployment," or NAIRU. The argument, going back to Milton Friedman and Edmund S. Phelps,[9] is that basic structural forces in the economy dictate an equilibrium rate of unemployment; this rate may involve considerably more unemployment than just the modest proportions of "frictionally" jobless traditionally associated with full employment.[10] In Europe, double-digit rates have been accepted by many now for some years as "natural." I have quipped with considerable accuracy that the difference between conservative and liberal economists in the United States may be characterized by the views of those, like Martin Feldstein, who see the natural rate at 6½% to 7%, and of those, like Alan Blinder, who suggest it is between 5½% and 6%. A few brave souls are willing, given our uncertainties and the standard errors of our estimates, to allow unemployment to edge down into the danger range. But certainly too few reject the notion as a dismal dogma, never unambiguously supported by the facts.

According to the NAIRU dogma, increased demand due to fiscal or monetary policy may only temporarily increase the rate of employment.

The theory rejects the old Phillips Curve notion of a tradeoff between inflation and unemployment, whereby increased demand may reduce unemployment but only at the cost of higher inflation. The NAIRU idea is that any such reduction in unemployment occurs only because inflation is temporarily higher than had been expected. This higher inflation leads workers, apparently voluntarily and not involuntarily unemployed, to make themselves available for work because they note the increase in wages before they become aware of the increase in prices. They hence respond to what appears to them to be higher real wages by supplying themselves for jobs. Employers, on the other hand, recognize that the prices they can get for their products are higher and are going up faster than wages. Real wages to them are lower and hence they eagerly hire the additional workers.

This happy situation, however, cannot last. As workers come to realize that prices have in fact risen more than wages, they demand still higher wages or quit their jobs if they don't get them. Employers, faced with wages catching up to prices, no longer see any profit in the additional workers and let them go. We are thus back where we started, at the natural rate of unemployment.

But then the cycle repeats itself. Unemployment can only be kept below its natural rate by constantly raising inflation above what has been expected, thus producing the "accelerating" inflation that gives the concept its name. If the natural rate is, say, the 5.8% that the Congressional Budget Office has recently calculated,[11] allowing it to stay at the 5.7% of July 1995 (or the 5.4% of several months earlier!) would have the annual rate of price increase rising from its current 2% or 3% to 4%, 6%, 10%, 20%, and on into an endless hyperinflation.

If we give up this effort to keep unemployment "too low," or the Federal Reserve is successful, after inflation has reached, say, 10%, in getting unemployment back up to the natural rate of 5.8%, this will not end the inflation. It will stop accelerating, but it will remain stuck at that rate of 10%. To lower inflation we will then have to go through the painful experience of high unemployment, that is, unemployment in excess of the natural rate. The clear policy implication, to Alan Greenspan and others, is that we must not allow unemployment to get too low in the first place. And that also means that we cannot permit the economy to grow too fast. Since 2.5% growth in real GDP is associated with a fairly constant rate of unemployment, any signs that the economy is growing or will be growing faster than that must be combatted by tighter fiscal policy (cutting government expenditures and deficits) and/or tighter monetary policy (holding down bank reserves and raising interest rates).

Is there any solid justification for all this? To answer that question, I have put the NAIRU idea through two series of tests. First, assembling the data used by the Congressional Budget Office, I used CBO's model to re-estimate the NAIRU. Second, I made a slight change to the model to better reflect a different, though plausible, scenario for the effect of low unemployment.

In testing CBO's model, I found, as did CBO, that, other things equal, inflation experienced in the recent past gets passed on into the present. I too found that high rates of unemployment lead to decelerating inflation and vice versa. Most importantly, I got their precise results for the estimate of the NAIRU, a number that varied closely around CBO's then estimate of 5.8%, depending on the measure of inflation that was used.

When I made projections for the future using this standard model, I found, as expected, that unemployment below the NAIRU led to accelerating inflation. But interestingly, even with the standard model, low unemployment did not lead to sharply accelerating inflation.[12] Most striking, however, are the results of the second test, in which I made a change to the standard model.

Suppose we accept that high unemployment lowers inflation, as it apparently does. A relation estimated with observations of both high and low unemployment may well show unemployment and inflation moving in opposite directions solely because of those high unemployment observations. But suppose high and low unemployment aren't mirror images, one causing inflation to rise by a point and the other causing it to fall the same amount. Suppose low unemployment does not raise inflation and maybe even lowers it.

There are many reasons why such an asymmetrical relationship is plausible. When unemployment is low, productivity tends to be high, since firms will be trying to make full use of previously idle labor. This will tend to lower average costs, and possibly even marginal costs.[13] Also, during periods of low unemployment workers will be putting in more overtime and more hours in general. This means that they will have higher weekly pay even at the same basic wage rate, so they may feel less need to insist on hourly pay increases. Both of these factors under competitive conditions will tend to hold down prices. It is also possible that at a time when high demand will be already producing high profits, firms with current control of the market will be reluctant to raise prices out of fear of encouraging new competition, which would lower profits in the long run.

Whatever the theoretical formulation, what are the facts? I have re-estimated the NAIRU equations by separating the data into two pools, one for periods when unemployment was above the conventionally measured estimate of the NAIRU, and one for periods when it was below. The results are dramatically different. During the first period, high unemployment had an even larger effect than previously estimated on reducing inflation. However, in the period of low unemployment, there was no evidence whatsoever that low unemployment leads to accelerating inflation.

I find in fact that, on the basis of the low-unemployment observations, 5.8% unemployment yields forecasts over the rest of the century of fairly constant and modest inflation. Lower unemployment, as shown in **Figure A**, actually traces a path of *lower* inflation.

FIGURE A
Low Unemployment and Inflation Simulation,1995-99

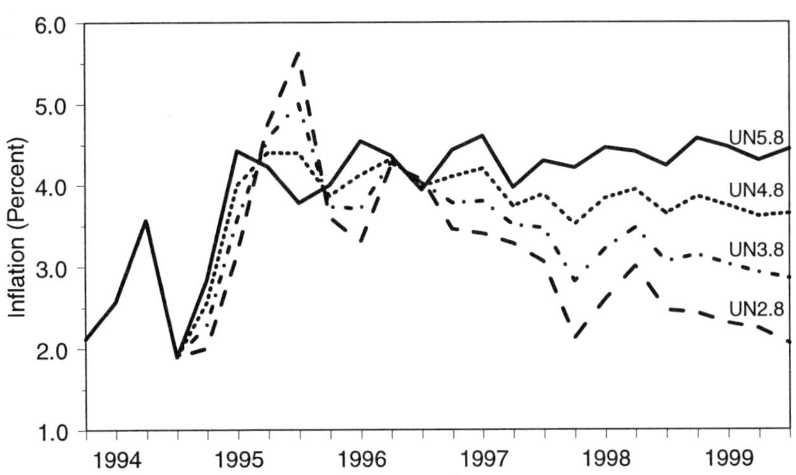

Source: Author's analysis of CBO data.

I am fond of stating that I would not bet my life—or the economy—on anyone's econometric estimates, including my own. I do not mean to substitute for the old dogma that low unemployment causes permanently accelerating inflation a new dogma that low unemployment can be relied upon to lower inflation. But I think these results[14] should give pause to those who have for some years been contributing to keeping economic policy in a nasty straight-jacket.

Perhaps we should proceed after all to implement the policies aimed at maximum and full employment that are mandated in the laws of the land.[15]

Notes

1. Congressional Budget Office (1995), p. 28.

2. Of that, 5.4% was held by the Federal Reserve, leaving only 46.4% held by the rest of the "public." See Office of Management and Budget (1995c), Table 7.1, p. 89.

3. And forecasts by the Organization for Economic Cooperation and Development (OECD) now warn of the likelihood of double-digit unemployment rates in Europe on into the next century.

4. I believe the concept was first developed by Herbert Stein, later chairman of President Nixon's Council of Economic Advisers, when he was with the business-supported Committee for Economic Development. It was later presented more widely by Walter Heller and Arthur Okun, chairmen of the CEA under Presidents Kennedy and Johnson.

5. There is nothing significant in the particular percentage chosen. It could be a full-employment figure, such as 4% unemployment. It could be a low employment figure, say 8% unemployment. The important point is that, by not varying with cyclical fluctuations, it sets aside those cyclical effects of the economy on the deficit.

6. Generally calculated at the 6% rate used for some time by the Bureau of Economic Analysis or at the fairly similar "standardized employment" rates provided by the Congressional Budget Office.

7. See Eisner (1986, 1989, 1991, 1992, 1994a, and 1994b), and Eisner and Pieper (1984, 1988, and 1992), for example.

8. This section is based on findings reported in considerable detail in Eisner (1995a). A brief popular presentation of some of the arguments is to be found in Eisner (1995b).

9. See Friedman (1968) and Phelps (1968).

10. People who quit their jobs or leave school to start work generally don't get a job immediately. This portion of the workforce (perhaps 2-3%) is referred to as the "frictionally" jobless.

11. Congressional Budget Office (1994), p. 62 for 1993; raised to 6.0%, based on new calculations of the unemployment rate, for 1994.

12. Thus, simulations over the period 1994 (fourth quarter) to 1999 (fourth quarter) of a major one percentage point reduction below its NAIRU in the married-male unemployment rate, used by the CBO in estimating its equations, had inflation rising about 3 percentage points after five years. This is not clearly an inadmissible tradeoff. One percentage point of married-male unemployment might well correspond to 1½ percentage points of total unemployment. By Okun's law this would correspond to some 3 percentage points of GDP, or about $200 billion of output. Would 3 percentage points of steady inflation be too much to accept for that much more output?

13. See Chirinko (1995).

14. Shown in considerable detail in Eisner (1995a).

15. The Employment Act of 1946 and the Balanced Growth and Full Employment Act (Humphrey-Hawkins) of 1978.

References

Chirinko, Robert S. 1995. "Non-Convexities, Labor Hoarding, Technology Shocks, and Procyclical Productivity: A Structural Econometric Approach," *Journal of Econometrics.*

Congressional Budget Office. 1994, 1995. *The Economic and Budget Outlook: An Update.* Washington, D.C.: Congressional Budget Office.

Eisner, Robert. 1986. *How Real Is the Federal Deficit?* New York: Free Press.

Eisner, Robert. 1989. "Budget Deficits: Rhetoric and Reality." *Journal of Economic Perspectives,* Vol. 3, Spring, pp. 73-93.

Eisner, Robert. 1991. "Our Real Deficits." *Journal of the American Planning Association,* Vol. 57, Spring, pp. 131-135.

Eisner, Robert. 1992. "U.S. National Saving and Budget Deficits." In G. Epstein and H. Gintis, eds., *The Political Economy of Investment, Saving and Finance: A Global Perspective.* Project of the World Institute for Development and Economic Research (WIDER), United Nations University. Helsinki, Finland. Manuscript copy.

Eisner, Robert. 1994a. "National Saving and Budget Deficits." *The Review of Economics and Statistics,* February, pp. 181-186.

Eisner, Robert. 1994b. *The Misunderstood Economy: What Counts and How to Count It.* Boston: Harvard Business School Press.

Eisner, Robert. 1995a. "A New View of the NAIRU." Northwestern University, presented to the 7th World Congress of the Econometrics Society, Tokyo, August 1995.

Eisner, Robert. 1995b. "Our NAIRU Limit: The Governing Myth of Economic Policy." *American Prospect,* Spring 1995.

Eisner, Robert and Paul J. Pieper. 1984. "A New View of the Federal Debt and Budget Deficits." *American Economic Review,* Vol. 74, March, pp. 11-29.

Eisner, Robert and Paul J. Pieper. 1988. "Deficits, Monetary Policy and Real Economic Activity." In K.J. Arrow and M.J. Boskin, eds., *The Economics of Public Debt.* Macmillan Press in association with the International Economic Association, London.

Eisner, Robert and Paul J. Pieper. 1992. "National Saving and the Twin Deficits: Myth and Reality." In J. H. Gapinski, ed. *The Economics of Saving.* Boston: Kluwer Academic Publishers.

Friedman, Milton. 1968. "The Role of Monetary Policy." *American Economic Review,* Vol. 58, March, pp. 1-17.

Office of Management and Budget. 1995a. *Budget of the United States Government, Fiscal Year 1996.* Washington, D.C.: U.S. Government Printing Office.

Office of Management and Budget. 1995b. *Budget of the United States Government, Fiscal Year 1996, Analytical Perspectives.* Washington, D.C.: U.S. Government Printing Office.

Office of Management and Budget. 1995c. *Budget of the United States Government, Fiscal Year 1996, Historical Tables.* Washington, D.C.: U.S. Government Printing Office.

Phelps, Edmund S. 1968. "Money-Wage Dynamics and Labor-Market Equilibrium." *Journal of Political Economy,* Vol. 76, August, Part 2, pp. 678-711.

CHAPTER 2

Public Investment

Budgeting the Old-Fashioned Way

by Todd Schafer

LISTEN TO C-SPAN FOR A HALF-HOUR STRETCH ANY TIME DAY OR NIGHT and you will hear words close to these: "You people out there have to balance your checkbooks—why can't the federal government?" The implication, of course, is that ordinary people like us have, out of necessity, developed the discipline to keep our finances in order, while the federal government recklessly spends its way into a $3.5 trillion debt. But the fact is, the federal government does balance its checkbook, in the same way we all do—by borrowing.

Borrowing is a way of life for most households. Despite our deeply held aversion to debt, we eagerly borrow for the big, important purchases—homes, cars, college—that allow us to prosper. We avoid borrowing (the banks probably won't let us anyway) and instead use cash for day-to-day expenses like food or movies. Here, the comparison with the government breaks down. Households (and businesses) borrow for particular things that will provide long-term benefits; the government borrows when it runs out of money. Perhaps the oft-repeated line should be: "You borrow when it makes sense—why doesn't the government?"

Sensible borrowing is crucial to securing a prosperous future for a household, business, or government. Without debt, cash would be required for every purchase. How many families could afford to purchase a home or send their children to college if they had to pay cash? Would these families be better off as a result—uneducated and renting but debt free? How many businesses would ever grow if they delayed making capital expenditures until cash was available? Debt in this sense is good. It allows us to make important investments in our futures.

Todd Schafer is a policy analyst specializing in the federal budget at the Economic Policy Institute.

The federal government undergoes no such deliberations in making its borrowing decisions. It decides how much to tax, how much to spend, and the difference is made up in borrowing. This "system" results in thoughtless budgeting, and it leaves us with a debt that doesn't necessarily produce higher national income in the future. Hence, we say, let the federal government borrow, but require it to keep its books in the same way that virtually every citizen, business, and state or local government does: credit for investment, cash for consumption.

Living for Today and Tomorrow

Lumping all kinds of spending together results not only in arbitrary deficit levels but also in distorted spending decisions that increasingly shortchange our future. In deciding which projects to fund, it is usually preferable politically to get as big a bang up front as possible. When investment and consumption compete for the same dollars, investment, with its bigger but slower payback, suffers.

For example, consider the tradeoff between a $1 million bridge that takes, say, four years to complete and an annual $100,000 farm subsidy. On the face of it, the subsidy payment is cheaper, and perhaps the better buy in an age of budget austerity. Over what would have been the 50-year life of the bridge, however, those subsidy payments will cost five times what the bridge did, while failing to offer any of its productivity benefits. Nevertheless, because the federal budget requires payment up front for every item, the price tag on the bridge may prove prohibitive.

The point is not that subsidy payments are without merit; rather, that it is a mistake to finance investments in the same way as consumption items. This distorted bookkeeping hampers the federal government's willingness to invest in itself and has dire consequences for our economic future.

Distorted Perceptions

Another bad consequence of the way the federal government keeps its books is that it distorts public perceptions about what shape the government is in. Because assets are ignored in federal budget accounting, the budget debate tends to focus only on the annual changes in liabilities and the debt. Drawing our attention only to this side of the ledger, politicians and talk-show hosts have propounded the disturbing assertion that every child born in America begins life with an $18,000-or-so debt. In reality, however, the value of the federal government's assets is comparable (government spending, if it is not wasteful, does buy something after all), so each child is born essentially debt-free.[1]

Deficits and surpluses as reflected in the current "cash flow" budget are not unimportant: they are essential tools for economic stability. Deficit spending when the economy is sluggish can spur production and create jobs; pulling back when the economy is chugging along nicely can keep it from overheating. But deficits alone do not tell us much about the long-term health of the economy. The more important question is what we buy with the deficit spending.

The Case for Public Investment

Economists agree that in order to reverse the decades-long slide in American living standards, we must become more productive. Since 1973, the year that wages began to slip, productivity growth has been barely a third of what it was before. Clearly, as productivity lagged, so did our paychecks.

The key to boosting productivity is investment. If workers are given better tools, they will be more productive. These tools come in two types—private and public—and common sense says we need both. Truckers, for example, need good trucks (private investment) as well as good roads (public investment) to work efficiently.

In 1995, more than 400 prominent American economists, including six Nobel Prize winners, signed a letter to Congress and the President warning of the economic dangers of neglecting the public infrastructure. A glance at the recent history of the world's major economies bears out what these economists have found: countries with the highest rates of infrastructure investment have the highest rates of productivity growth (**Figure A**).[2]

Our own recent history tells the same story. During decades when the United States built up its infrastructure (as in the 1960s) productivity climbed; when we neglected it (as in the 1980s) productivity suffered (**Figure B**).

FIGURE A
Public Investment and Productivity in the G-7, 1978-90

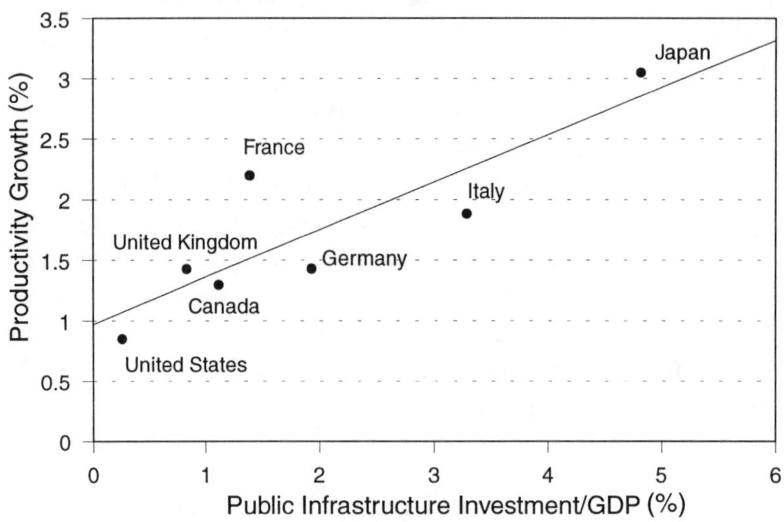

Source: Update of Aschauer (1990) analysis.

FIGURE B
Thirty-Five Years of Public Investment, 1965-2000

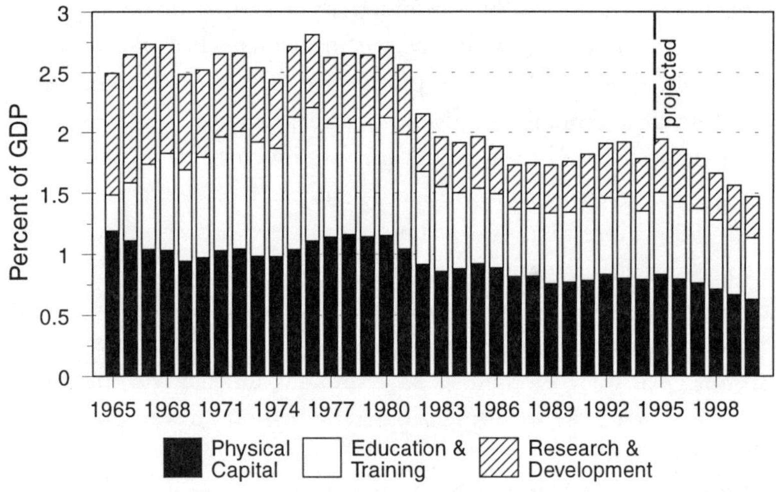

Source: EPI analysis of Administration's FY96 budget proposal.

Note: The GOP alternative, embodied in the FY96 budget resolution, would produce an investment level of less than 1.3% of GDP. The majority of the additional cuts would come from education and training.

According to a survey prepared by the Economic Policy Institute in 1991, an additional $60 billion per year is needed to revive our historical investment standards.[3] Achieving the levels of investment of our major international competitors would require double that sum. An update of that earlier survey—adjusting for inflation, growth, and changes in investment outlays—would produce comparable numbers today.

INVESTMENT IN THE FEDERAL BUDGET

How could the investment shortfall be so great? Hasn't "cut and invest" been a theme since the early days of the Clinton Administration? Such were the initial goals, but in the context of a shrinking discretionary budget—from 9.1% of gross domestic product in 1992 to 7.5% in 1996 and to a projected 6.6% in 2000—cutting has applied to investment as well. Thus far, "cut and invest" has succeeded merely in keeping investment at the historically low points hit during the 1980s.

Unfortunately, the budget outlook for the rest of the century is gloomy. According to the Administration's own FY96 budget path, not including any further cuts aimed at achieving a balanced budget, federal investment as a share of GDP is projected to fall steadily through the turn of the century, to a level markedly lower than in the depths of the Reagan Administration. Subsequent cuts by the Republican Congress during the FY96 budget debate will produce the lowest levels of investment since early in the Eisenhower Administration.

Given our current approach to budgeting, this trend is inevitable. Much as the Administration may try to spare "investment" from the budget knife, competition with other spending priorities will interfere. And since the Congress and White House have agreed that shrinking the deficit is our No. 1 priority, the theme of "shared sacrifice" has come to include investment.

Like a household or business, the federal government must find a way to finance its needed investment. And like a household or business, the federal government should look to its credit line.

Investment Budgeting: From Tax-and-Spend to Finance-and-Invest

The federal budget equals about one-fifth the size of the U.S. economy, so there is no disputing the broad economic role it plays. The important decision in this context concerns the proper size of the federal deficit and the debt. That is, we need to ask not, "how do we get rid of the deficit?" but rather, "how big should the deficit be?"

According to Robert Eisner (in the previous chapter), there is a simple answer: we need a deficit big enough to ensure healthy growth but small enough to prevent debt from accumulating even faster. As a rule of thumb, Eisner recommends that we keep the ratio of debt to GDP stable or let it fall gradually. In today's dollars, that means a deficit of roughly $200 billion.[4] The Eisner recommendation leads to our first rule of budgeting:

- *Budgeting Rule One:* The federal budget should run a deficit that stabilizes or gradually shrinks the debt-to-GDP ratio over the long term, thus insuring that both the debt burden is forever tolerable or diminishing and that the economy gets sufficient economic support.

The second economic function of the federal budget is to determine spending priorities. Some federal functions—such as providing a social safety net, for example—address today's economy; other functions—such as providing and maintaining the nation's physical, human, and technological infrastructure—concern themselves with the economy of the future. As noted above, it is a mistake to finance both government functions in the same way. Consumption or operating expenditures should be paid for in cash, and investment should be financed with debt. Investment budgeting, an accounting framework that provides for this distinction, is a means to ensure that the future is not shortchanged.

Investment budgeting allows investment projects to be financed over their useful lives. When a business is deciding whether to upgrade its computers, for example, the overall purchase price is only one consideration. The business also determines whether the monthly (or quarterly) cost of financing the purchase is justified by the expected monthly (or quarterly) efficiency gain.

The federal government needs to be equally rational in its bookkeeping. Rather than being stymied by the sticker price of a new bridge or education program, the Congress should compare the payoff to the cost. Besides asking ourselves whether we can afford to make an investment, we should also be asking ourselves whether we can afford *not* to, since the payoff easily may be bigger than the costs.

Thus, the federal government needs to follow the lead of business and most state governments by setting up separate accounts for investment and operating expenditures. The operating account should be set up on a pay-as-you-go basis, with income roughly equaling outlays over time.[5] This is not to say that new consumption-spending priorities must be ruled out. Rather, this accounting method requires that new consumption priorities be paid for, either with new revenues or reduced spending elsewhere.

The investment account—$138 billion of federal investment expenditures in FY96[6]—would be financed by borrowing. For our purposes, then, a budget deficit in FY96 of $138 billion would be considered "balanced." This leads to our second new budgeting rule.

- *Budgeting Rule Two:* The budget should be divided into an investment account and an operating account. The operating account should be on a pay-as-you-go basis, roughly balanced over time. The investment account should be financed by borrowing, constrained only by the rule that the overall deficit not raise the amount of the national debt relative to GDP.

Taken together, these two rules would create federal budgets that look dramatically different from today's. While the FY96 deficit level is on target—below the $200 billion needed to keep the debt stable at about 52% of GDP—the makeup of the budget would need to change. Since all borrowing must occur only in the investment account, we would need to increase investment spending by about $60 billion (the difference between current investment and the allowable deficit) and decrease operating expenditures by the same amount. Coincidentally, this level of investment would return total federal investment to its pre-Reagan level.

The largest complication here is identifying $60 billion in savings from the operating budget. But the sources of such funding exist; they can be found in (1) a major overhaul of the nation's health care system (see the chapter in this volume on health care by Edith Rasell); (2) cuts in defense spending (see the chapter on defense conversion by Michael Oden and Ann Markusen); (3) an expansionary monetary policy that would dramatically reduce the interest burden and spur growth (see the chapters by Robert Eisner and James Galbraith); and (4) new taxes or closing of existing loopholes.

The proposal above is not, strictly speaking, a capital budget, because it does not require that depreciation of existing capital be captured in the operating account. Moving to such a system might be feasible over an extended period, but doing so in the near term would force dangerously contractionary budgets and violate Budgeting Rule One: the debt-to-GDP ratio should be stable or *gradually* lowered.

Moreover, it is appropriate that the federal budget differ somewhat from the capital budget of a household or business. As Richard Musgrave, the dean of American public finance economists, once wrote, "...as distinct from the balance sheet of a private firm, the purpose of a public capital budget is *not* to test the financial soundness of the government by balancing assets against liabilities (public debt) but to measure the government's contribution to the economy's capital stock."

This proposal would not, in itself, automatically lead to a conservative or liberal economic policy. Conservatives have resisted such budgeting principles because the current focus on the deficit gives them a convenient target with which to attack efforts to expand spending on domestic programs. Yet some of the best work on capital budgeting and government balance sheets has been done by conservative economists, who see these techniques as a way of keeping down entitlement spending.

Liberals tend to be unenthusiastic about capital budgets because they see a bias for "bricks and mortar" over human capital and technology. This plan answers that concern by counting investments in human capital—that is, education and training—and civilian R&D in our definition of investment. Liberals may also detect a bias against entitlements, but entitlement spending need not suffer in this plan. Investment budgeting does not preclude entitlement spending; it merely requires that it be paid for. In fact, pressure to constrain entitlement costs could actually result in healthy reforms that expand the scope of existing programs. Consider health care, the only truly problematic entitlement area. As Edith Rasell argues in her chapter on health care, the only way to control costs over the long-term is to expand the public program. In short, investment budgeting might force not smaller entitlement programs but better ones.

Finally, investment budgeting makes no real distinction between the relative merits of any two potential expenditures. It does not, for example, tell us whether any given farm subsidy is less or more valuable than any given bridge. It simply accounts for the different costs in a way that underscores the fact that the bridge will not have to be replaced every year.

Next Steps

Because this proposal is a dramatic departure from our current budgeting practices, we need to move toward it gradually. A proper goal would be to have the system in place by the year 2000. But our investment needs are pressing now. As a transition to an investment budget, the federal government should establish an Investment Bank of the type long advocated by financier Felix Rohatyn and economist Carol O'Cleireacain. Based on the widely accepted business tradition of financing physical capital investments over the life of the capital, this system would:

- create an off-budget fund, financed by the sale of bonds backed by a fixed, long-term, dedicated funding stream.
- undertake a major capital improvement program over a shorter period to be financed by the fund.

This arrangement would permit a much-needed investment catchup effort within the confines of fiscal responsibility. (It could be amended to provide a second dedicated revenue stream to finance investments in human capital.) Over the life of the bank, the program would pay for itself, including interest. To facilitate the transition to full investment budgeting, the bank could start out with $15 billion in FY97, increasing the amount to the needed $60 billion by FY2000. At that time, the bank could be incorporated into the overall investment budgeting scheme.

In a 1992 proposal, O'Cleireacain recommended that the dedicated funding stream be generated by a gradual increase in the gasoline tax. While this would have the advantage of mirroring the current funding method of the Highway Trust Fund, we would opt for a more progressive method. Possibilities include a limitation on the tax benefit of itemized deductions in the personal income tax or a small tax on securities transactions. The political difficulties facing any new tax—even one targeted on the well-to-do—are substantial. However, public opinion polls have shown that people support new taxes that are earmarked for a specific public good.

Conclusion

Politicians of both parties go to great lengths to appear "fiscally responsible." Perhaps responsibility can be redefined to accurately reflect the realities of investment and debt, and perhaps then the federal government can be allowed to operate on a sound business basis, an outcome so fervently desired by fiscal conservatives. The height of irresponsibility is the notion that a business or government cannot "afford" to invest. Such is the thinking that undoes corporate titans and leaves our grandchildren debt free and dirt poor.

Notes

1. Schafer 1994.

2. Research into the economic effects of investment in human capital (i.e., education and training) and civilian research and development have found similar productivity payoffs.

3. Faux and Schafer 1991.

4. Based on a publicly held national debt of $3.6 trillion and a GDP of $7.0 trillion this year. Anticipating GDP of $7.4 trillion next year allows us to add $200 billion to the national debt and still keep the ratio the same.

5. We say "roughly" to preserve the flexibility of the federal government to intervene with fiscal contractions or expansions during economic swings.

6. Some would argue that we should include another $91 billion in military expenditures for hardware, R&D, etc. We oppose such an approach, since these purchases offer little in long-term productivity growth for the private economy.

References

Aschauer, David. 1990. *Public Investment and Private Sector Growth.* Washington, D.C.: Economic Policy Institute.

Baker, Dean and Todd Schafer. 1995. *The Case for Public Investment.* Washington, D.C.: Economic Policy Institute.

Eisner, Robert. 1994. *The Misunderstood Economy: What Counts and How to Count It.* Cambridge, Mass.: Harvard University Press.

Erenburg, Sharon. 1993. *The Relationship Between Public and Private Investment.* Working Paper No. 65. Annandale-on-Hudson, N.Y.: Jerome Levy Economics Institute.

Faux, Jeff, Dean Baker, and Todd Schafer. 1994. *Back to Investment: A Proposal to Create a Capital Investment Fund.* Briefing Paper. Washington, D.C.: Economic Policy Institute.

Faux, Jeff and Todd Schafer. 1991. *Increasing Public Investment: New Budget Priorities for Economic Growth in the Post-Cold War World.* Washington, D.C.: Economic Policy Institute.

Office of Management and Budget. 1995. *Budget of the United States Government, Fiscal Year 1996, Historical Tables.* Washington, D.C.: U.S. Government Printing Office.

Schafer, Todd. 1994. *America's Inheritance: More Than Just Debt.* Briefing Paper. Washington, D.C.: Economic Policy Institute.

CHAPTER 3

SOCIAL SECURITY
Don't Mess With Success

by Dean Baker

THE DRIVE TO BALANCE THE FEDERAL BUDGET HAS FOUND AN EASY target in the programs that benefit the elderly. And why not? Social Security and Medicare combined consumed 32% of federal spending in 1994; by 2030, we are warned, these two programs will devour 64% of spending unless something is done to rein them in. It follows that the consequent burden for future generations will be enormous. For example, the "generational accounts" in the President's budget show future generations paying 84% of their labor income in taxes over the course of their lifetimes, more than double what current generations pay now. We have also been warned that retiring baby boomers will soon bankrupt Social Security, leaving nothing for "Generation X-ers" and their progeny.

The bottom line from the budget cutters is that, because of our irresponsible spending today, elderly people in the future will have to accept a far lower standard of living than they enjoy now. Apparently the technological wonders of the 21st century will not be wondrous enough to allow for a decent retirement for American workers.

But the facts are otherwise. There is no reason to deny retirees the benefits they have worked a lifetime to acquire.

- By the Social Security Administration's own pessimistic projections, the fund will have a positive balance for the next 35 years. With minor adjustments, it can remain in the black indefinitely. Furthermore, if the fund used projections that were more in line with economic reality, the perceived threat to the program would disappear altogether.
- There is no real basis for the claim that government programs that

Dean Baker is a macroeconomist at the Economic Policy Institute.

benefit the elderly are placing an excessive tax burden on future generations. On the contrary, future generations should be able to enjoy substantially higher after-tax incomes than do current generations.

Social Security is a social insurance program that Americans can point to without apology. Unfortunately, both Democrats and Republicans have done their constituents a gross disservice by denigrating the health of the program and obscuring the benefits it provides.

SOCIAL SECURITY: THE FUND IS SOUND, THE CRITICISMS AREN'T

Every year the Social Security Administration provides projections of the balance and cash flow of the Social Security trust fund for the next 75 years. These projections are based on assumptions about population growth, economic growth, immigration, life expectancies, and other relevant variables. According to the 1995 report, the trust fund will have a positive balance until 2030. This means that the sum of all the taxes paid into the fund and the interest these deposits earn will exceed all the benefits paid out until the year 2030. After 2030 there will still be money to pay benefits: taxes will continue to come in, although they will be insufficient to meet the full benefit level specified in current law. Meeting such a shortfall would require either a tax increase or benefit reduction at that point. The fund would not, therefore, *go bankrupt*, as is often claimed,[1] but would require an adjustment of some sort. For example, a series of payroll tax increases of 0.1% per year beginning in 2010 and continuing to 2040 (for a total of 3% of payroll) would keep the fund in the black indefinitely, with no cut in benefits whatsoever. Would a tax hike of this size impose an onerous burden? Applied to the Social Security projections, such tax increases would still allow our children's and grandchildren's *after tax* wages to grow 0.9% a year, so that in 2040 wages should be about 50% higher than they are now. This hardly seems like impoverishment.

The dire projections for Social Security appear even less so when one looks at the assumptions upon which the projections are based. In preparing its report, the Social Security Administration has relied on assumptions that are so negative as to be almost absurd. For example, the size of the labor force relative to the size of the retired population is projected to fall, from five workers for every one retiree now, to 3.5 workers per retiree in 2030. Such projections imply an enormous labor shortage, where workers have their pick of jobs. Remarkably, the projections do not see the economy responding in typical supply-and-demand fashion, that is, with either increased wage growth or increased immigration. If the projected labor shortage led to either the bidding up of wages of the available workforce or to increased immigration to fill unwanted jobs, then Social Security obligations could be met with no tax increase at all.

Some critics of Social Security ignore the fact that the fund has accumulated a large surplus over the last decade, and that this surplus is continuing to grow. Instead they focus only on the annual income-benefit flow. Currently the flow is strongly positive—annual Social Security taxes now exceed annual benefit payments by approximately $60 billion. This annual surplus will dwindle when the baby boom generation starts to retire, and it should turn into an annual deficit by around 2013. At that point, Social Security will no longer be reducing the overall government deficit. Instead, it will begin drawing on the money it loaned to the federal government over the previous three decades.

It is possible that the government's obligation to pay back the money it borrowed from the Social Security fund could pose a problem in the same way that paying back the money borrowed from private creditors could pose a problem. Just as private creditors do, the Social Security fund lends money to the government and receives government bonds in exchange. An inability on the part of the government to make good on these bonds and pay back its debt would be a problem of the government's overall fiscal policy, not of the Social Security fund. The fund simply would be drawing on the money it saved with the government in anticipation of the day when baby boomers started to retire.

Three Bad Remedies to a Non-Problem

If the Social Security fund is basically sound, then there is no reason to look to the program as a place for budget cuts. In fact, since the fund is already running a surplus, cutting benefits without cutting taxes means increasing our use of designated Social Security taxes to finance other areas of the budget. This kind of shell game—generating even bigger surpluses in Social Security in order to fund regular government spending—would be extraordinarily dishonest, and it is doubtful that it would be politically possible if the public were aware of it.[2]

Nonetheless, the budget cutters are on the attack. The three proposals most often mentioned are:

(1) Raising the retirement age. Since people are living longer, shouldn't they take some of the burden off Social Security by working longer? Many baby boomers probably don't know it, but this change has already been made. The retirement age is scheduled to rise from 65 to 66 over the period 2000-2005, then to 67 in the period 2017-22. Having these changes take place earlier is unfair for two reasons. First, it is cruel to push back a person's retirement date just as they approach it. For example, this could mean telling a worker preparing to retire at 65 in 1998 that he or she will have to wait two more years. Second, life expectancies vary enormously by race and class. Raising the retirement age would disproportionately deny benefits to the poor and minorities (the life expectancy of black males, for example, is only 65) and to people performing demanding physical work who have to stop working at an earlier age.

(2) Reducing or denying benefits for the well-off. If people are well off, the argument goes, they don't need giveaways from the government. There are three reasons why means testing for Social Security is a bad approach. First, in contrast to means-tested welfare programs, people *earn* Social Security benefits by virtue of their having paid into the fund, just as they earn interest on government bonds by lending the government money. Moreover, the claim that people are receiving benefits in excess of their contributions is false. For example, the accumulated tax payments plus interest (calculated at a 3% real rate of growth) of a person retiring in 1994 who worked for 45 years and always earned the average wage would finance that worker's benefits for 16 years. The level increases to 21 years for a person retiring in 1999 and to 26 years for a person retiring in 2004. Since wealthy people have paid into the Social Security fund like everyone else, it makes no more sense to deny them their Social Security benefits than it does to deny them interest on their bonds. In any case, the benefit structure of Social Security is already quite progressive: the wealthy typically get a much lower return on their tax payments than do

the poor or middle class.

Second, it would be difficult to construct a form of means testing that would raise significant revenue for anyone except the tax shelter industry. Evading the cutoff lines would be quite simple. For example, a retiree with substantial interest income could escape means testing by investing in assets that yielded capital gains instead.

Third, means testing would undermine support for the program. Presently, Social Security enjoys extremely wide support because virtually everyone benefits from it. At the same time, it is by far our most successful anti-poverty program, raising approximately 15 million people above the poverty line. If a significant segment of the population were excluded from its benefits, or found themselves confronting a convoluted means-testing formula, support for the program would plummet. As Social Security took on more of the characteristics of a welfare program and less those of a retirement plan, the quality of the service and the value of the benefits would be likely to deteriorate dramatically. If the experience of the last 15 years has taught us anything, it is that progressives cannot hope to protect programs that are perceived as welfare for the poor. Means testing is the first step toward transforming a remarkably popular and successful national retirement plan into a woefully inadequate band-aid for the indigent elderly. If we want to get more revenue out of the wealthy there is a simple way that doesn't jeopardize Social Security: tax them.

(3) Reducing the adjustment for inflation. Some powerful Washington policy makers, chief among them Federal Reserve Board Chairman Alan Greenspan, have put forth the argument that the consumer price index (CPI) overstates inflation and that, therefore, government payouts like Social Security that are based on the CPI are too high. Shaving a percentage point off the annual cost-of-living increase in Social Security and other programs would cut billions from federal spending with relatively little political pain, since most recipients probably wouldn't realize their benefits had been cut. (In current Washington political jargon this wouldn't even be a cut, just a "reduction in the growth of benefits.")

But contrary to the wishes of Greenspan and others, there is little clear evidence that the CPI actually overstates inflation. In fact, most research on the issue has indicated that, if anything, the CPI *understates* the increase in the cost of living for the elderly, since that group spends a high proportion of its income on two categories of expenditures for which prices are increasing rapidly: health care and housing.

Furthermore, under-adjusting for inflation would lead to a cumulative decline in benefits the longer a person lives. The original level of benefits a person receives when he or she retires is in no way affected by the inflation measure (rather, it is based on the average wage prevailing at the time). However, if a person lives 30 years into retirement and receives 1% less each year because he or she is not fully compensated for inflation, by the 30th year the real value of the benefits will have fallen by nearly 30%. Such a decrease would be sufficient to push many of the elderly into poverty as they approach the end of their lives. Does the government really want to be creating such incentives for an early death?

Altering the inflation adjustment for Social Security is just one more bad solution to a non-problem. The basic point is that Social Security isn't broke, so we shouldn't let them "fix" it.

Generational Accounts: Frightening the Kids for Nothing

Most of the techniques used by economists are complex and obscure and never get beyond academic conferences and journals. However, sometimes their equations escape from the lab and terrorize the population at large. Such is the case with "generational accounting." It is utterly harmless as a tool used by economists, in an academic setting, to find new and unusual ways to analyze the budget. But in the hands of budget cutters, wielded to create fears about horrific future tax burdens, it is a menace to society.

Generational accounting is a technique for measuring the net lifetime tax burdens for particular age groups. Here is a rough idea of how it works: let's say you are 35 years old, a member of the generation born around 1960. Generational accounting adds up all the taxes, of all types, you will pay over your lifetime (assuming no changes in government policy), and subtracts from that the total value of the government benefits, like Medicare, welfare payments, and Social Security, you are likely to receive. That net amount, divided by your lifetime labor income (not your income from saving or investment, but just what you earn from working), is your lifetime net tax burden. For someone born in 1960, the latest estimates from the Office of Management and Budget (1994) peg the lifetime tax burden at 35%. It is also possible to calculate an average lifetime net tax burden for all future generations.

This accounting exercise has been included as a chapter in the President's official budget analysis since the 1993 budget. The most recent numbers show gradually increasing lifetime net tax burdens, from 31% for someone born in 1930, to the 35% mentioned above for 1960, to 37% for 1970, and eventually to an astronomical 84% for all future generations. The lesson we are expected to learn from the generational accounts is clear: unless we can control government spending, government spending will bury us.

There are many reasons why these numbers should not be taken seriously. As might be surmised from the description of generational accounting above, the technique is extremely sensitive to the assumptions one makes about the future (for example, with how much confidence can you estimate the value of your own income in 2025?) and to how one defines government benefits. In some key areas the generational accountants are quite wide of the mark, and substituting more realistic assumptions into the analysis brings the estimates of lifetime net tax burdens out of the disaster range.

The most basic assumption is the rate of discount used in the analysis. A rate of discount is a way of making future taxes or earnings comparable to what they're worth now. Economists usually discount money at a point in the future, because it is usually possible to get some return on the money through time. For example, if the going real rate of interest (over and above inflation) is 3%, and you put aside $100 this year, you will have $103 next year. Thus, having $100 this year is about as good as having $103 next year. To look at the discount from the opposite perspective—how much you need today to have $100 next year—you would discount next year's money by 3% (divide it by 1.03), to get a value of $97.09.

While discounting is a standard economic technique, the rate chosen is very important, particularly when it is used to discount *all* future earnings, as is the case with generational accounting. In deriving their estimate of an 84% tax burden for future generations, the generational accountants use a 6% real discount rate. This means that, after adjusting for inflation, they still discount earnings by 6% per year. This is an extremely high rate, which has the effect of devaluing the future. For example, at a 6% discount rate, the amount of money the people in the United States earn over the next 17 years will be worth more than what the generational accountants project people living in the United States will earn *for the rest of time.*[3]

By comparison, the average real interest rate on government debt over the last 15 years has been approximately 3%; over the whole postwar period it has averaged less than 2%. Switching from a 6% real discount rate to a 3% rate lowers the lifetime net tax burden for future generations from 84% to approximately 45%. At a 2% rate it falls to less than 38%, roughly where it is now. But there are yet other problems with the assumptions.

The generational accountants treat the government's Medicare expenditures as though the government were handing cash to the elderly. Yet education expenditures, from Head Start spending to funding of state universities to subsidies for student loans, are not counted as benefits to the young. The generational accountants acknowledge that the correct procedure would be to treat educational expenditures in the same manner as health care, but they have not yet applied this method themselves.[4] When this error is corrected, the lifetime future tax burden falls approximately 32 percentage points, from 84% to 52% of future labor income.

Finally, the generational accounting story includes a scenario for health care disaster that can never come to pass. The projections in the official generational accounts imply that by the year 2030 a family of four earning the median income will pay 97% of its income for health care. A couple over age 65 earning the median would pay 134% of its income for health care. With that kind of health care burden, taxes may be the least of our problems. Health care costs are indeed rising rapidly, well beyond the ordinary rate of inflation, but the economy would collapse before costs reached such a point. In any event, the problem is health care, not the government programs that pay for it. One of the tragedies of the current obsession with cutting entitlements is that the looming disaster of exploding health care costs has been removed from public view. If health care costs could be reined in to the point where they grow only with the aging of the population and the overall inflation rate—and wouldn't this make a great agenda for the budget conscious—then the lifetime tax rate for future generations falls by 29 percentage points, from 84% to 55%.

When the change in these three assumptions are taken together (i.e., a more reasonable real discount rate, treating education in the same way as health care, and removing the health care disaster scenario) the lifetime tax burden falls 64 percentage points, from 84% to 20% of future labor income. These corrections should allow our children and grandchildren to sleep more soundly, indeed even more soundly than we do today.

The Curse of Success

Ultimately, the real problem with Social Security is not that it doesn't work, but rather that it works so well. It is a government-run program that does almost exactly what it is supposed to do. With administrative expenses that are less than 0.9% of benefits, it is run with a minimal amount of bureaucracy and is subject to very little fraud and abuse. As a result of the program, tens of millions of Americans have enjoyed a decent retirement. Thus, it is a prime target for conservatives and neo-liberals. After all, it might be dangerous if people thought the government could do some things right.

There is no reason to fundamentally alter Social Security. The fund should be sound for the indefinite future, and at worst small adjustments will be needed beginning in 15 or 20 years. The problems that may or may not exist with the rest of the budget should not be used as a pretext to deny benefits to people who have paid for them in good faith.

Notes

1. A business that, when faced with expenses exceeding revenues, could always adjust one or the other to make ends meet would never be described as "bankrupt," yet this word has inexplicably caught on as a way to describe the plight of Social Security.

2. The fact that the Social Security levy is among the most regressive of federal taxes makes the use of its surplus, rather than more progressive income taxes, to fund general expenditures particularly odious.

3. To see how this could be so, use a calculator to compute the discounting of wages along the lines of the equation offered above. If $30,000 is the average wage now, at a 6% discount earning the same wage next year would be worth $28,302 this year ($30,000/1.06). The same wage earned 100 years from now would be worth just $88 this year ($\$30,000/1.06^{100}$).

4. The concept of generational accounting was developed in a series of technical papers, including Auerbach, Gokhale, and Kotlikoff (1991). The authors' comments about education spending appear in that paper in a footnote on page 72.

The way the generational accounts are currently calculated, higher expenditures for education *increase* the lifetime net tax burden of future generations by increasing the debt that is handed down to them.

References

Auerbach, A.J., J. Gokhale, and L.J. Kotlikoff. 1991. "Generational Accounts: A Meaningful Alternative to Deficit Accounting." In David Bradford, ed., *Tax Policy and the Economy*. National Bureau of Economic Research, Volume 5. Cambridge, Mass.: MIT Press.

Baker, Dean. 1995. *Revising the Consumer Price Index: Correcting Bias or Biased Corrections?* Briefing Paper. Washington, D.C.: Economic Policy Institute.

Baker, Dean. 1995. *Robbing the Cradle? A Critical Assessment of Generational Accounting.* Washington, D.C.: Economic Policy Institute.

Mishel, Lawrence, and Jared Bernstein. 1994. *The State of Working America 1994-95.* Economic Policy Institute Series. Armonk, N.Y.: M.E. Sharpe.

CHAPTER 4

HEALTH CARE REFORM
It's Time for Single-Payer

by Edith Rasell

REMEMBER HEALTH CARE REFORM? IN THE EARLY DAYS OF THE CLINTON Administration it was as ubiquitous as the weather—everybody talked about it, but in the end, nothing was done. Now, there is talk about slashing the Medicare and Medicaid programs, but hardly anyone even mentions comprehensive reform and, because of our inaction, the crisis has only worsened.

In the absence of major reform, policy makers and politicians are turning once again to incremental changes in the health care system. Insurance industry reforms and "medical savings accounts" are put forth as ways to rein in costs and improve coverage in the private sector. Cuts in Medicare and Medicaid are proposed as a way to curb mushrooming federal spending. But the problems in the U.S. health care system—lack of universal health insurance coverage, high and rising costs, and inequitable financing—are not the result of minor aberrations that can be alleviated by fine tuning or by limiting access to care. Rather, they are the predictable and unavoidable result of a system in which health care and health insurance are supplied primarily through a market, that is, through a process of buying and selling. Attempts to solve our health care problems using market-based approaches or reforms that only tinker at the margins are doomed to failure.

Beyond our shores, our industrial competitors have devised regulatory mechanisms to prevent many of the problems common in the United States. A single-payer, Canadian-style system, as has been proposed for the United States, would provide universal insurance coverage and ac-

Edith Rasell is a health economist at the Economic Policy Institute.

cess, contain costs, and improve equity in the financing of health care while preserving the private practice of medicine and choice of provider. Given our growing numbers of uninsured and the federal and state budget crises stemming in large part from rising health costs, it is essential that such a system be implemented soon.

Health Expenditures and the Federal Budget

Between 1989 and 1993, Medicaid spending grew an average of 16.1% a year.[1] This rapid growth was due to expanded criteria for eligibility, the recession (which raised the number of people who were eligible), and rising prices and volumes of services. Medicare spending rose rapidly as well, growing 10.3% a year due to increasing numbers of elderly, rising prices, and greater volumes of services received. Federal expenditures for Medicare and the federally funded portion of Medicaid grew from $119.6 billion in the 1989 fiscal year to $206.4 billion in FY1993.[2] Annual federal receipts over this period rose by $162.8 billion.[3] (None of these figures is adjusted for inflation.)

If current trends continue, health care spending will rise much faster than inflation and will consume a growing share of national income and the federal budget. Between 1995 and 2005, federal health care spending is projected to grow 9.6% a year (compared to an expected overall inflation rate of 3.0%), pushing the share of national income devoted just to federal health care spending from 3.8% to 6.0%.[4] During that time the federal deficit is projected to grow from 2.5% of gross domestic product to 3.6% (**Figure A**); this entire increase could be avoided if Medicare and Medicaid spending grew at a more moderate rate. In other words, containing health expenditures would eliminate the problem of a growing federal budget deficit.

High quality health care can still be provided with lower rates of spending increases. Between 1980 and 1992, the seven largest industrialized countries had average annual growth in health expenditures, measured as a share of GDP, of 1.7%. If this rate prevailed in the United States between 1995 and 2005, federal government expenditures on Medicare and Medicaid would rise from 3.8% of GDP in 1995 to 4.5% in 2005, *saving 1.5% of GDP in 2005* compared to current projections.

FIGURE A
Health Care Drives the Deficit Projections, 1995-2005

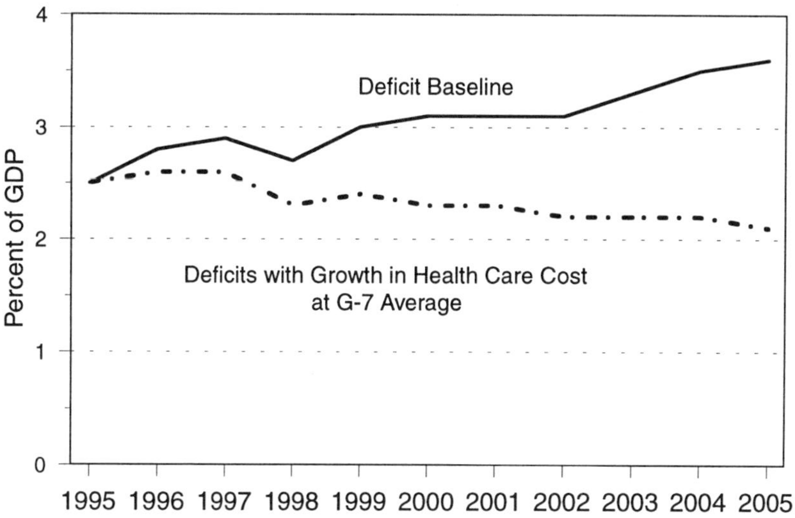

Note: "Deficit Baseline" reflects CBO baseline prior to the FY96 Budget Debate.

Source: EPI analysis of CBO data, 1995.

These savings would allow the federal budget deficit to fall below the 1995 level of 2.5% of GDP to 2.1% in 2005.[5]

But the federal government cannot unilaterally reduce health expenditures by this magnitude without creating serious problems for Medicare and Medicaid beneficiaries and for the privately insured as well. Shifting costs to beneficiaries would create a hardship for many elderly who already are paying large shares of their incomes for health care (the average elderly household spent 24% of its income for health care in 1992, not counting expenditures for nursing homes[6]). If the government attempts to save money by reducing payments to providers, hospitals and doctors tend to respond by raising rates for the privately insured and increasing the volume of services performed. It has also been suggested that Medicare and Medicaid could cut back on the number of services covered, but this is an undesirable option at a time when benefits need to be increased (for example, to cover prescription drugs). If access and quality are to be maintained, significant savings in Medicaid and Medicare can be achieved only through comprehensive reform encompassing both the public and private insurance systems.

Shifting beneficiaries to health maintenance organizations (HMOs) will not solve the problem either. Enrolling all Medicare beneficiaries in HMOs would indeed yield a one-time drop in expenditures of about 7%,[7] but since the rate of spending growth is the same for HMOs as in the fee-for-service sector, the rate of increase in health care spending would likely continue unchecked after this one-time savings.

Another proposal for containing costs is the adoption of a Medicare voucher system. The elderly would use a voucher to shop for a private insurance policy. Proponents argue that this system would encourage cost consciousness among Medicare beneficiaries and provide an incentive for insurers to supply competitively priced policies. Unfortunately, however, making people more price conscious usually means creating barriers to care for low- and middle-income individuals and results in greater efforts by insurers to avoid accepting high-cost users. Moreover, since higher-income elderly could afford to supplement their vouchers with their own funds, political pressure from the elderly to maintain the buying power of the voucher and the quality of care it would purchase would likely be reduced. Over time, inflation or federal cutbacks could erode the value of the voucher and the quality of the services it would buy, potentially leaving the less well-off with inferior coverage. Government efforts such as these to contain costs in public programs will hurt the beneficiaries of care without addressing the overriding, national problem of rising health care expenditures. By shifting the high costs of medical care from its hands to the indigent and elderly, the government does not resolve the crisis but merely turns it over to those who can least afford to deal with it.

Efforts for Incremental Reform

The two most popular private-sector measures being considered by policy makers are insurance reforms and medical savings accounts. Neither is likely to bring universal access, affordability, and equitable financing, nor contain costs.

Insurance reform. As it was proposed by the House Republican leadership in early 1995, insurance reform would require health insurers to sell policies to anyone who could buy them. To make insurance affordable to those in relatively poor health, there would be restrictions on the differences in premiums charged to those who were ill or at high risk for illness and those who were healthy or at low risk. In addition, exclusions for pre-existing conditions would be limited.

Insurance reform has worthy goals: to make insurance available and affordable to all, and to provide coverage for existing medical conditions. But while insurance reform may increase the availability of insurance for those who are ill, the overall effect is likely to be negligible or even negative as relatively healthy people drop out of the system because of higher prices.

The reform proposals would allow everyone, whatever the condition of their health, to pay an average or community rate for their insurance coverage. This method differs from experience rating (the predominant pricing method used today[8]), in which premiums are based on an individual's likely use of services. In the move from experience rating to community rating, costs would fall for those who were ill but rise for those who were healthy.[9] This would more evenly distribute health costs and reduce the financial penalty associated with poor health. However, since the purchase of insurance is optional, the increase in rates charged those who are healthy and with little need for health care will lead some of them (or their employers) to drop coverage. If the inexpensive-to-insure people drop out of the common pool, then per-person costs will rise for those remaining. The net effect would likely be higher average premiums for those with insurance coverage and lower rates of insurance coverage overall.[10] This scenario is especially likely because those who drop coverage know that, if they do get sick, the insurer must sell them coverage at the community rate.

Although Congress is still debating insurance reform, 45 states have implemented similar plans since 1990. A study of 12 states that enacted insurance reforms before July 1992 concluded that these measures are unlikely to solve the problems of affordability and availability of insurance.[11]

Medical savings accounts. A medical savings account (MSA) is essentially a tax-advantaged savings account combined with a catastrophic health insurance policy. The insurance component is a policy with a large deductible, possibly $2,000 to $3,000. The policy would provide coverage for large health expenditures that exceeded the deductible (i.e., "catastrophic" illnesses), but would not cover routine or moderate amounts of care.

The difference in the cost between the inexpensive catastrophic policy and the more costly standard policy would be placed in a tax-free savings account to be used to pay for day-to-day health care. Any money not spent on health care could be withdrawn for other purposes after taxes (and probably penalties) were paid or could be withdrawn without penalty after the depositor reached retirement age. Thus, MSAs could be seen as another type of tax-advantaged savings vehicle, like IRAs, that would be used primarily by those with high incomes.

Once the funds in the MSA were spent, additional medical costs would have to be paid out of pocket until expenditures exceeded the deductible and coverage under the insurance plan was triggered. People with few medical expenses will end the year with money remaining; those with higher expenditures will exhaust the account and face large out-of-pocket payments. Proponents of this plan argue that people spending "their own money" for the first few thousand dollars of health care each year would be more likely to shop around for the best prices, go to the doctor less often, and be more skeptical about obtaining every test or procedure suggested by their doctors. Overall health spending would go down as a result.

However, the plan has major drawbacks. Because most health care services are used by a small segment of the population (the 10% of the population in the poorest health spends 72% of all health care dollars), most spending would be made by people who had exceeded their deductible[12] and were no longer spending money out of their MSAs. In other words, they would have no incentive to shop around or forgo treatment. In 1994, if everyone had had a catastrophic policy with a $5,000 deductible, 71% of spending would still have been done by people who had exceeded their deductibles.[13] Even if the 90% of the population who are low-cost users reduced their use of health care by 10% or found price reductions of 10%, total health care spending would drop less than 3%. Unless people had further reductions each year, after this one-time drop the MSA plan would probably have no effect on the rate of increase in expenditures.

MSAs may also adversely affect health outcomes.[14] When people forgo or delay seeking health care services because of fees, they do not just eliminate unnecessary services. Instead, they also cut back on services that are medically necessary[15] and on preventive care that could reduce future expenditures and improve quality of life.[16] Moreover, among the 25% of the nonelderly population in the poorest health, having access to care without having to pay out-of-pocket fees has been shown to reduce the risk of death by 10%.[17]

The people who would be most disadvantaged by MSAs and by cost sharing in general are those with limited incomes or with chronic illness and relatively high annual health expenses. High-income families that had used up the money in their savings accounts would still be able to purchase health care as needed until the deductible was reached and the insurance policy began to pay for care. But low- and middle-income families would be less able to afford such out-of-pocket expenditures, and their access to care would be limited.

In addition, MSAs would probably result in further fracturing of the common insurance pool. Families that anticipated high expenditures requiring large out-of-pocket spending would probably opt to buy standard policies. The healthy, by contrast, would probably opt for the tax-advantaged status of the MSA. As with insurance reform, this splitting of the population into the sick and the well would result in higher rates for standard insurance policies and lower rates for catastrophic policies. Once again, those in poor health would be financially penalized.

The presumption behind MSAs and all types of cost-sharing plans is that overuse of doctors' services in the United States is an important cause of high and rapidly rising health expenditures. However, it is hard to make the argument that Americans overuse services when we average *fewer* visits to the doctor per year than do people in any other major industrialized country, where health expenditures are lower.[18]

Problems Inherent in a Market-Based System

The problems Americans face with regard to health care—large numbers of people without insurance, lack of affordable policies, and high costs—are not minor aberrations that can be fixed with piecemeal adjustments like insurance reform or medical savings accounts. Rather, they are the inevitable result of trying to provide health care and health insurance through a market system of buyers and sellers. It is to these three problems that we now turn.

Access to care. Between 1989 and 1993, the number of uninsured rose from 34.7 million to 41.2 million. The increase would have been even larger had not the number of people covered by Medicaid risen 50%, from 21.1 million to 31.6 million, over the four years. In addition, another 29 million people were underinsured in 1993.[19]

Since seniors age 65 and above enjoy nearly universal coverage and access through Medicare, uninsurance and underinsurance are largely problems for the population under age 65. In 1993, 39% of the under-65 population received no insurance coverage through an employer.[20] While the majority of these had either public insurance or private insurance not received through an employer, fully 18% of the under-65 population was uninsured in 1993. Nearly all of these—85%—were workers or family members of workers.

People with very low incomes who are uninsured and also meet additional criteria are eligible for Medicaid, which in 1993 provided care for 13% of the nonelderly population. The program primarily serves families eligible for Aid to Families With Dependent Children, the disabled of all ages, and the low-income elderly. But many low-income people are not eligible for the program because they are not disabled or do not have children. In 1993, approximately 50% of nonelderly people with incomes below the poverty level were covered by Medicaid, another 18% had private coverage, either through an employer or purchased directly from an insurer, and 33% were uninsured. Among people with incomes between 100% and 200% of the poverty line (up to an annual income of $23,044 for a family of three), 31% were uninsured and 17% had Medicaid coverage.

Perhaps because low-income people usually have little political clout, the Medicaid program is frequently under political attack, and its funding is often in jeopardy. It is severely underfunded at present, and in many cases the fees paid by Medicaid to doctors and hospitals are far lower than those paid by private insurers or by Medicare. As a consequence, Medicaid-eligible beneficiaries often cannot find doctors who will treat them.

Any health care system in which those without political influence are segmented into a separate system will likely have an inequitable outcome. An equitable system would be one that served people of every class and race in the same facilities with the same equipment and providers, and for the same fees.

Affordability. A major reason people lack health insurance is cost. Unlike police and fire protection, education, and access to roads, health insurance is provided not as a right (as in many other countries) but, as a rule, only to those who purchase it. Medicaid fills in some of the gaps left by the market system, but, as described above, many people with Medicaid still lack equal access to care.

Most economists agree that, when insurance is received on the job, workers' wages and salaries are reduced to offset, in large part, the employer's cost. Thus, the benefit is actually being paid for by the worker, and in 1995 the cost was about $5,000 for a family. Low-wage workers, many of whom are uninsured, would likely find this unaffordable. For example, a worker earning $7 per hour in a full-time, full-year job without health insurance would earn $14,560 annually. If the employer began to provide family health insurance and reduced wages to offset the cost, the worker's annual earnings would fall to $9,560, a reduction of 34%. Can society reasonably expect a family to spend 34% of income (plus copayments, coinsurance, or deductibles) for health care? In fact, approximately 35% of under-65-year-olds live in households with incomes of $25,000 or below; they would need to spend 20% of income or more to buy premiums.[21]

If we think all families should have access to health care, then a system that makes it dependent upon buying a premium is not workable. Inevitably, many people will be left uninsured, and the problem will worsen if health costs rise more quickly than do incomes, as has been the case for many years.

Cost containment. U.S. expenditures for health care are the highest in the world. In 1992, the last year for which comparative data are available, Americans spent 13.6% of national income on health care, compared with an average of 8.1% spent by other industrialized countries. Average family expenditures for health care (including out-of-pocket expenditures, premiums, and tax payments that are used to pay for health care) have risen from $3,503 (in 1992 dollars), or 15.1% of income, in 1977[22] to $6,877, or 18.2% of income, in 1992.[23] The share of income spent on health care is much higher for families with low incomes than for those with high incomes.

Health expenditures in the United States have been rising much faster than expenditures on other goods and services. There are a number of reasons for this trend. One is the aging of the population, which raises demand for health care; another is increasing affluence—as a nation's per capita GDP rises, so does its per capita demand for health care (**Figure B**). Yet both of these phenomena are occurring in other industrialized countries, thus they cannot explain why expenditures in the United States are so much higher and rising so much more rapidly. What is unique to the United States is that health care services are provided in large part through a relatively unregulated market system.

There are important differences between the market for health care and the market for other goods and services. For most products, price determines whether they will be bought and if so in what quantities. Both prices and sales volumes are constrained by competition and the interaction between buyers and sellers. In most markets, sellers of goods and services face an automatic check on price increases. If they raise their prices too much, people stop buying.

But for at least two reasons, the price and sales of health care services are not restrained by the usual market forces. First, for many people, not buying a recommended health care service is not an option. If a doctor recommends a particular medicine or procedure, most people will follow the recommendation, even if it means going without other things to pay for it. In many cases, the price of the test or procedure plays a small role in the decision about whether to buy it.

The influence of market forces on health care is also influenced by the fact that most people have health insurance. Having health care coverage is a priority for many people, despite the expense. But when someone has an insurance policy, the cost of actual care is only a fraction of the total cost and may be zero. Thus, the effect of price on determining

FIGURE B
Health Care Expenditures per Capita Compared to GDP per Capita,* 1991

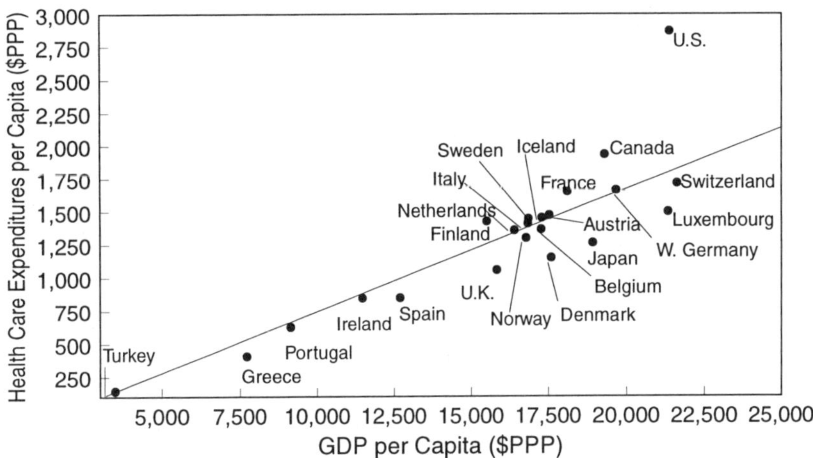

*Converted using purchasing power parities for GDP.

Source: Author's analysis of OECD data.

if the service will be purchased is diminished. Insurers often compete to offer lower-cost policies, but comparison shopping is difficult because the terms of the policies and the services covered vary widely. Moreover, the easiest way for insurers to compete in price is to keep their rates down by avoiding high-cost users.

For these reasons, the market does not work well to restrain health care expenditures. If our solution is to make the market system work better to reduce or slow the rate of growth in spending, we need to make people more sensitive to prices, that is, make price an important determinant of whether people buy a particular service. This concept is fundamentally at odds with the principle that people should have access to all the health care services they need, regardless of ability to pay.

There is a fundamental incompatibility between facilitating access to needed services and the ability of market mechanisms to control expenditures. The reluctance of U.S. policy makers to consider nonmarket approaches that preserve insurance coverage without large deductibles, copayments, and coinsurance, but that also control costs has stymied health care reform and cost containment in the United States for decades.[24] What is needed to enhance access and affordability while also containing costs are nonmarket, regulatory mechanisms that have proved effective in the Medicare program and in other industrialized countries.

CAN MANAGED CARE CONTAIN COSTS?

Managed care has been watched for years for its cost-containment potential. Managed care combines the financing and delivery of health care (the functions of insurance companies and doctors) with efforts to contain costs and improve quality. In a managed-care setting, patients may be required, for example, to obtain authorization from someone other than their personal physicians before obtaining a particular test or being admitted to a hospital. Hospital stays are monitored to eliminate unnecessary days. Most people under age 65 are covered by insurance plans that manage care in one way or another.

Managed-care plans, such as HMOs and preferred provider organizations (PPOs), take managed care one step further. They contract with limited numbers of physicians to provide care to enrollees, and they monitor these physicians to reduce provision of inappropriate services. (By contrast, indemnity plans, which often manage care, allow enrollees to seek care from any physician.)

In some locations, managed-care plans are less expensive than indemnity plans, in part because managed-care plans are more likely than indemnity plans to enroll relatively healthy people. Also, some managed-care plans use their market clout to extract discounts from doctors and hospitals, thus shifting costs from enrollees in managed-care plans to people in indemnity plans. Managed-care plans also reduce the use of services by about 8%,[25] but this reduction does not directly translate into a proportional reduction in costs since administrative costs are higher in managed-care plans than in indemnity plans. Nonetheless, if everyone enrolled in managed-care plans, national health expenditures probably would be lower in the first year. But because these plans have not demonstrated any effectiveness in reducing the rate of growth in expenditures, costs would continue to grow afterwards at the same rapid rate as before. Moreover, in some HMOs there continue to be concerns with quality of care and access to covered services such as mental health care. With this uncertain evidence, we cannot rely solely on managed-care plans to contain health expenditures.

In the rush to boost enrollment in managed-care plans, we must be careful to monitor and regulate the quality of care delivered. Managed-care plans achieve some of their savings by denying care. Without careful monitoring, restrictions on inappropriate or unnecessary care could become limits on needed and appropriate care as well.[26] To ensure high-quality care in existing managed-care plans, Congress should immediately enact laws to monitor the quality of care delivered, provide for consumer oversight and grievance procedures, ensure due process for enrollees and providers, and require reporting and disclosure requirements with speedy enforcement provisions and stiff penalties for violations and noncompliance. But even at its best, managed care is no substitute for comprehensive health system reform that would provide universal coverage and affordable and equitable financing, as well as cost containment and high-quality services.

A Successful Reform Strategy: Single Payer

Despite the inability of the United States to solve its problems of cost, access, and affordability, other industrialized countries have developed systems that offer universal coverage along with much lower health care expenditures, more equitable financing, and better health outcomes than are available in the United States. In large part, these countries use similar mechanisms to achieve these ends. They include universal health insurance coverage provided without regard to health status or financial ability to buy a premium; tax-based financing for health care, with taxes tied progressively to income; and regulatory measures to contain costs.

A single-payer Canadian-style system, which we propose for the United States, would use these measures to address the current ills of the American system. Everyone would have access to all medically necessary services provided by physicians in private practice or in managed-care plans. Health insurance would be provided to everyone in the same manner that Medicare now provides coverage for all people over age 65. To make the plan affordable, costs must be assessed in relation to income; an easy way to do this is to fund with tax revenue that portion of the health care system currently financed out of pocket and through premiums. Since taxes are usually paid in relation to income (people with low incomes generally pay less than do people with high incomes), payments for health care would be affordable to all.

Medical care would still be provided as it is now, primarily by private practitioners in private offices; people would have free choice of provider and of plan type (fee for service or HMO), in much the same way as they do in the current Medicare program. But instead of 1,500 different companies providing insurance, and instead of providers billing each firm to receive payment, only one entity would provide insurance and pay claims (a "single payer"). This greatly simplified administrative system would save approximately $90 billion in 1995 alone.[27] Medicare offers a good analogy. In that system, overhead costs are approximately 2% of claims paid;[28] for private insurance claims overhead totals 12-14%.[29]

The single-payer system would contain costs by negotiating budgets with providers. It would institute a fee schedule for outpatient services and a global budget for providers, somewhat similar to that now used in Medicare, and hospitals would receive an annual sum for expenses. In order to avoid the problem of expensive duplication of equipment and services (the current situation has been described as a medical arms race), purchases of major equipment and construction of additional facilities would have to be approved by regional planning boards.

Adoption of a single-payer system would preserve what is best in American health care while also providing security through universal coverage, affordability, and cost containment. It would also relieve the pressure on the federal budget: along with reducing the deficit, Congress could use the health care savings to address other pressing national concerns.

Conclusion

Many people believe that American medicine is the best in the world, and for many people it is. But disparities in health outcomes by class and race are large and growing.[30] On many health indicators the United States ranks below other industrialized counties; on some, we rank lower than some countries in Latin America and Eastern Europe.[31] Comprehensive health care reform is needed to bring greater access and higher-quality care to the most disadvantaged members of our society.

But given existing national economic and political realities, Americans face the danger that the problem of high expenditures and lack of insurance coverage will be "solved" by segmenting people into plans of varying cost and quality. Such plans hope to realize savings by allowing those of us who can't afford anything better to receive less costly, poorer-quality care. Meanwhile, those of us with higher incomes will still be free to purchase higher-quality, more expensive care. Total health care spending may indeed decline, but only because the people who can afford to spend little or nothing will vastly outnumber the well-to-do.

The danger in proposals for incremental health care reform is that the existing segmented structure will simply be expanded to cover more people. The goal of health care reform should be the elimination of inequities based on class and race, not the promotion of inequity in the name of cost containment or universal coverage. The single-payer system would provide treatment to everyone within a single system, regardless of class or race, and contain costs while preserving the high quality care for which the U.S. system is known. It is the best—and only true—solution to the health care crisis in the United States.

NOTES

1. Levit, Katherine R. et al. 1994, p. 285.
2. Office of Management and Budget 1995, p. 242.
3. Council of Economic Advisors 1994.
4. Congressional Budget Office 1995.
5. Author's analysis of Congressional Budget Office 1995.
6. Rasell and Tang 1994.
7. Christensen 1995.
8. Policies sold to small firms and individuals are usually experience rated. However, firms that self-insure (approximately half of all workers are employed in self-insured firms) are essentially experience rated as well. The proposed insurance reforms would likely affect policies sold to small firms and individuals only, not self-insured firms.
9. Sometimes, insurance reform packages also limit the share of premiums that can

be spent on insurers' nonmedical expenditures such as administration or profits. If a company with high administrative costs and/or profits were required to reduce these expenditures, premiums would also be reduced. In a case like this, it is possible that the community-rated premium, even for a healthy enrollee, could be lower than the pre-reform premium.

10. If the healthy have other sources of health insurance outside the common pool, then coverage rates may not decline.

11. Markus, Ladenheim, and Atchison 1995.

12. Aaron and Schwartz 1993.

13. Author's calculations based on Council of Economic Advisors 1994.

14. The following arguments are also reasons why cost sharing in standard insurance policies—copayments, coinsurance, and deductibles—should be avoided.

15. Lohr et al. 1986; Siu et al. 1986.

16. Lurie et al. 1987.

17. Brook et al. 1983.

18. Organization for Economic Cooperation and Development 1993.

19. Bodenheimer 1992.

20. Employee Benefit Research Institute 1995, p. 37.

21. Author's analysis of Bureau of the Census data.

22. Rasell, Bernstein, and Tang 1993.

23. Rasell and Tang 1994.

24. The exception is Medicare and Medicaid, which have instituted regulatory controls. But as will be discussed below, this approach is limited when the private sector is largely unregulated.

25. Christensen 1995, p. 8.

26. Recent reports on managed-care plans serving Medicaid beneficiaries in Florida are just one example. See Schulte and Bregal 1994.

27. The U.S. General Accounting Office (1991) estimated administrative savings from a single-payer system of $67 billion in 1991. Between 1991 and 1995, health expenditures have risen at an average annual rate of 7.66% in nominal terms (assuming the 1993-4 and 1994-5 increases were the same as in 1992-3). If excess administrative expenditures rose at the same rate as total spending (this probably is an underestimate—see Woolhandler and Himmelstein 1991), in 1995 administrative savings would total $91 billion.

28. Social Security Administration 1994.

29. Sheils, Young, and Rubin 1992; Woolhandler and Himmelstein 1991; U.S. General Accounting Office 1991.

30. Rasell 1994.

31. Zarate 1994.

References

Aaron, Henry J. and William B. Schwartz. 1993. "Managed Competition: Little Cost Containment Without Budget Limits." *Health Affairs,* Vol. 12 (Supplement), pp. 204-15.

Bodenheimer, Thomas. 1992. "Underinsurance in America." *New England Journal of Medicine.* Vol. 327, No. 4, pp. 274-8.

Brook, R.H., J.E. Ware Jr., and W.H. Rogers et al. 1983. "Does Free Care Improve Adults' Health? Results From a Randomized Controlled Trial." *New England Journal of Medicine,* Vol. 309, No. 23, pp. 1426-34.

Christensen, Sandra. 1995. "Managed Care and the Medicare Program." Washington, D.C.: Congressional Budget Office. Memorandum.

Congressional Budget Office. 1995. *The Economic and Budget Outlook: Fiscal Years 1996-2000.* Washington, D.C.: U.S. Government Printing Office.

Council of Economic Advisors. 1994. *Economic Report of the President.* Washington, D.C.: U.S. Government Printing Office.

Employee Benefit Research Institute. 1995. "Sources of Health Insurance and Characteristics of the Uninsured: Analysis of the March 1994 Current Population Survey." *EBRI Special Report SR-28.* Issue Brief No. 158. Washington, D.C.: EBRI.

Levit, Katherine R., Arthur L. Sensenig, Cathy A. Cowan et al. 1994. "National Health Expenditure, 1993." *Health Care Financing Review,* Vol. 16, No. 1, pp. 247-94.

Lohr K.N., R.H. Brook, and C.J. Kamberg et al. 1986. "Use of Medical Care in the Rand Health Insurance Experiment: Diagnosis and Service-Specific Analyses in a Randomized Controlled Trial." *Medical Care,* Vol. 24 (Supplement), pp. S31-38.

Lurie, N., W. Manning, C. Peterson, G. Goldberg, C. Phelps, and L. Lillard. 1987. "Preventive Care: Do We Practice What We Preach?" *American Journal of Public Health,* Vol. 77, No. 7, pp. 801-4.

Markus, Anne R., Kala Ladenheim, and Lisa Atchison. 1995. "Small Group Market Reforms: A Snapshot of States' Experience." Intergovernment Health Policy Project, George Washington University, Washington, D.C.

Office of Management and Budget. 1995. *Historical Tables: Budget of the United States Government.* Washington, D.C.: U.S. Government Printing Office.

Organization for Economic Cooperation and Development. 1993. *OECD Health Systems: Facts and Trends, 1960-1991.* Vol. I. Paris: OECD.

Rasell, Edith. 1994. "Health Care: Expenditures Exceed Results."In Mishel, Lawrence and Jared Bernstein. *The State of Working America 1994-95.* Armonk, N.Y.: M.E. Sharpe.

Rasell, Edith and Kainan Tang. 1994. *Paying for Health Care: Affordability and Equity in Proposals for Health Care Reform.* Washington, D.C.: Economic Policy Institute.

Rasell, Edith, Jared Bernstein, and Kainan Tang. 1993. *The Impact of Health Care Financing on Family Budgets.* Washington, D.C.: Economic Policy Institute.

Schulte, Fred and Jenni Bregal. 1994. "Florida's Medicaid HMOs: Profits From Pain." *Fort Lauderdale Sun Sentinel,* December 11-15.

Sheils, John F., Gary J. Young, and Robert J. Rubin. 1992. "O Canada: Do We Expect Too Much From Its Health System?" *Health Affairs.* Vol. 11, No. 1, pp. 7-20.

Siu, A.L., F.A. Sonnenberg, and W.G. Manning et al. 1986. "Inappropriate Use of Hospitals in a Randomized Trial of Health Insurance Plans." *New England Journal of Medicine.* Vol. 315, No. 20, pp. 1259-66.

Social Security Administration. 1994. *Annual Statistical Supplement to the Social Security Bulletin.* Washington, D.C.: U.S. Government Printing Office.

U.S. General Accounting Office. 1991. "Canadian Health Insurance: Lessons for the States." HRD-91-90. Washington, D.C.: U.S. GAO.

Woolhandler, Steffie and David U. Himmelstein. 1991. "The Deteriorating Administrative Efficiency of the U.S. Health Care System." *New England Journal of Medicine.* Vol. 324, No. 18, pp. 1253-8.

Zarate, Alvan O. 1994. "International Mortality Chartbook: Levels and Trends, 1955-1991." Hyattsville, Md.: U.S. Public Health Service.

CHAPTER 5

TAX REFORM
A Progressive Flat Tax

by Robert Eisner[1]

OUR TAX SYSTEM IS A MESS. WE WASTE BILLIONS OF PERSON-HOURS AND hundreds of billions of dollars administering, complying with, and seeking to avoid or evade taxes. Eliminating the current system would indeed add measurably to unemployment by destroying the livelihood of hundreds of thousands of tax preparers and accountants, lawyers, and lobbyists. It would also rid the economy of countless distortions that lead to the misallocation of resources between work and leisure, between saving and consumption, and among forms of saving and consumption and investment goods.

There is a great deal that reasonable people must find unfair about our present system. It fails over and over again with regard to our usual criteria of equity both within and across income groups. People with the same incomes pay vastly different amounts of taxes, and many people with very high incomes pay little or nothing. The presumed progressivity of our tax system is far less than is generally presumed. If we include all income, we find that the very rich pay smaller proportions of their income in taxes than do the moderately rich.

Furthermore, some marginal tax rates are excessively high, although I see the problem somewhat differently than do those who seem only to note the marginal income taxes on the top 1% or 2%. The problem is worse for wage income than for other income, and it is much worse at the very low end of the income distribution. The marginal effective rate of taxation and loss of benefits for work by many of the very poor on welfare, at least without the earned income tax credit, has been over 100%. And it is now simi-

Robert Eisner is the William R. Kenan professor emeritus of economics at Northwestern University and a past president of the American Economic Association.

larly high for some of those presumably wealthy retirees—with over $35,000 in income!—between the ages of 65 and 70 on Social Security.

Finally, income taxes are only part of the problem: much too little attention is paid to payroll taxes for Social Security and Medicare, which now account for 36.7% of all federal receipts, exceeded only by the 43.2% from individual income taxes.[2] Most Americans probably pay more in these payroll taxes than they do in income taxes. Unnoticed as they are, they are not only not progressive, they are substantially regressive: they allow no deductions or exemptions, they are in large part limited to the portions of incomes under $61,200, and they touch labor income only, thus excluding completely the interest, dividends, profits, and capital gains received almost entirely by the rich and super-rich.

The So-Called "Flat Tax"

We must present a new tax system that is fairer, more efficient, and less painful. But how to proceed? The Tax Reform Act of 1986 offered some improvement by removing a number of egregious loopholes, but some $450 billion of "tax expenditures" remain.[3] Serious discussion has now moved to a radical innovation, the so-called "flat tax." First developed in detail and presented to the public by Robert Hall and Alvin Rabushka some 13 years ago,[4] it has gained important political support with its inclusion in a bill introduced in Congress by Richard Armey, now the majority leader of the House of Representatives.

In either the Hall-Rabushka, now updated,[5] or the similar Armey version, the flat tax would eliminate all deductions other than exemptions or personal allowances relating to filing status or number of dependents. It would replace current individual and corporate income taxes and all of their rates as well as all exclusions and deductions with two new taxes, one on wage income and one on business. And as Hall and Rabushka have repeatedly pointed out, their flat tax is a consumption tax.[6]

The Armey proposal[7] would set the "flat" rate on both wages and business initially at 20% (but drop it to 17% in 1997 on the basis of other spending reductions and the expected increase in productivity and resultant tax revenue increases). Hall-Rabushka would set the rate at 19%. The wage tax would apply to all wages, salaries, and pensions. The Armey bill would allow indexed deductions on the wage tax initially totaling $34,700 for a family of four; the Hall-Rabushka "personal allowances" would come to $25,500 for a family of four. There would be no further deductions—not for state and local taxes, IRAs, charitable contributions, mortgage interest, excess health costs, or moving expenses. You name it; they would all be gone.

The business tax would apply to gross revenue from sales minus allowable costs, which would include purchases of goods, services, and materials; wages, salaries, and retirement benefits; and purchases of capital equipment, structures, and land. Note that capital acquisitions would be "expensed"; there would be no depreciation or separate capital accounts. Sales of capital equipment, structures, and land, however, would be included in gross revenue. Income from investment would not be included, but banks and insurance companies would, in Hall-Rabushka, have their sales grossed up to include the value of services furnished in lieu of interest payments. Fringe benefits (other than contributions to pensions) would not be deductible, nor would employer contributions for Social Security and state and local taxes. Neither interest payments nor dividend payouts would be deductible, but neither would be taxable at the individual level; there, only wages and pensions (and not Social Security benefits) would be taxed.

Hall-Rabushka would explicitly eliminate inheritance taxes. Both plans would eliminate all capital gains taxes (other than that portion of net business taxes that might result from the sale of assets for an amount higher than what was originally deducted).

The elimination of withholding taxes in the Armey bill would appear to invite considerable evasion by wage-earners and consequent revenue loss. Armey argues that taxpayers would consider his flat tax so fair and simple—returns could be filed on a postcard—that they would voluntarily mail in their checks to the Internal Revenue Service each month! Hall and Rabushka do provide for withholding.

Hall and Rabushka claim that their flat tax of 19% with their personal allowances is revenue-neutral as compared to current law. If so, the Armey bill, with its much higher deductions, is not revenue-neutral at its initial rate of 20%, let alone at 17% in two years. This is indicated implicitly by Hall and Rabushka (in their book *The Flat Tax*), and I have confirmed that if the Hall-Rabushka proposal is revenue-neutral, the

Armey bill would require a "flat" rate of about 23% (22.87%, precisely calculated) to avoid adding to the deficit.

Even this rate would seem attractive on its surface to many taxpayers, particularly when they are told of their large personal deductions; that $34,700 for a family of four would appear to relieve huge numbers of people of any tax liabilities and let most of the middle class off with modest taxes at worst. The large deductions also offer sponsors of the flat tax the opportunity to claim that their wage tax is highly progressive, since the actual proportions of wage income taxed are very low, if not zero, for most wage earners.

But all this is vastly misleading. The proposed flat taxes arrive at their low rates essentially by replacing much of the current income tax with what amounts to a sales tax on virtually all current, domestic consumption. Current individual and corporate income taxes bring in revenues equal to 15.71% of what the IRS defines as "total income"; this breaks down into 9.77% from the non-business portion of personal income taxes and 5.95% from current business income taxes. The Hall-Rabushka proposal would raise the business proportion to 9.07%, and the Armey bill would raise it to 10.91%.[8]

But these vastly increased business taxes, like sales taxes generally, would certainly be passed on in higher prices, so anything individuals saved in income taxes they would lose in the taxes on their domestic consumption. And, as is well known, such taxes are highly regressive. What is more, the conversion of the individual income tax to a wage tax relieves the wealthy, who receive the bulk of capital income, of a major portion of their current tax burden.

Detailed analysis of Statistics of Income[9] data for 1993 (the year on which Hall and Rabushka base their calculations) and of Joint Committee on Taxation estimates of the burden of a consumption-sales tax[10] allows us to estimate the proportions of total income, by adjusted gross income class, that would be subject to current income taxes and to the Hall-Rabushka and Armey flat taxes. The results are shown in **Table 1**. Ignoring the under-$10,000 income class, for which the results are probably seriously distorted by substantial amounts of largely transitory negative income, we see that the current income tax system is progressive over all classes.[11] Hall-Rabushka taxes would be considerably higher than current taxes for all income groups between $20,000 and $100,000, essen-

TABLE 1
Current and Flat Taxes as Percent of Total Income, by Adjusted Gross Income Class, 1993

AGI Class (in Thousands of Dollars)	Current Total Tax (Percent)	Hall-Rabushka Total Tax (Percent)	Armey Total Tax (Percent)
Under 10	21.95	30.89	37.18
10 Under 20	10.18	9.87	11.88
20 Under 30	12.48	13.91	12.91
30 Under 40	13.62	15.62	14.77
40 Under 50	14.04	16.51	15.76
50 Under 75	14.83	16.97	16.36
75 Under 100	16.56	17.54	17.14
100 Under 200	18.65	16.15	16.12
200 and Over	24.36	12.55	12.69
All Incomes	15.71	15.71	15.71

Source: Author's calculations based on IRS data, 1994.

tially the much-mentioned "middle class." They would be much lower for the highest income groups: 16.15% of total income as against 18.65% for the $100,000 to $200,000 class, and 12.55% compared to 24.36% for the $200,000 and over class. The Armey flat tax version would also have considerably higher taxes than current law for the middle-income classes, although somewhat less than the Hall-Rabushka flat tax. For the $200,000 and over class, the Armey total tax would be 12.69% of total income, compared to Hall-Rabushka's 12.55%. Both of these rates are little more than half of the current total tax figure of 24.36%.

There are other serious objections to the proposed flat taxes. They would entail double taxation for state and local governments, since their taxes are taxed again in the new business income tax. The elimination of deductibility of all fringe benefits, without any substitution of other subsidies, would entail large new net health cost burdens for most taxpayers. The elimination of mortgage interest deductions would eliminate a major subsidy to the investment in owner-occupied housing that has contributed greatly to investment in our future and to the security of most of at least the upper middle classes and their neighborhoods. The lack of a provision for the earned income tax credit would eliminate one of our most important, innovative efforts to help the poor by making work more rewarding. Removing all taxation of capital income suggests new distortions in favor of capital and against labor. And there are serious transition problems as well.[12]

A Better "Flat Tax"[13]

There is a simple way to achieve the ideal of sweeping tax reform that meets all or almost all of the faults in the current income tax system but that avoids most of the drawbacks of these flat tax proposals. It would substitute for the current corporate and individual income taxes and payroll taxes one comprehensive flat tax on all kinds of real income, including capital gains. Like the Armey and Hall-Rabushka proposals, it would eliminate all the myriad deductions and complications of the current system and would include similar, large personal exemptions. It would lower the highest marginal rates, particularly on wage income, but would be truly progressive.

Despite the potential support generated by Congressman Armey's position and the interest expressed by presidential candidates moving into the 1996 campaign, it is doubtful that many, including Mr. Armey, would view his flat tax proposal as within the realm of current political reality. In addition to obstacles that will be raised by all those likely to suffer from the loss of their own deductions and "preferences," one may expect substantial opposition because of the regressivity of the Armey proposal, which would make a large majority of taxpayers worse off. The Eisner program would no doubt also face serious political obstacles, but it can be endorsed not only for its vast simplification of the tax system but also for its ability to reduce the taxes of most Americans.

First, we should eliminate the corporate income tax, lock, stock, and barrel. To quote Hall and Rabushka, "Businesses do not pay taxes, individuals do."[14] Let us then tax individuals directly so that we can get a reasonable idea of who is paying the taxes and how much. We would include all of the earnings related to business activity—real interest, dividends, and real, accrued capital gains of owners—in individual income. Among the many advantages of eliminating the corporate income tax would be elimination of the double taxation of dividends, which biases the financial structure of corporations in the direction of internal financing and raising outside capital by debt rather than equity. Taxing real rather than nominal interest is an obviously desirable move that limits the tax to what is actually income and permits lenders to receive positive after-tax returns in periods of substantial inflation. Taxing real capital gains as they accrue, with full offset for losses, would end the lock-in effect on holders of equity and hence improve the efficiency of capital markets. It would also make moot the step-up of basis at death. And it would eliminate the absurd and pernicious taxation of nominal capital gains that reflect only general inflation.[15]

Second, let's eliminate payroll taxes for Social Security. Putting their proceeds in trust funds is an accounting fiction. Besides, our separate set of payroll taxes discriminates against labor income (which is also taxed in the individual income tax) and allows no deductions and hence no progressivity. To assuage the feelings of those who might be concerned by the loss of Social Security "trust funds," we could earmark to those funds an appropriate portion of the comprehensive income tax. The problem of maintaining "solvency" of the funds in future years can then readily be met by increasing the allocations of taxes to those funds.[16]

We should also remove all taxes on Social Security benefits. Recipients will generally have paid taxes on their income, which are credited to the personal Social Security accounts out of which they receive benefits.

We should, unlike Hall-Rabushka, retain estate and gift taxes as an instrument of our dedication to a free and fluid society, in which people are led to succeed by their own efforts and the influence of inherited wealth is moderated.[17] We should eliminate all other taxes that cannot be justified as user taxes or taxes to attempt to equate individual and social cost. I would hence maintain—and increase—gasoline and cigarette taxes and, with a bit of hesitancy, maintain but not necessarily increase taxes on alcoholic beverages. (I refuse to believe that, taken in moderation, the latter are bad!)

We would then fold all other federal taxes into our new, comprehensive income tax. As with Hall-Rabushka and Armey, other than the standard personal and dependent deductions or allowances, all of the myriad deductions, loopholes, and "tax expenditures" would be eliminated. In a number of cases, however, these would be replaced by up-front government spending. Among our recommended Treasury subsidies would be those for replacement (and expansion) of the earned income tax credit, state and local taxes and taxable bonds (as a substitute for tax-exempt bonds), health care, owner-occupied housing, education and training, and basic research. Together, these might come to no more than $200 billion, as compared to revenue losses from tax expenditures in the current tax code, as reported above, of some $450 billion.[18]

There are important externalities in the activities that would be subsidized, particularly in light of other aspects of the interface between government and the private sector. But to realize these positive externalities, the Eisner program would not reduce the measure of comprehensive income subject to taxation. In fact, it would add imputations for rental income produced in owner-occupied housing, plus some of the other corrections in the Bureau of Economic Analysis National Income and Product Accounts, such as the value of food and fuel consumed on farms, board, meals and services furnished by employers to employees without charge or below cost, and services provided consumers by financial institutions in lieu of interest payments. The comprehensive base, with the inclusion of all real capital gains and interest on government securities, would exceed the total for national income.[19]

With the taxation of all capital income, including interest on state and local bonds, dividends, and real, accrued capital gains, as well as generous personal allowances (included in both Hall-Rabushka and Armey) and the maintenance of an expanded earned income tax credit, there really would be progressivity in the cherished "flat tax," albeit, as in Hall-Rabushka and Armey, really at two rates: zero and some positive number. Under the Eisner program, given its larger base, particularly with the inclusion of all capital income, we could, despite the elimination of payroll and other taxes, maintain revenue neutrality with the Armey personal deductions ($34,700 for a family of four) and a flat rate of 31.63%. This flat rate tax, it will be recalled, will replace current individual and corporate income taxes and payroll taxes. It is to be compared with a rate of 36.72% (22.87% plus 13.85% in payroll taxes for Social Security and Medicare) that the Armey bill would impose in direct taxes on labor income.[20] If we use the smaller personal deductions of Hall-Rabushka ($25,500 for a family of four), we would need a flat tax of only 27.10%, compared with the total of 32.85% in direct taxes that their proposal would place on labor income. The financing of the $200 billion in subsidies proposed above would increase the flat tax rates to 37.63% with the Armey exemptions and to 32.23% with the Hall-Rabushka exemptions. In either case we would have a more progressive tax structure than we have now.[21] Except for the additional reporting necessary for fair and effective taxation of real capital gains, this comprehensive, flat tax offers all of the simplification advantages of the Hall-Rabushka and Armey plans. And it quite eliminates the monstrous system we have now.

But it does it in a way that is fair, flatter, and not at all foolish.

NOTES

1. This chapter draws heavily upon Eisner (1995). In preparing that paper I was indebted to Tom Petska and the staff of the Statistics of Income Division of the Internal Revenue Service for making available and offering some guidance to a number of SOI documents bearing on the components of income and their taxation. I was also indebted to Eric Toder and the professional staff of the Office of Tax Analysis of the Treasury Department for advice as to a number of published documents and general information bearing on the issues discussed in this paper. And I am grateful for the research assistance of Jim Gill and Jay Hoffman, who have helped process a variety of statistical tabulations. The current paper has benefitted as well from comments by Jane Gravelle.

2. Budget Tables (1995), Table 2.2, p. 24.

3. Calculated by adding item-by-item estimates. See Budget Perspectives (1995), Table 5-6, pp. 64-65.

4. In the *Wall Street Journal,* December 10, 1981, and then, in book form, in Hall and Rabushka (1983).

5. Hall and Rabushka (1995).

6. See, for example, *The New York Times,* op-ed page, February 8, 1995, where they write: "...the deduction for purchases of capital goods (plant and equipment) makes the tax a consumption tax. Why do the family and business taxes add up to a consumption tax? Consumption is total income minus investment in new capital. Any tax imposed on income minus investment is a consumption tax."

Hall and Rabushka add that "a national sales tax on consumption of goods and services" would be "economically equivalent." A national sales tax would, however, lack the element of progressivity that they introduce by deducting wages and pensions from the base of the business tax and then offering substantial personal exemptions to their taxation at the individual level.

7. In H.R. 4585 (1994).

8. Calculations explained in detail in Eisner (1995).

9. SOI (1994) and *SOI Bulletin,* Fall 1994.

10. JTC (1993), Table 3, p.55.

11. That is, over all adjusted gross income classes broken down in these tabulations. As we move to very high incomes, over $1,000,000, we may find regressivity developing to the extent that larger and larger proportions of income are received in the form of lightly taxed capital gains. The inclusion of non-taxable interest in "total income" would also decrease the measure of progressivity or increase the regressivity as we move into upper income groups.

The 22.87% rate necessary for revenue neutrality in the Armey proposal would yield a tax of 37.18% of total income in the under $10,000 income class, as shown in Table 12 of Eisner (1995). This result, derived from the Joint Committee on Taxation estimates based on Survey of Consumer Finances saving rates, reflects substantial negative transitory income, contributing to zero and negative total incomes. Lifetime income figures would certainly show lower proportions of income taxed in the lowest income classes and somewhat higher proportions of income taxed in the upper income classes.

12. All this is spelled out in Eisner (1995).

13. This section is taken largely from Eisner (1995), with permission of the American Enterprise Institute.

14. Hall and Rabushka (1995), p. 121.

15. Taxation of real, accrued capital gains can be easily accomplished for owners of listed securities. Corporations would simply report to their stockholders (and to the IRS) the averages of the highs and lows for stock prices on the last trading day of each year. The IRS for its part would make known the inflation percentage to apply to the initial prices of securities held for the entire year. More detail, in terms of adjustments by month for securities acquired during the year, could readily be added. Computing accrued capital gains for assets for which transaction prices were not established could be accomplished by relying on taxpayer declaration of values at the end of each year. To the extent the taxpayer misestimates them, he or she would compensate—with appropriate interest or other penalties—at realization or death. This method would apply as well to owners of unincorporated businesses, who would be taxed only on what they take out of their businesses and their real, accrued capital gains. There would be no business tax returns of any kind, no elaborate depreciation calculations—nothing! Individuals would be permitted to deduct out-of-pocket expenses incurred in connection with earning their income.

Some may anticipate difficulties in collecting taxes on income or capital gains that are not distributed. But taxpayers should generally be able to borrow against their assets, if necessary, to meet their tax obligations currently. And the IRS can ease matters further by offering taxpayers the opportunity to pay portions of their current tax obligations, plus a suitably high interest charge, in later years.

Noncorporate income is already taxed at the individual level. Taxation of real, accrued capital gains of noncorporate enterprise and on real estate or other assets would be more difficult. One possibility, to encourage taxpayers to report their gains as they accrue, would be to assume that gains on realization in excess of previously reported accruals would be taxed, with interest, as if they had occurred evenly over prior years. It would probably be best, however, to exclude owner-occupied homes from taxation of capital gains as they accrue, while preserving current rules pertaining to taxation at sale.

16. This of course has nothing to do with providing the real resources necessary to care for those retired. But raising payroll taxes does nothing for that, either. Those not working, well into the 21st century or at any other time, can only be supported by the output of the human and physical capital then available. That means not accounting gimmicks but public and private investment over prior years in education, research, health, infrastructure, housing, and plant and equipment. It means having a fully equipped and fully employed labor force in which there are minimum discouragements to work.

17. Armey's H.R. 4585 makes no mention of estate and gift taxes, thus implying that they would be retained. This is put in some doubt, however, by his avowal that his bill is essentially an implementation of the flat tax proposal of Hall and Rabushka, who call explicitly for their abandonment (Hall and Rabushka (1995), pp. 126-7, for example).

18. See again Budget Perspectives (1995), Table 5-6, pp. 64-65, which lists total revenue losses for tax expenditures in the income tax, but does not total them, presumably because of interaction of the revenue effects of the various tax expenditures.

19. An indication of just how much a truly comprehensive income tax base would exceed the base in current law may be gleaned from Nelson (1987). She derives a measure of "family economic income" that exceeds 1983 adjusted gross income (based on the pre-1986 tax law) by almost 50% and somewhat exceeds personal income for that year as well. Hall and Rabushka (1995) arrive at a total of $5,003 billion for the 1993 bases of their business and wage tax before allowances. This total, without capital income, comes close to the 1993 figures of $5,131 billion for national income and $5,375 billion for personal income.

20. We should add to this the 22.87% business tax on the 6.2 percent employer contribution for Social Security, or 1.42%, which would bring the total to 38.14%.

21. These figures are estimated, roughly, by assuming that the comprehensive base could be built up to about $5,600 billion (calculated in terms of 1993 figures). The exemptions under the Armey plan come to $2,263 billion, and under Hall-Rabushka to $1,705 billion. Total income and payroll taxes to be replaced amount to $1,055.5 billion. Adding our $200 billion of direct expenditures produces a total of $1,255.5 billion that needs to be raised either on Armey's $3,337 billion base, implying a 37.626% flat rate, or on Hall-Rabushka's $3,895 billion base, for a rate of 32.23%. Without the additional direct expenditures, the taxes to be raised are reduced to $1,055.5 billion and the flat tax rates to 31.632% and 27.099%.

If it were desirable to introduce more progressivity, we could adopt a third tax rate, say 46% with the Armey exemptions, for really high incomes—perhaps over $350,000. If such a rate were adopted, it might be advisable to add an averaging feature for taxable income to avoid penalizing those whose incomes fluctuate from year to year across marginal rates. This would certainly be a trivial complication as compared to either Hall-Rabushka or Armey. Their "flat tax" on wages would actually have, as we have pointed out, two rates: 19% (or 20% or 22.87%) and zero. There is hence a need to avoid penalties for those who are at the zero rate one year, not using up their personal deductions, but then at the positive flat rate the next. Neither Hall-Rabushka nor Armey provides for negative taxes or refunds so that taxpayers with incomes that fluctuate above and below the zero rate point can avoid being penalized.

References

Eisner, Robert. 1995a. "The Proposed Sales and Wages Tax: Fair, Flat or Foolish?" Prepared for an American Enterprise Institute Conference on "The Flat Tax: An Alternative to the Current Income Tax," Washington, D.C., January 27. (Version of February 12, 1995 prepared for publication in American Enterprise Institute conference volume.)

Hall, Robert E. and Rabushka, Alvin. 1983. *Low Tax, Simple Tax, Flat Tax.* New York: McGraw-Hill.

Hall, Robert E. and Rabushka, Alvin. 1995. *The Flat Tax.* Stanford, Calif.: Hoover Institution Press.

Internal Revenue Service. 1994. *Individual Income Tax Returns, 1993: Early Tax Estimates.* Washington, D.C.: U.S. Government Printing Office.

Internal Revenue Service. 1994. *SOI Bulletin.* Washington, D.C.: U.S. Government Printing Office (Fall).

Nelson, Susan C. 1987. "Family Economic Income and Other Income Concepts Used in Analyzing Tax Reform." In Office of Tax Analysis, Department of the Treasury, *Compendium of Tax Research 1987.* Washington, D.C.: U.S. Government Printing Office.

Office of Management and Budget. 1995. *Budget of the U.S. Government: Analytical Perspectives, FY1996.* Washington, D.C.: U.S. Government Printing Office.

Office of Management and Budget. 1995. *Budget of the U.S. Government: Historical Tables, FY1996.* Washington, D.C.: U.S. Government Printing Office.

U.S. Congress. 1994. *H.R. 4585.* 103rd Congress, 2d Session, in the House of Representatives. Introduced by Mr. Armey (June 16), with additional sponsors (August 4).

U.S. Congress, Joint Committee on Taxation. 1993. *Methodology and Issues in Measuring Changes in the Distribution of Tax Burden.* Washington, D.C.: U.S. Government Printing Office.

SECTION II

Working America

Overview
Working America

by Lawrence Mishel

THE STORY OF THE MIDDLE-CLASS SQUEEZE OF THE 1980S IS WELL KNOWN. Middle-class incomes stagnated as real wages declined for males. Only the continuing rise in two-earner families and the increase in wives' hours of paid work prevented a significant erosion of middle-class living standards during that decade. Meanwhile, the number of families living in poverty grew while income and wealth soared among the top 1% of households. All of the progress toward greater equality achieved during the postwar period was reversed.

Things have gotten worse in the 1990s. The income of households at the middle of the family income distribution fell in every year from 1989 to 1993, the latest year for which data are available (see **Figure A**). This is the first time in the postwar period that family incomes fell four years in a row—falling not only in the recession years but in the first two years of the current recovery as well. The income of this median, or typical, family fell from $40,000 in 1989 to $37,300 in 1993—a decline of nearly 7%. The economy also set records for the breadth of the decline in living standards, with incomes falling steadily for the "bottom" 80% of families from 1989 through 1993.[1]

Recent wage data suggest that the family income situation can only have worsened in 1994 and 1995. Real weekly wages of men at the midpoint have continued on a downward trajectory, and even women's earnings, which rose slowly in the 1980s, have fallen since 1993.

A number of the more popular explanations for these disastrous developments do not stand up to scrutiny. Big government is a popular scapegoat. The Republican House Majority Leader, Dick Armey, has

---

Lawrence Mishel is research director at the Economic Policy Institute.

FIGURE A
Median Family Income, 1947-93*

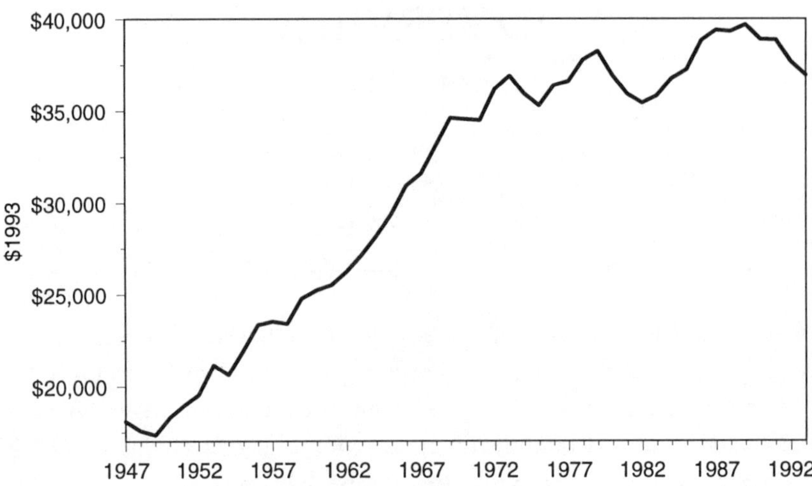

* Data for 1989 and 1992 were revised using Census weights. Data for 1990 and 1991 are interpolations based upon this revision.

Source: U.S. Bureau of the Census (1994).

claimed that people are working harder and getting less because the government is taking a bigger bite out of their paychecks. In reality, it's not an increased tax burden that is squeezing the middle class—it's *pre-tax* income that has collapsed. Both the Congressional Budget Office and the conservative National Tax Foundation report that federal tax rates on the middle class were stable or declining in the 1980s. And in 1995, when all the effects of the early Clinton budgets are included, effective tax rates are projected to decline for all but the most prosperous one-fifth of families.

If anything, the size of government, as measured by shares of total employment, spending, or regulatory costs, has been stable or shrinking since 1979, when the wage implosion began. Unfortunately, according to a recent *Business Week* poll, the public seems to believe the big government, high taxes story—a wrong diagnosis that leads to misguided "cures."

Another favorite explanation, popular among editorial writers, is that slow productivity growth is the villain. Certainly, productivity growth has been slower since 1973 than it was in the earlier postwar period. And more rapid productivity growth would have produced a bigger economic pie. But the real problem lies in how the pie is being sliced. Productivity (output per hour) has grown 25% since 1973, a weak performance by historical standards but quite enough to enable workers to achieve real wage growth of about 1% a year. But this productivity performance has not resulted in gains for most workers. In fact, the hourly compensation (wages and benefits) of the median worker has not grown in over 20 years, and the hourly compensation of the median male worker has been declining 1% each year since 1979 (see **Figure B**).

Technology is the favorite culprit cited by economists. According to this explanation, technology has raised the demand for skills more rapidly than our colleges can graduate skilled workers. As a result, the wages of more-skilled workers have been bid up. In contrast, the wages of low-skilled workers have suffered because there is less demand for them. Economists readily acknowledge that there is little direct evidence to support the technology story. Rather, they have attached a technology label to

FIGURE B
Productivity and Average & Median Compensation, 1973-94

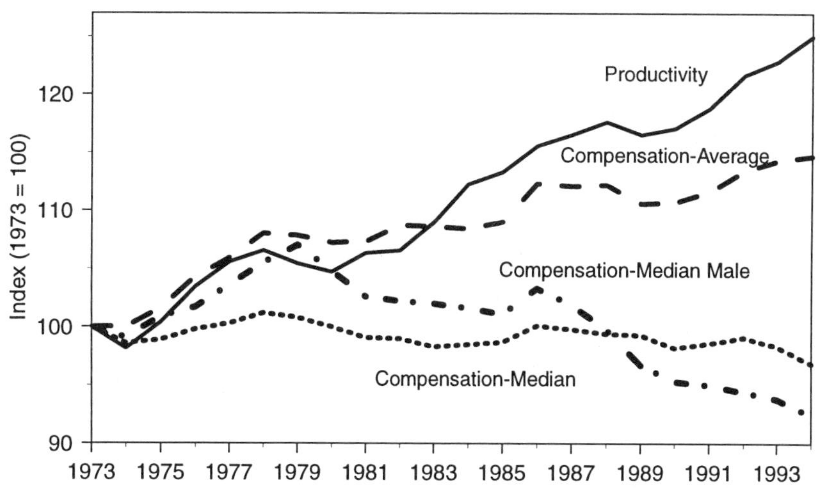

Source: Author's analysis.

whatever cannot be otherwise explained.

The technology story strains credulity. We are asked to believe that the effects of technology are powerful enough to raise wage inequality while at the same time they are not strong enough to raise productivity growth significantly. We are asked to describe a labor-market process that has lowered the real wages of male college graduates since 1987 as the "bidding up of skilled workers' wages." And we are asked to label workers with a high school degree, and even those with one to three years of college, as "low skilled." And, of course, technological change in the workplace is not new. For the technology story to make sense, technology has to have had a greater impact on labor markets in recent years than in earlier periods. My recent research with Jared Bernstein shows no acceleration in the rate of introduction of new technologies.

Most wages have been falling, despite rising productivity, for one simple reason. Workers—union and nonunion, college- and non-college-educated, white-collar and blue-collar—have lost bargaining power relative to their employers. Corporate America today has the power to respond to increased domestic and global competition by cutting labor costs. Profit rates on capital have recently reached record highs, fueled by lower wages and lower taxation of profits (see **Figure C**). If the profit rate in the early 1990s had been at the high level that prevailed in the early postwar period instead of at its current record level, then hourly compensation would have grown nearly twice as fast over the 1989-94 period and been 4% higher in 1994.[2] Unfortunately, this high profitability is not the result of any acceleration of productivity growth (i.e., increased efficiencies) or any investment boom that is, or will be, generating higher overall income growth. That is, higher profits are not associated with any social gain, only the dampening of wage growth.

Public policies have generally accommodated or reinforced the pursuit of a "low-wage path" to competitiveness by failing to pursue full employment, fair trade, higher minimum wages, or renewal of the labor movement. Certainly, current policy proposals will do little to reverse wage erosion and the accompanying pressures on family incomes. The long-term effects of deficit reduction on productivity are uncertain, slight, and at least a decade away. Clinton's Council of Economic Advisers estimated the payoff for the Administration's sizable deficit reduction package at 2.5% more consumption after 20 years. Republican proposals for

FIGURE C
Profitability, 1948-95*

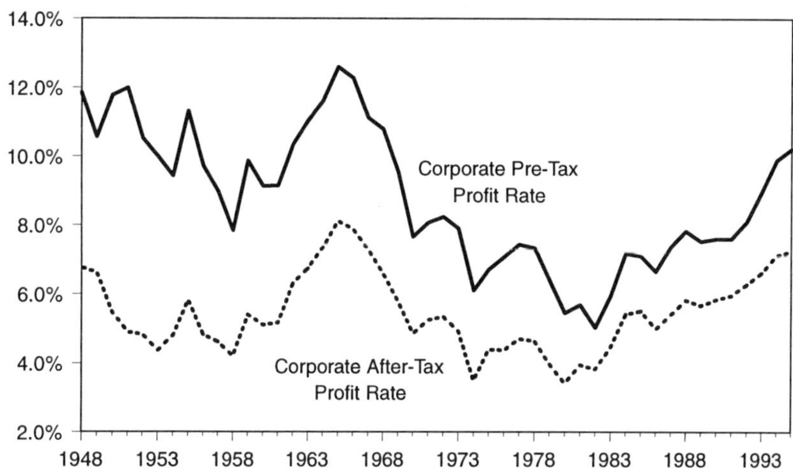

Estimated from the first quarter of 1995.

Source: Baker (1995).

deregulation and tax reduction will do nothing to upgrade the quality of jobs or to translate productivity growth into middle-class wage gains.

Rising wage inequality and the middle-class squeeze can be attributed to two clusters of factors.[3] First, the combined effect of globalization of markets and the continued expansion of employment in the lowest-paid portion of the service sector together explain at least a third of the wage problem. The Bureau of Labor Statistics attributes 25-30% of the growth of wage inequality to sectoral shifts alone. In addition, import pressure has lowered wages for many industrial workers and undercut the wages of non-college-educated workers generally.

The other prime culprit, responsible for another third of the wage problem, is the weakening of labor-market standards and institutions that improve the bargaining power of workers. The erosion of the minimum wage, a nearly 30% drop in value from its 1979 level, has particularly affected wage levels for women. Deunionization and the weakening of union bargaining power has had a particularly adverse effect on non-college-educated men. This erosion of wage-setting institutions can explain roughly another third of wage deterioration. Other factors that are harder to quantify, such as the growth of contingent work, have also had an impact.

The articles in this section propose policies that redress the decline of wages by raising skills, empowering workers, and changing the dynamics of how wages are set.

According to Ray Marshall, achieving high-performance production systems requires extensive employee involvement in what are "management" functions in mass production systems. Marshall proposes a set of complementary policies to improve the performance of companies and the wages and working conditions of employees.

Industrial relations policy affects both the representation of workers within the firm and the political representation of working families in the wider society. Paula Voos moves beyond conventional labor law reform to propose innovations that increase both employees' stakes in their firms and firms' stakes in their employees.

Peter Berg writes that, while training is part of the answer, current proposals miss the crucial target: the frontline labor force. Any strategy to achieve a high-skill, high-wage workforce cannot be limited to those *out of work.* If it is, it's more of an adjustment program, not a national strategy for high performance.

Marshall argues that one of the most important measures in the interest of workers and firms is the development of a consensus for a high-performance strategy, since market forces will tend to perpetuate the low-wage trajectory. William Spriggs and John Schmitt make the case that raising the minimum wage from its current level of $4.25 per hour to $5.75 would help us along the high-wage path by blocking the low-wage route.

Jared Bernstein and Irwin Garfinkel argue that welfare reform is really a labor-market issue. Because of declining labor-market prospects, they say, welfare caseloads have nowhere to go but up. Thus, strengthening low-wage labor markets is integral to welfare reform.

NOTES

1. Mishel and Bernstein 1994.
2. Baker 1995.
3. Mishel and Bernstein 1994.

REFERENCES

Baker, Dean. 1995. *Trends in Corporate Profitability: Getting More For Less?* Washington, D.C.: Economic Policy Institute.

Mishel, Lawrence and Jared Bernstein. 1994. *The State of Working America 1994-95.* Economic Policy Institute Series. Armonk, N.Y.: M.E. Sharpe.

CHAPTER 6

WORK ORGANIZATION
The Promise of High-Performance Production Systems

by Ray Marshall

FROM ROUGHLY 1940 TO 1970, AMERICAN WORKERS EXPERIENCED A LONG period of equitably shared economic growth and the highest wages in the world. The production system that helped produce these outcomes was widely emulated and had been established throughout Europe by the mid-1950s.

Today, the basic conditions undergirding this production system have been eroded by internationalization and technological change. New systems are emerging in response to these changes, but, with a few exceptions, American companies are lagging behind their international competitors in adopting new work systems, and the United States has been slow to develop the institutions and policies needed to deal with these new conditions.

High-performance work systems provide a foundation that can enable us to halt the erosion of real wages for most workers and restore a more equitable distribution of the benefits and costs of economic development. This chapter outlines the trends in new systems of work, describes the production system and supporting institutions that might restore equitable growth in real incomes, and concludes with the policies and institutional changes required to encourage and support such a system.

Ray Marshall holds the Bernard Rapoport Centennial Chair in Economics and Public Affairs at the LBJ School of Public Affairs at the University of Texas/Austin and is former U.S. secretary of labor.

The Way Things Used To Be

The economy that evolved in the United States during the first two-thirds of the 20th century had three distinguishing characteristics: a heavy natural resource orientation; supporting policies and institutions, especially pragmatic public-private partnerships to build the education, transportation, and other infrastructures that facilitated rapid economic growth and sustained the system during the 1930s when private demand faltered; and the mass production system. Mass production was made possible by a large and growing internal market for standardized products. The system's main economic advantage in basic industries was its ability to achieve economies of scale with a combination of relatively high fixed-capital costs, a few highly educated and skilled workers, and a heavy reliance on front-line workers who needed little more than basic literacy and math skills. This system's efficiency was demonstrated by Henry Ford's assembly line, which reduced the cost of a touring car from $850 to $360 in about six years just before World War I. Actually, the mass production system's advantages had already been demonstrated long before Henry Ford popularized it with his highly successful Model T. Andrew Carnegie, for example, used mass production techniques to reduce the cost of steel from $36.52 to $12 a ton between 1878 and 1898.[1] The advantages of the mass production system caused its management practices to be widely emulated in governments and schools as well as in industry.

The mass production organization of work was rationalized by Frederick Taylor's scientific management system, which sought to give management almost complete control by modeling the "one best" method for performing a task and transferring ideas, skills, and knowledge to management and machines. Only managerial, professional, and technical workers needed higher-order thinking skills. Most workers could perform the "one best" method with routine skills and basic literacy and numeracy. Management's control of the work was facilitated by detailed rules and regulations enforced by supervisors and inspectors.

Despite its productivity, the mass production system had a number of problems that were addressed in various ways by the end of the 1940s. Because of large capital requirements and high fixed costs, mass production companies were vulnerable to competition that could depress prices to below-average costs for long periods. Mass production companies consequently used their oligopolistic positions (in which a few firms control the market) to develop policies that "stabilized" prices, and they adjusted to changes in demand by varying both the utilization of their plant and equipment and employment. With fixed prices for oligopolies and competitive prices for workers and farmers, who often were squeezed by falling prices and high costs, production was periodically greater than consumption, leading to recessions.

After the Great Depression, the United States and other industrialized countries addressed the business cycle problem through "Keynesian" policies designed to reduce unemployment by stimulating demand. Many analysts thought that U.S. performance during World War II demonstrated the efficacy of these policies. The Keynesian system also justified unions, collective bargaining, and such income support systems as unemployment compensation, pensions, and agricultural price supports as ways to stabilize demand.

Another major problem for the mass production system was how to structure the relationships between workers and managers in systems where employers held overwhelming power relative to workers. In every industrial country, these relationships were worked out in industrial relations systems. The American system, established mainly during the 1930s and 1940s, had some features that resembled those of other industrial countries, but some that were unique. Shared characteristics included a Keynesian demand-management approach to economic policy; a commitment to a "free" labor movement;[2] and the involvement of representatives of labor, management, and specialized government agencies as the main actors in the system.

The common ideas holding the traditional system together included the right of workers to organize and unions' acceptance of the prevailing economic and political system. The traditional system also sought to protect working conditions and stimulate efficiency by "taking labor out of competition."

In addition to these features it had in common with other industrial nations, the American industrial relations system was distinguished by the following:

- *Exclusive representation,* whereby the union that is recognized as the bargaining agent represents all employees, whether or not they are union members. The legal right of workers to vote for or against unions in government-supervised elections has strongly influenced the American industrial relations system, creating competition between the union and nonunion sectors and between unions and employers for the workers' allegiance.

- *Decentralized bargaining,*[3] with heavy emphasis on wages, hours, and working conditions in particular firms, industries, and labor markets. But pattern bargaining has been very important—wage comparisons between companies and occupations are major elements in wage determination—with only a loose relation to economic conditions in particular firms or industries in the short run.
- *Greater hostility to unions by employers,* perhaps due to the greater political power of unions in other countries, which makes them a greater threat to hostile employers; the greater individualism and fluidity in the American system; and a laissez-faire political system that gives great weight to private property and business freedom from governmental constraints.
- *A nonsocialist political orientation.* American unions are unique in that they have not formed a labor party; less class consciousness has caused the American labor movement to organize mainly around the job for economic reasons rather than around the working class for political reasons. And the American political system has made it very difficult to organize third parties.

In large establishments, the American industrial relations system was closely related to the mass production organization of work and Taylorism. The alienating nature of that work, with its elitist management practices, invited an organized adversarial response from workers. And the oligopolistic pricing arrangements easily accommodated collective bargaining after the New Deal encouraged both administered prices and legal protections for workers to organize. While American industrial unions always found highly competitive industries very difficult to organize, after the 1930s they were more successful in unionizing oligopolies and regulated monopolies.[4]

THE NEW ECONOMY: GLOBAL COMPETITION AND HIGH-PERFORMANCE WORK ORGANIZATIONS

Toward the end of the 1960s, there were growing signs that America's economic system was in trouble. The main forces for change were technology and increased international competition, which combined to weaken the mass production system and its supporting institutions. In this more competitive world dominated by knowledge-intensive technology, the keys to economic success have become human resources and more effective production systems, not natural resources and traditional mass production economies of scale. Economies of scale are still very important, but they now must be considered in a global context, and they are called upon to recoup much more extensive research-and-development costs than before. Although no consensus has formed for a new economic policy model, two things are reasonably clear: the policies that supported the old economy have lost their effectiveness, and human capital must be the centerpiece for economic success in the new economy.

Technological change and the internationalization of competition have greatly weakened unions and traditional industrial relations systems. Except for the older craft unions, U.S. union strength was concentrated mainly in oligopolies and regulated industries, which became less viable in a more competitive economy. Similarly, technological change weakened U.S. unions by reducing the size of firms, dispersing employment to nonunion areas, and shifting the composition of employment away from highly unionized, blue-collar industrial workers toward relatively unorganized white-collar and service workers. Moreover, global joblessness and shortages of highly mobile capital and technology greatly strengthened the positions of multinational corporations relative to national unions.

THE CHOICE: HIGH-PERFORMANCE SYSTEMS OR LOW WAGES

With the internationalization of national economies, countries, companies, and people must yield to the imperatives of global competition if we are to thrive. The most basic of these imperatives is that we can compete in only two ways: reduce wages and incomes, or increase productivity and quality. Most high-wage industrial countries have either implicitly or explicitly rejected the low-wage option because it implies lower and more unequal wages—which is exactly what most workers in the United States have experienced in the past 20 years. The only workers whose incomes have increased since 1979 are the college-educated. Young male high school graduates' earnings were 30% lower in 1991 than in 1979. Among all male college graduates, earnings increased only for those with advanced degrees; young male college graduates actually earned 8% less in 1993 than they did in 1979, with most of the drop coming after 1987.[5]

The U.S. experience illustrates why most other industrialized countries have rejected the low-wage option—they see that lower and more unequal incomes threaten their political, social, and economic health. The only way for those following the low-wage option to improve total incomes is to work more, a reality that clearly limits economic progress.[6] The high-wage, high-productivity option, by contrast, could create very steep learning and earning curves, and therefore holds greater promise for personal, organizational, and national advancement.

What must we do to pursue the high-productivity option? Worldwide experience suggests that we must first develop national consensus for that option and then support the policies and strategies to achieve it. Because competitive market forces alone tend to produce low-wage outcomes, national strategies are necessary to create environments that discourage the low-wage alternative and encourage companies to organize for high performance. Indeed, sustainable high-performance systems are highly unlikely without the kind of supporting social and economic policies discussed below.

In a 1990 report based on more than 2,800 in-depth interviews at 550 companies in a broad cross section of industries, the Commission on the Skills of the American Workforce (CSAW) found that, relative to six other countries (Japan, Singapore, Germany, Sweden, Denmark, and Ireland), few American companies have moved to the high-performance option.[7] The CSAW found that 95% of major American companies cling to the mass production organization of work. Other studies[8] have produced much higher estimates of companies that have introduced flexible work arrangements, but that is not the same as high-performance systems as defined in this chapter. Before discussing why most American companies have been so slow to abandon the traditional organizational forms, it would be useful to outline the characteristics that most effective high-performance systems are developing in the United States and other countries. Although there is as yet no agreement on the definition of high performance, the following section outlines the characteristics of such a system.

Characteristics of High-Performance Organizations

Productivity, flexibility, and quality. In a competitive global information economy, success requires emphasis on factors that were much less important in traditional mass production systems. These new factors are quality, productivity, and flexibility.

Quality, best defined as meeting customers' needs,[9] becomes more important for two reasons. First, as the mass production system matured and personal incomes rose, consumers became less satisfied with standardized products. Second, a more competitive environment is largely consumer driven; the mass production system was more producer driven, especially after governments and oligopolies "stabilized" prices.

Productivity and flexibility are closely related to quality. The difference is that now productivity improvements are achieved through the more efficient use of all factors of production, not, as in the mass production system, mainly through economies of scale and shifts from low-productivity industries (such as agriculture) to high-productivity industries (such as manufacturing). The mass production system can be enormously wasteful in the utilization of capital (especially inventory) and people, but in the past this feature could be more than offset by economies of scale. Once technology reduced traditional scale advantages, mass production companies were left with labor and capital inefficiencies.

Flexibility enhances productivity by facilitating the shift of resources from less to more productive outputs, and it improves quality by facilitating quick responses to diverse and changing customer needs. Moreover, flexibility in the use of workers and technology improves productivity by reducing the waste of labor and machine time.

Worker participation and decentralized production systems. The fundamental issue, of course, is how to achieve quality, productivity, and flexibility. The answer is to create high-performance production systems, the defining characteristic of which is extensive employee involvement in what were considered "management" functions in mass production systems. Indeed, high-performance systems blur the distinctions between front-line "managers" and "workers."

A number of features of high-performance systems encourage decentralized, participative structures. First, workers must have more knowledge and skill, which in turn makes them less tolerant of monotonous, routine work and authoritarian managerial controls.[10] Second, quality, productivity, and flexibility are enhanced when production decisions are made as close as possible to the point of production. Mass production bureaucracies strive for quantity, managerial control, and stability, not flexibility, quality, or productivity in the use of all factors of production. Mass production systems are based on managerial information monopolies and control of workers; in high-performance systems, workers must be free to make decisions. To accomplish this, information must be shared, not monopolized.

Several features of the high-performance system reduce the efficacy of hierarchical management systems. First, because machines perform more of the direct work and front-line workers assume more of the indirect work formerly done by managers and administrators, fewer inspectors, schedulers, and other indirect workers are needed. Second, because workers manage more of their own work, individually or in teams, fewer supervisors are needed. Thus, the flow of information, a major function of Tayloristic managers, can be controlled by computers and other information technology, which can provide everybody a common database or "score," to use an orchestra analogy. The role of managers therefore shifts from "bossing" or supervising to teaching, building consensus, and supporting front-line workers, who assume more responsibility for quality, productivity, and flexibility.

One of the most important differences between high-performance and Tayloristic mass production systems is the attitudes of managers and workers toward one another. Taylorism assumes that workers are naturally lazy and must be forced to work for fear they will lose their jobs or be reprimanded. Taylor's system, in addition, was based on the belief that most front-line workers should not have to think and, indeed, were incapable of the higher-order thinking done by supervisors educated in "scientific management." This attitude naturally bred resentment and distrust of management by workers and unions. Labor's distrust was made worse by declining upward mobility for skilled, non-college-educated workers. High-performance managements, by contrast, foster trust and respect between workers and managers by assuming that most workers want to do a good job that enhances their self-worth and gains them the respect of management and their co-workers. High-performance managers believe, in addition, that skilled, motivated workers and effective work organizations are the keys to success; they believe that workers understand their jobs, are capable of higher-order thinking, and are motivated by positive reward systems.

Higher-order thinking skills. High-performance systems therefore require front-line workers to have different thinking skills than those needed in Tayloristic systems. One of the most important of these skills is the ability to analyze the flood of data produced by information technology; this skill requires workers to understand and utilize models, metrics, and other quantitative tools. Workers who are able to impose order on chaotic data can use information to add value to products, improve productivity and quality, solve problems, and improve technology.

High-performance work also is apt to be group work, requiring more communication, interpersonal skills, and teamwork. In addition, high-performance workers manage their own work, solve problems without assistance, and deal with ambiguity. These skills are necessary because productivity, quality, and flexibility require close coordination between what were formerly more discrete components of the production process (e.g., research and development, design, production, inspection, distribution, sales, and services). These functions were more linear in the mass production system, but are more interactive in dynamic, consumer-oriented production systems where rapid response times offer significant advantages.

Another important high-performance skill is the ability to learn. Indeed, since high-performance systems rely heavily on the substitution of ideas, skills, and knowledge for physical resources and hard work, learning—both internally and externally—along with participation, becomes a distinctive feature of a high-performance production system. Learning not only is more important in high-performance than in mass production systems, it is also very different. The simplification of tasks and the standardization of technology and production in Tayloristic systems limit the amount of learning needed or achieved. For line workers, mass production systems stress learning almost entirely by observation and doing. More learning is required in a dynamic, technology-intensive workplace, and more of that learning must be achieved through the manipulation of abstract symbols, simulations, and models. Learning in productive workplaces also is more communal and cooperative than was true in mass production systems. Well-educated, well-trained, highly motivated workers are much more flexible and productive, especially in supportive systems that stress equity and internal cohesion. Indeed, humans are likely to be the most flexible components in a high-performance system.

Development and use of leading-edge technology. Another feature of high-performance workplaces requiring greater employee involvement and higher-order thinking skills is the need for constant improvements in technology—or what the Japanese call "giving wisdom to the machine." Technology is best defined as how things are done. The most important fact about technology is not the physical capital itself but, as noted above, the ideas, skills, and knowledge embodied in machines and structures. Technology becomes standardized when the rates at which ideas, skills, and knowledge can be transferred to machines or structures become very small. Some American companies have responded to competitive pressures by combining high technology and low skills through automation.[11] General Motors, for example, spent over $70 billion on plant and equipment for a system based largely on this theory and was less competitive in 1986 than when the process started in the late 1970s.[12] The most productive systems, therefore, have highly skilled workers who adapt, develop, and use leading-edge technology in particular production systems. And the shorter life cycle of products and technologies in a dynamic and competitive global economy provides important advantages to continuous innovation and creativity.

The need to pay more attention to quality and productivity is another reason for front-line workers' increased involvement in production decisions. Flexible, highly skilled employees can provide better service than do workers who can offer only narrow specialized service. In manufacturing systems, moreover, even the most sophisticated machines are idiosyncratic and therefore require skilled workers who can adapt them to particular situations. While the mass production system's long production runs allowed companies to amortize the cost of startup defects over those long runs, systems with short production runs cannot afford many startup defects; these systems must therefore rely on workers to override machines that malfunction or produce defects. Quality-driven systems also require more inspection by workers on the basis of visible observation so that defects are prevented rather than detected at the end of the production process.

Positive reward systems. Because organizations ordinarily get the outcomes they reward, the explicit or implicit incentives of a system are basic determinants of its outcomes. High-performance systems stress positive rewards. Mass production incentives, by contrast, tend to be more negative—fear of discharge or punishment; they also are more individualistic and implicit. As noted below, mass production incentives sometimes actually are perverse in that they impede productivity enhancements.

Positive rewards enhance flexibility as well as productivity and quality. Group incentives and job security encourage flexibility by simultaneously overcoming resistance to the development and use of broader skills and providing employers greater incentives to invest in education and training to develop those skills. Similarly, properly structured bonus compensation systems provide greater incentives for workers to improve productivity and quality. The ability to participate in production decisions is itself a positive reward. In essence, the high-performance system substitutes clearly defined goals and objectives and positive rewards for the mass production system's rules, regulations, supervisors, and administrators.

It would be hard to overemphasize the importance of equity, trust, internal unity, and positive rewards for high-performance, knowledge-intensive workplaces, because all parties must be willing to "go all out" to achieve common objectives. In mass production systems workers often are justifiably afraid to improve productivity for fear they will lose their jobs. Similarly, the fragmentation of work within mass production systems gives workers little incentive to control quality—it is somebody else's responsibility. A high-performance system, by contrast, makes quality control everybody's responsibility.

The role of labor organizations. Workers are unlikely to go all out to improve productivity and quality unless they have an independent source of power to protect their interests in the process. Moreover, the relationships between workers and managers are inherently adversarial as well as cooperative. (Indeed, adversarial relations often work well because they provide processes to resolve inherent differences.) Workers therefore need an independent source of power to promote their interests in these adversarial relationships. It is not at all inconsistent for workers and their leaders to cooperate with management to increase performance and to bargain with management over the distribution of a company's gains. The challenge, of course, is to maximize common interests and prevent conflicts from becoming "functionless" by making all parties worse off.

Workers and managers often clash over inherent conflicts in the components of a high-performance system. Management typically wants to restrain wages, for example, whereas workers want to increase them. Workers value job security, while management stresses "flexibility," a tool that can threaten earnings, inhibit work rules to protect safety and health, and lead to "outsourcing" and the use of temporary contingent workers. How such clashes are resolved determines the extent to which incentives remain positive. The nature of the relationship between unions and management therefore is an important determinant of whether unionized firms can be high-performance organizations. Thus, logic as well as much evidence suggests that, with mutual acceptance and respect between unions and managers, unionized firms can achieve higher performance than can nonunion firms.

These, then, are the characteristics of a high-performance production system. However, before we discuss their application to American companies, several points should be stressed:

- *The high-performance work system is an ideal type and does not necessarily define a particular enterprise or industry.* Since it is a system, the components are interrelated and cannot be considered in isolation from each other; they work together in a complementary way to improve productivity, quality, and flexibility.

- *A system that depends heavily on cooperation and motivation will be more viable and successful than one that is controlled by, or conveys unfair benefits to, some stakeholders relative to others.* For example, a so-called "lean production system"[13] that is controlled mainly by managers can maximize short-run profits by forcing workers to work harder and smarter, downsizing, squeezing suppliers, and shifting production to low-wage countries. But such a strategy in the long run will receive less support from workers and communities, who are very important stakeholders influencing an organization's long-run viability. Indeed, a major reason for the greater emphasis on high-performance work systems in other countries relative to the United States is that most other industrialized democratic countries deny managers the low-wage option followed by so many American companies. While all production systems are evolving, and each has problems to overcome, the lean management-controlled Japanese production system is likely to be less viable in the long run than the German and Scandinavian models, which are more worker friendly.

- *A high-performance system is effective in a variety of organizational forms, industries, and firm sizes—its efficacy is not restricted to large manufacturing firms.* For example, the Italian "flexible specialization" model achieves high-performance outcomes (flexibility, productivity, and quality) through networks of small firms and local governments that meet all of the characteristics, including strong unions, of a high-performance system.

- *The full high-performance production system model as defined in this chapter has never been evaluated.* However, partial evaluations of its main components suggest that:

  (1) human capital investments produce high returns,[14] and at least 60% of productivity improvements come from "advances in knowledge" or "innovation,"[15] most often developed through individual and group learning in the production process;[16] in fact, studies of matched plants between countries confirm the positive correlations between productivity and workforce skills,[17] which often permit better coordination of work, smaller ratios of supervisors to workers, lower rates of machine breakdown, a higher level of machine technology, and more timely delivery of products;[18] and

  (2) worker participation greatly improves productivity and quality, especially when combined with positive reward systems; the more intensely workers are involved in production decisions, the greater the productivity improvements.[19]

- *In general, productivity is higher in union than in nonunion workplaces;* unionized employees are more likely to be involved in workplace innovations such as teamwork and gainsharing that yield higher productivity; and unions strengthen the effectiveness of more cooperative worker-management processes. However, the strength of the union effect depends heavily on the degree of trust between unions and managers.[20]

Some of the most important effects of strong political labor movements like those in Europe, Scandinavia, and Australia are to resist low-wage policies, provide political support for the high-performance option, and establish mechanisms to achieve the necessary restructuring of production processes. The Australian Labor Party, for example, explicitly developed a high-performance strategy in the 1980s and has supported specific activities to achieve this objective, including the decentralization of collective bargaining, higher investments in education and training, stronger social safety nets, work restructuring, and a more cooperative industrial relations system.

With respect to the Australian experience, an extensive evaluation by John Mathews concluded:

> Unions showed they could play an important role in all these change programmes. After coming in from the cold, where previous mass production attitudes had cast them, they were able to play a positive role in terms of an understanding of the change process, providing a means through which options could be tested and explored, and in some cases, an avenue through which support for change could be mobilized....If there is a single lesson to be wrung from the Australian case studies, it is surely that industrial relations can make or break programmes of organizational change.[21]

High Performance in the United States

The United States and other countries are in the process of adjusting to a more knowledge-intensive and competitive global economy. There is evidence that the United States and its business and labor organizations are adjusting to these realities more slowly than have their counterparts in other countries.[22] It is not at all clear why this is true, but several hypotheses can be advanced. One is that the United States had more success with the old economy than most other countries. We therefore developed institutions, attitudes, and policies that were deeply rooted in the mass production, natural-resource-oriented economy, making change difficult. The hierarchical organization of schools, governments, and companies is one such example.

Second, the strength of laissez-faire attitudes creates resistance to the consensus-based strategies required to force companies to organize for high performance. Indeed, the U.S. economic environment contains many incentives for companies to pursue low-wage alternatives. In Europe and Japan, in contrast, consensus-based public policies (the empowerment of workers, social support systems, labor standards, or full-employment and education policies) discourage low-wage strategies and encourage companies to organize for high performance.

Third, deeply entrenched institutions in the United States strongly impede change. Companies' internal reward systems often cause them to adopt policies and procedures that satisfy the short-run interests of some stakeholders but not others. And even if managers see that transforming hierarchical systems may be in their long-run interest, there can be serious risks of losing market share to cost-cutting competition or becoming targets for takeovers by other companies. The ownership of Japanese and German companies by suppliers and banks (prohibited by U.S. law since the 1930s) and worker representation on company boards in Germany make takeovers less likely and focus management attention on the long-run interests of workers and other stakeholders.[23] Unions also face serious obstacles in evolving from adversarial to more collaborative relationships. Members are likely to be dubious of collaboration between their leaders and the managers they have distrusted for so long. And U.S. unions are less likely than those in Australia or Europe to have the necessary institutional security or resources needed to support change.

In addition, because American schools have been oriented toward providing students with the skills required for routine mass production work, front-line workers in the United States are less likely than their German or Japanese counterparts to possess the higher-order thinking skills required for high-performance work. The United States does not have efficient job training processes like those in Europe and Japan or those being created in Australia, and front-line workers receive much less education and training on the job than do their counterparts in other countries. A consistent finding in studies of the transition to high-performance work is the need to invest 5% or more of payroll to train workers at every level.[24]

Finally, since worker participation is an indispensable prerequisite of a high-performance system, American employers' strong resistance to sharing power with workers makes it difficult to create the most effective high-production systems.

The most important measure the United States could take to accelerate the move to high performance would be to develop consensus for a high-performance strategy and the necessary policies to achieve it. A strategy is required because, under present conditions, market forces alone will perpetuate the low-wage trajectory and continue to polarize incomes. Such a course would continue to weaken national unity and undermine democratic institutions.

Measures that would block the low-wage option include:

- Strengthening the social safety nets—especially health care—and family support systems that currently force unemployed workers to reduce wage levels by taking whatever jobs they can find.
- Raising minimum wages to allow workers to support themselves and their families and to create incentives for jobless people to work. Measures like the earned income tax credit are useful, but they act like wage subsidies for employers and therefore do not substitute for minimum wages.
- Strengthening the right of workers to organize and bargain collectively.

Measures to facilitate the movement to the most beneficial forms of high performance for workers and the country include:

- Creating systems to support high performance, including: market systems that promote economic growth and competition; supportive networks of high-performance suppliers; ready access to leading-edge technology; ready access to financial capital at competitive rates; and high-quality factors of production, including modern equipment and highly trained workers.[25]
- Transforming schools and other learning systems into high-performance organizations. A major precondition for this outcome is to establish high-performance standards for learners moving from one system to the next, especially from schools and training programs into the workforce.[26]
- Reforming corporate law and financial institutions to require or encourage participation by workers and other stakeholders on corporate

boards, and removing the risks to companies of taking longer strategic perspectives and making the investments required for the transformation to high performance.[27]

- Facilitating the process of change through institutions to give information, tax incentives, and technical assistance to companies wishing to reorganize or establish themselves as high-performance production systems. The United States should learn from the Australian experience and make labor relations a more important requirement for the Baldrige award.[28]
- Modernizing international institutions and policies to encourage all countries to pursue high performance. The high-performance option does not mean, of course, that all countries have the same standards or procedures, but rather that the operating principle should be for all countries to adopt minimum international labor standards and compete mainly by maintaining and improving those conditions, not by suppressing wages and working conditions.
- Improving the labor relations climate by (a) implementing the recommendations of the Commission on the Future of Worker-Management Relations (1994) to strengthen workers' right to organize, thus reducing the negative effects of acrimonious organizing campaigns and union-avoidance strategies by companies; and (b) mandating joint participatory processes, like occupational safety and health. The experience in other countries suggests that giving workers the right to decide on participatory processes improves labor relations, especially where the participation is backed by strong labor organizations, and where collective bargaining and adversarial relationships are separated from more cooperative or less adversarial labor-management processes to improve performance.
- Creating strong incentives for companies to provide education and training for front-line workers. The CSAW recommended a mandatory training obligation of 1% of payroll; the Clinton Administration raised this to 1.5%. However, this proposal met stiff resistance from business. The federal government should work out an acceptable incentive system with unions and major business groups, but if that fails, Congress should mandate a training obligation of at least 1.5% of payroll—which would be low by international best-practice standards.

Conclusion

Besides getting the credit for introducing mass production to American manufacturing, Henry Ford also stands out in business lore for being one of the first major capitalists to realize that workers had to receive high enough wages to buy the products that were being mass produced. In many ways, the realization that production works best when it is an interactive, dynamic process has stopped there. It is as if Americans believe that the systems of production that carried them through the first two-thirds of the century will sustain them again, perhaps after this downturn or after some rough adjustments to international competition.

In the meantime, while businesses in the United States lower wages and incomes to keep their profits up, our international competitors have turned their attention to productivity. The low-wage strategy implies lower and more unequal incomes, with all that this implies for democratic institutions and social harmony, as well as economic performance. The low-wage strategy also limits improvements in incomes to hard work and the use of more physical resources, which is inherently self-limiting. By contrast, the high-productivity option substitutes ideas, skills, and knowledge for physical labor and resources. We do not know where this option leads, but it puts people on steeper learning and earning curves and therefore could lead to higher and more equitably shared incomes.

A national strategy for high-performance production thus offers a route by which both American business and American workers can return to a high-productivity path toward greater market share, profits, and wages. It is difficult to imagine anything more important to America's economic future.

Notes

1. Marshall and Tucker 1992, p. 4.

2. A free labor movement is free from control by outside political or religious organizations and emphasizes democratic control by its members and the right to strike.

3. Decentralized bargaining means that collective bargaining is mainly at the firm, industry, or local levels. In some countries bargaining is more national or regional in scope and is more likely to be industry-wide than in the United States. However, some

U.S. industries—bituminous coal mining, steel, and long-distance trucking—have had industry-wide bargaining, although it has been weakened or broken up since the early 1970s. Pattern bargaining has been more common in the United States; with this type of bargaining, the unions select a firm to set the pattern to be used in attempting to secure similar conditions in other firms in the industry.

4. Marshall 1967.

5. Mishel and Bernstein 1994, p. 109.

6. According to Juliet Schor (1991), the average American worker works about one month more now than in the 1960s for about the same real wage.

7. CSAW 1990.

8. For example, Osterman 1993.

9. Quality often refers to zero defects, but this is not as appropriate, for competitiveness purposes, as meeting customers' needs. Timely delivery or convenience might be as useful to customers as zero defects. Some firms have extended the "meeting customers' needs" concept to include "customers" within the firm.

10. This was a major factor in the introduction of the socio-technical system in Sweden.

11. Keller 1989; Smith 1995.

12. Smith 1995.

13. Womack, Jones, and Ross 1990.

14. Middleton, Ziderman, and Adams 1993, p. 42.

15. Baumol, Blackman, and Wolff 1989.

16. Hulten 1993; Lillard and Tan 1986; Denison 1985.

17. Mason and van Ark 1992.

18. Prais and Wagner 1988, pp. 34-37.

19. Dertouzos, Lester, and Solow 1989; Blinder 1989/90; Economic Policy Council 1990; Krafcik 1988; Adler 1991; Levine and Tyson 1990.

20. Freeman and Medoff 1984, pp. 162-63; Eaton and Voos 1992; Kelley and Harrison 1992; Freeman and Rogers 1993; Mishel and Voos 1992; Marshall 1987; Belman 1992, pp. 45-46.

21. Mathews 1994, pp. 258, 261.

22. CSAW 1990; Appelbaum and Batt 1993.

23. Smith 1995.

24. CSAW 1990; Marshall and Tucker 1992.

25. Porter 1990.

26. Marshall and Tucker 1992; CSAW 1990.

27. Porter 1992; Smith 1995.

28. The Baldrige Award for quality is named for Malcom Baldrige, secretary of commerce in the Reagan Administration. This award was inaugurated in 1988. Most of the Baldrige criteria for quality improvements are based on improvements in management (85%) and a relatively small percentage (15%) for improvements in human resource practices.

REFERENCES

Adler, Paul. 1991. "Capitalizing on New Manufacturing Technologies: Current Problems and Emergent Trends in U.S. Industry." In National Academy of Engineering and Commission on Behavioral and Social Sciences and Education, National Research Council, ed., *People and Technology in the Workplace.* Washington, D.C.: National Academy Press.

Appelbaum, Eileen and Rosemary Batt. 1993. *High Performance Work Systems.* Washington, D.C.: Economic Policy Institute.

Baumol, W.J., S.A. Blackman, and E.N. Wolff. 1989. *Productivity and American Leadership: The Long View.* Cambridge, Mass.: MIT Press.

Belman, Dale. 1992. "Unions, the Quality of Labor Relations, and Firm Performance." In Lawrence Mishel and Paula Voos, eds., *Unions and Economic Competitiveness.* Armonk, N.Y.: M.E. Sharpe.

Blinder, Alan. 1989/90. "Pay Participation and Productivity." *The Brookings Review,* Winter, pp. 33-8.

Commission on the Skills of the American Workforce. 1990. *America's Choice: High Skills or Low Wages.* Rochester, N.Y.: National Center on Education and the Economy.

Denison, Edward. 1985. *Trends in American Economic Growth: 1929-1982.* Washington, D.C.: Brookings Institution.

Dertouzos, Michael L., Richard K. Lester, and Robert M. Solow. 1989. *Made in America: Regaining the Productive Edge.* Cambridge, Mass.: MIT Press.

Eaton, Adrienne and Paula Voos. 1992. "Unions and Contemporary Innovations in Work Organization, Compensation, and Employee Participation." In Lawrence Mishel and Paula Voos, eds., *Unions and Economic Competitiveness.* Armonk, N.Y.: M.E. Sharpe.

Economic Policy Council of the United Nations Association. 1990. *The Common Interests of Employees and Employers in the 1990s.* New York: Economic Policy Council.

Freeman, Richard and James Medoff. 1984. *What Do Unions Do?* New York: Basic Books.

Freeman, Richard B. and Joel Rogers. 1993. "Who Speaks for Us? Employee Relations in a Non-Union Market." In Morris Kleiner and Bruce Kaufman, eds., *Employee Representation, Alternatives and Future Directions.* Madison, Wis.: Industrial Relations Research Association.

Hulten, Charles R. 1993. "Growth Accounting When Technical Change Is Embodied in Capital." *American Economic Review,* September, pp. 964-80.

Keller, Maryann. 1989. *The Rude Awakening.* New York: William Morrow.

Kelley, Maryellen and Bennett Harrison. 1992. "Unions, Technology, and Labor-Management Cooperation." In Lawrence Mishel and Paula Voos, eds., *Unions and Economic Competitiveness.* Armonk, N.Y.: M.E. Sharpe.

Krafcik, John. 1988. "Triumph of the Lean Production System." *Sloan Management Review,* Fall, pp. 41-52.

Levine, David I. and Laura D. Tyson. 1990. "Participation, Productivity, and the Firm's Environment." In Alan S. Blinder, ed., *Paying for Productivity: A Look at the Evidence.* Washington, D.C.: Brookings Institution.

Lillard, Lee A. and Hong W. Tan. 1986. *Private Sector Training: Who Gets It and What Are Its Effects?* Santa Monica, Calif.: Rand Corporation.

Marshall, Ray. 1967. *Labor in the South.* Cambridge, Mass.: Harvard University Press.

Marshall, Ray. 1987. *Unheard Voices: Labor and Economic Policy in a Competitive World.* New York: Basic Books.

Marshall, Ray and Marc Tucker. 1992. *Thinking for a Living: Education and the Wealth of Nations.* New York: Basic Books.

Mason, Geoff and Bart van Ark. 1992. "Education, Training and Productivity: An Anglo-Dutch Comparison." Paper presented to the ESRC Study Group on the Economics of Education, London Business School, January 17.

Mathews, John. 1994. *Catching the Wave: Workplace Reform in Australia.* Ithaca, N.Y.: ILR Press.

Middleton, John, Adrian Ziderman, and Arvil Van Adams. 1993. *Skills for Productivity.* New York: Oxford University Press.

Mishel, Lawrence and Jared Bernstein. 1994. *The State of Working America 1994-95.* Economic Policy Institute Series. Armonk, N.Y.: M.E. Sharpe.

Mishel, Lawrence and Paula Voos. 1992. "Unions and American Competitiveness." In Lawrence Mishel and Paula Voos, eds., *Unions and Economic Competitiveness.* Economic Policy Institute Series. Armonk, N.Y.: M.E. Sharpe.

Osterman, Paul. 1993. "How Common Is Workforce Transformation and How Can We Explain Who Adopts It?" Paper for Allied Social Science Association meeting, Anaheim, Calif., January.

Porter, Michael. 1990. *The Competitive Advantage of Nations.* New York: Free Press.

Porter, Michael. 1992. "Capital Choices: Changing the Way America Invests in Industry." Report to the Council on Competitiveness, co-sponsored by Harvard Business School.

Prais, S.J. and Karin Wagner. 1988. "Productivity and Management: The Training of Foremen in Britain and Germany." *National Institute Economic Review,* No. 123, February, pp. 34-47.

Schor, Juliet. 1991. *The Overworked American: The Unexpected Decline of Leisure.* New York: Basic Books.

Smith, Hedrick. 1995. *Rethinking America.* New York: Random House.

Womack, James P., Daniel T. Jones, and Daniel Roos. 1990. *The Machine That Changed the World.* New York: Rawson Associates.

CHAPTER 7

LABOR LAW REFORM
Closing the Representation Gap

by Paula Voos

WORKING AMERICANS, INCREASINGLY "THE ANXIOUS CLASS," ARE NOW on a "downward escalator" according to Labor Secretary Robert Reich. As real wages and incomes fall, our anxiety is heightened, some argue, by a growing "representation gap"—a lack of voice in the economic and political arenas as well as in the workplace.

Independent labor organizations—unions—have historically been the key institutions offering workers representation in the work environment. Unions are imperiled in the United States today. Yet in a world of increased competition, labor organization is more important than ever for achieving our most important economic and political goals: a high and rising standard of living, a vital middle class, political democracy, employee voice in the workplace, a high quality of worklife, and individual liberty.

Unions are human organizations and, like corporations, universities, government, and other human endeavors, sometimes suffer from poor leadership, inertia, financial irregularities, and internal strife. Despite occasional failings, however, unions have enormous potential. They allow employees with relatively little individual bargaining power to come together to raise their compensation and voice their concerns. This contributes to a strong middle class and a more equal distribution of income. They facilitate meaningful employee participation and voice on the job—indeed, unionization is the one means today whereby employees can initiate involvement in corporate decision making. Labor organizations guarantee individual rights at work by insisting that individuals can only be disciplined or discharged for a valid reason. And by representing employees in a political world often dominated by monied

Paula Voos is professor of economics and industrial relations at the University of Wisconsin.

interest groups, unions promote a pluralistic democracy. Given the positive role unions can play in all these areas, public policy should be reoriented to encourage employees to organize and to allow their organizations to thrive.

Recently, some have claimed that what is needed in the workplace is not necessarily stronger union representation but rather enhanced opportunities for employee voice. Indeed, such economic voice is highly desired by employees and should be provided by our industrial relations system. However, in a competitive environment, voice on economic issues will tend to be ineffective unless employees can organize across firms and eliminate competition based on low wages, lack of health insurance and other benefits, unsafe working conditions, or other low labor standards. Hence, independent labor organization—that is, which is controlled by employees and has the potential of reaching across employers—is likely to become more, not less, important in the future.

The Need for Economic Representation of Employees

It is well known that unions raise wages and benefits of represented employees. Virtually all of the standard fringe benefits observed in the economic system today—pensions, health insurance, paid vacations—were the product of collective bargaining. In a recent survey, 41% of all employees said that raising wages and benefits was the most important thing unions do; 22% chose gaining more respect and fair treatment on the job; and 14% chose providing more say in workplace decisions.[1] Clearly, Americans expect unions to provide them with effective economic representation.

Labor organizations raise wages at a relatively small cost to economic efficiency in the society as a whole.[2] In part this occurs because of their other economic effects. Unions reduce the turnover of employees and thereby enhance the retention and accumulation of skills, encourage employer provided training, and improve working conditions like health and safety.[3] Where they represent employees, unions probably increase productivity, but less than they increase compensation.[4] At the same time, labor organizations reduce profits[5] and reduce inequality in the distribution of income.[6]

Since the late 1970s, income inequality has been widening in the United States and real wages have been falling, especially for non-college-educated men. A polarized society with a small middle class is one in which norms of human decency, social stability, and political democracy will be more difficult to maintain. Reducing or counteracting these trends will require a variety of public and private policy initiatives, including improved education and training, employee involvement for higher productivity, economic policy designed to bolster demand, an increased minimum wage, social programs for those not able to participate in the labor market, and so forth. A number of studies have shown that declining union membership and strength can account for at least 20% of the overall growth in wage inequality.[7] Expanding unionization, especially among lower-wage service and retail employees, would make an important contribution toward counteracting this trend.

Traditionally unions have been able to raise wages and improve benefits by standardizing them across competing employers, forcing employers to compete not through low wages but on the basis of quality, customer service, and productivity (this has been called "taking wages out of competition"). In a world of increased global competition and increased capital mobility, this basic union strategy has become more difficult, particularly in manufacturing industries in which goods are traded worldwide. The result has been downward pressure on union wages and levels of organization in the 1980s.[8] Nonetheless, there are several factors that continue to make it possible for unions to provide economic representation to employees and improve their compensation.

In manufacturing, the increased importance of near-market location, with just-in-time production and inventory-control processes, and the increased economic importance of rapid product development have given U.S. producers an edge over foreign competitors that can counterbalance somewhat higher labor costs. A second factor in manufacturing is the overall lessening in importance of labor costs to total competitiveness—transportation costs, inventory costs, costs of delay or slow delivery, and a high-quality product are increasingly important in comparison to labor costs. Third, organized employers and their employees are often able to bargain for increased productivity, and increased productivity can offset higher labor costs.

But what about the non-manufacturing sectors? Increasingly, employees work in services, including retail trade, where labor costs are often a substantial portion of total costs. Eliminating competition based on low wages, obtaining health insurance and pension coverage, and eliminating the use of underage employees are essential for effective economic representation. Fortunately, competition in services is often local or regional. Nursing homes, taxi services, automobile repair shops, supermarkets, beauty shops, and so forth have to be organized only on a metropolitan basis, not nationally or internationally, to eliminate competition based on low labor standards. This requires organizations that reach across competing employers.

Voice for Employees Within the Firm: An Alternative to Unions?

Over the last few years there has been a growing public policy discussion that emphasizes employee involvement and participation as vehicles of employee voice, as well as sources of increased productivity, competitiveness, and potentially increased compensation. Many employers and some academics contend that "employee empowerment" through involvement, as opposed to outside labor organization, offers the bright future of industrial relations. How well does employee involvement in the nonunion firm compare to unionization as a vehicle of voice? And what about government-mandated forms of employee representation, such as the works councils in Western Europe, or health and safety committees? Would they be a better vehicle of voice for the future than independent labor organization?

There are essentially three perspectives on employee involvement, voice, and independent labor organizations. The first, the unitary perspective, is common among nonunion employers and some human resource management academics, but is rejected by virtually all industrial relations scholars and by most labor economists, even the ones who are not particularly prounion. The second, which might be termed the participatory democracy approach, is adopted by some industrial relations scholars who view employee involvement as having a major potential for providing voice in the 21st century. Finally, the partnership perspective welcomes the limited participatory democracy and voice provided by employee involvement in nonunion situations, but it emphasizes that it is not an adequate substitute for independent labor organization and representative democracy.[9]

The unitary perspective. Employers have argued that, with good management, there is no need for employees to have independent representation or voice.[10] If there is a problem of inadequate upward and downward communication in an organization or of "alignment of vision" between the corporation and its employees, employee involvement programs, they say, can be constructive. Unlike unions, which typically provide indirect participation through representation, direct employee involvement "empowers" groups of workers to take the initiative in improving productivity, quality, and other work-related tasks. The firm and its employees are envisioned as a family, and indeed the "outside" labor union is resisted precisely because it is seen as disrupting this constructive relationship and introducing an artificial adversarial atmosphere. If employees are managed well, according to this perspective, they will neither need nor want representation from an outside labor organization. Employee participation structures, supplemented by the human resources department, are adequate vehicles of employee "voice" in the organization, where voice is perceived as "upward communication." James Sweet, vice president for human resources for the nonunion W. H. Brady Company, sums up this point of view regarding communications:

> When employee-management relations are operating at a high performance level, you don't need a union....You don't need a third party to interrupt the flow of communication.[11]

The unitary perspective is often used to justify anti-union activities.

Industrial relations scholars and labor economists have long rejected the unitary vision of the corporation and have insisted that employers and employees have inherently conflicting interests, such as those between raising wages and raising profits. Furthermore, industrial relations scholars argue that individuals in an authority relationship (managers and those they manage) often disagree over the limits of legitimate authority. For instance, friction arises over what is reasonable for the employee to do or over the amount of time needed for an assignment. Thus, the unitary perspective cannot provide a basis for public policy because it denies precisely the conflicts that policy makers have to address.

The participatory democracy perspective. This approach accepts that employers and employees have different interests, and argues that priority should be to provide some level of voice for all employees, whether or not they are represented by a union, precisely for this reason. Upgraded employee involvement processes and increased choice between union representation and a variety of employer-provided programs might be one option. Other participatory democracy theorists say that this is not sufficient, and that we need a government-mandated system of representation, comprising either works councils or committees devoted to particular topics like health and safety or training (see box).[12]

In this perspective, employee participation programs provide a voice to employees in a (limited) range of issues such as how the work is done, how quality is assured, how safety can be improved, and so forth. Involvement in this view is an opening wedge for greater freedom and voice within the largely authoritarian world of employment. The thinking is that, once employers set up participatory structures, they will have to agree to some employee suggestions or else lose all credibility and effectiveness of those structures in enhanced productivity, continuous quality improvement, and other corporate goals. In this view, participation goes beyond "upward communication"; it evolves toward greater freedom and influence for employees.

This vision has a number of problems and limitations. First, there cannot be real voice without free speech—the ability to criticize management without fear of retaliation. However, while the existing law on "concerted activity" theoretically applies to employee involvement, in reality freedom of speech is limited in nonunion firms today. Where employers have the right to set pay and determine promotions unilaterally, and employment is "at will," many employees will legitimately fear criticizing current practices.[13]

Second, as long as employee involvement concerns issues affecting participating employees themselves, there is no problem with participatory democracy. However, as employee involvement moves to larger (or strategic) issues in the corporation, where employees represent other employees as well as themselves, problems emerge. As long as the company appoints the representatives, and the employees represented cannot recall representatives who do not promote their interests, voice is not democratic.[14]

Is Employee Choice the Answer?

Company-sponsored employee involvement programs, works councils, arms-length union representation, union-management partnerships, minority representation, and "full-service unions," which provide training and placement assistance for workers organized by occupation, all may be good vehicles of representation in some situations. Tom Kochan, for instance, argues:

> We need a wide range of alternative forms of participation and representation that are available to the workforce, given its present and future diversity and the diverse types of employment arrangements that are evolving. So I don't see any single "one best" model, nor do I think the different models are mutually exclusive (Kochan 1995).

Kochan would not support classic employer-dominated employee representation plans (company unions). Others, however, would add them to the list of options, as long as workers have a free choice to organize into independent unions and had additional legal protection to insure fair dealing. Kaufman (1995), for instance, proposes that company unions be legal as long as the employer provides a legally enforceable employee handbook, including some formalized system of dispute resolution. The key argument is that as long as employees can exercise free choice—can unionize without fear of reprisal, or can quit—undesirable employer behavior will be constrained and alternative forms of representation kept "honest."

The choice perspective would be more persuasive if employees could easily unionize. Even then, however, company unions would fail on all fundamental criteria of employee voice (little protection for free speech, no right to elect employee representatives, no right to information, no right to consult over particular issues or to have advice heeded, employer domination). Even if the free speech issue were to be solved, company unions would still be vehicles of employer, not employee, voice. **—PV**

Third, it is difficult to "empower" people if they do not have some independent power already. Employee involvement programs are typically advisory; there is no employee power other than suggestion or persuasion. Employee involvement programs can be changed or canceled at any time by employers, an outcome made more likely by high turnover of top executives and frequent corporate mergers and takeovers. While employees may be outraged, there is little they can do about it except quit or unionize.

These three considerations are most problematic for employer-provided programs. There is some evidence that employees themselves recognize this and demand voice that is considerably more independent, influential, and extensive than that provided by the usual involvement program (see box). What about works councils, or some other form of government-mandated committee involving all employees for any employer, union or nonunion? With guarantees of free speech rights, democratic selection of representatives by employees, and mandated discussion of particular decisions now seen as exclusively "managerial," works councils would greatly expand the representation of employees in decision making by firms. However, most proposals for councils contain a "peace" proviso that would limit the rights of councils to press for higher wages and benefits. Works councils do not, and probably cannot, provide effective economic representation on compensation—in Germany they work precisely because economic issues such as collective bargaining are dealt with in other forums. Works councils may have promise, but American workers also need effective economic representation.

The partnership perspective. This approach emphasizes the importance of labor organization for achieving greater worker representation and voice within firms. It sees employee involvement programs as desirable, especially when they are teamed with labor organization, but it puts the primary public policy emphasis on fostering unionization.

Unions are an effective vehicle for representative or indirect participation in decision-making by employees in all types of firm decisions for precisely the reasons employee involvement processes are not. Unions protect employee free speech through "just cause" provisions in contracts, in which employees cannot be discharged except for valid reason.[15] Furthermore, unions increase democracy within largely nondemocratic workplaces. By law, local union officers must be democratically elected, and hence can be voted out of office if they do not serve members' interests; most unions go beyond the minimum legal requirements by providing contract ratification votes and other avenues of democracy. Unions cannot be disestablished by the employer; they have independent existence. They increase the bargaining power of employees by allowing individuals with limited individual bargaining power to use collective action. This power insures that employers heed employee voice, and it gives employ-

What Do Employees Want?

The Worker Representation and Participation Survey, directed by Richard Freeman and Joel Rogers, provides some information on what American employees now want with regard to involvement, voice on the job, and representation.

- Most employees (63%) want more influence or decision-making power on the job than they have now.
- A substantial minority of nonunion employees (32%) say they would vote for a union to represent them in the job where they now work.
- Most employees believe that management cooperation is key to successful workplace organization. By 78% to 17% they agree with the statement "employee organization...can only be effective if management cooperates" with it.
- Cooperation implies substantive influence to employees. Only 22% think management is being cooperative "if a company always listens to what employees have to say, but doesn't follow their advice."
- They prefer to select their own representatives. Asked how committee members should be selected, nonunion workers overwhelmingly chose against management selection, with a plurality favoring employee election (50%), another large group desiring self-selection by volunteers (36%), and 9% favoring management selection.
- They strongly prefer an organization where either management or employees can raise problems over one where management decides what should be discussed (91% versus 7%).
- They strongly prefer a situation where employees and management have to agree on decisions, as opposed to management making the final decision (81% versus 17%).
- A majority prefers an organization in which employees can meet on their own to discuss workplace problems (50%) as opposed to one in which all meetings are held with employees and management together (47%).

In sum, while only a minority of employees would vote for a union at the present time, a much greater number are attracted to workplace organizations with considerable independence and capacity to influence workplace decisions.

The survey was based on a representative sample of 2,400 employees in privately owned firms with more than 25 workers conducted in fall 1994; a second smaller wave (800) was conducted in February 1995. **—PV** ees a firm basis for cooperative partnership with management. Finally, unions allow workers to join together across corporations to assist one another in improving their economic position by negotiating industry-wide or market-wide agreements.

On the whole it appears that participatory democracy (employee involvement) and representative democracy (collective bargaining) are complementary in a workplace context.[16] It is well documented that works councils are more effective in countries in which collective bargaining is well developed, as in Germany, than in countries in which it is weak, as in France.[17] Similarly, employee involvement is both more likely to yield good results for employees and more likely to be sustained in an organized environment, particularly one in which the union is supportive of the involvement effort and assists in managing it.[18] Unfortunately, the flip side of the fact that the existence of unions makes employee participation more likely is that the decline of unions limits the growth and sustainability of employee involvement in the United States.

In summary, employee involvement in the nonunion workplace offers advantages, but it will never be a substitute for collective bargaining. In fact, it has the greatest potential to be adopted and sustained in the organized workplace, since there its advantages can be complemented by the use of representative democracy to move participation to higher, "strategic" issues, to give workers voice in the very operation of the involvement process, and to reap the advantages of productivity bargaining for continuous improvement.

The Political Representation of Employees

Representation in the political system comes not only through elected government officials but also through a system of lobbying and political mobilization through voluntary interest groups. Obviously, employees like other citizens are free to vote, to join one voluntary association or another, to make donations to causes or campaigns, and to be affiliated with a political party. Additionally, labor unions play a role as political representatives of working Americans, both union and nonunion.[19] Today organized labor uses both political action and lobbying to advance a broad political agenda on behalf of many working and middle-income families. In fact, organized labor has often been more successful with regard to its broad agenda than it has been with regard to direct union interests.[20]

In recent years, many Americans have questioned the influential role organized groups play in the political system. But such associations are inevitable in a democracy; there should rather be concern if these forces are not balanced out. Labor representation tends to balance the influence of business interests and wealthy individuals in the political process. Today, the economically advantaged have considerable representation through campaign finance and lobbying activities. In contrast, working- and middle-income Americans perceive themselves to be underrepresented. Organized labor is one of the few political groups representing the economic interests of working families.

While employee involvement programs and works councils may enhance employee voice in the workplace, they cannot provide workers with political representation in the broader society. To help ensure that workers have effective economic and political voice, government policy needs to encourage labor organization where it is desired by employees.

Public Policy to Enhance the Representation of Employees

Two types of policy initiatives are needed to insure that employees who desire union representation are able to organize. One might be termed "conventional labor law reform," which is oriented toward fixing a number of widely recognized problems in the current representation election system. The second type of initiative might be termed "visionary." It looks to a whole new system of organizing (and representation) for emerging employment situations, particularly those in the service sector. Visionary proposals often focus on adapting the current union representation system to a more competitive economic environment.

Conventional reform proposals are important because most union organizing in the near future is likely to be of the familiar sort—industrial organization of essentially stable units of employees—and because existing unions are likely to be around for a while. Yet there are serious problems in the fit between the current representation election process and the portion of the economy marked by small employers, subcontracting, contingent employment relationships, and so forth. Hence, both conventional and visionary reforms are needed.

Conventional labor law reform. Conventional labor law reform would address current problems with the representation election process. These include employer discharge and discrimination against union supporters (discharge occurs in perhaps one in four representation elections today), unequal access and debate (union organizers and supporters have much less ability to present their views before an election), lack of coverage of the law (perhaps one in four employees are now excluded from protection), and a process marked by excessive delay.[21] Even when employees vote to unionize, they are unable to get a collective bargaining agreement about one-third of the time. This outcome is probably related to the fact that it is perfectly legal for employers to permanently replace economic strikers.

These problems have been the subject of both modest, centrist reform proposals, such as those offered by the Carter Administration and by the recent Commission on the Future of Worker-Management Relations[22] (of which I was a part), and more sweeping and inclusive attempts to give employees ready access to representation. Our list of priorities for conventional labor law reform (see box) is in the latter spirit.

Visionary labor law reform. Beyond conventional labor law reform, it is important to consider how to modify the entire union organizing process in order to meet the needs of employees in competitive, local market environments. Labor organization in such environments needs to be market-wide in order to eliminate competition based on low wages, lack of benefits, and low labor standards. Organization might be occupational in nature.

This type of union structure has been impeded by a labor law focused on elections in very small units, units that often cannot be the basis of effective representation because of the fluidity of employers and employees and the lack of representation in the rest of the market.[23] Moving to a system that lets individual employees decide if they want to be members of a union would provide a better basis for the growth of occupational or "associational" unionization in competitive markets. Increasingly, the labor movement is talking about this possibility under the guise of "minority representation" or "members-only representation."

Priorities for Reform of Conventional Labor Law

Return choice to employees and make the process less bureaucratic

- Certify based on authorization cards where there is a "super-majority" (for example, 60%).
- Hold representation elections in other units quickly (say, within two weeks) by hearing challenges after the election.

Reduce unfair labor practices

- Require that the National Labor Relations Board get injunctions to return workers to work where there is prima facie evidence of unlawful discharge.
- Increase penalties for unfair labor practices (for instance, by making them similar to those for violations of employment law).

Encourage bargaining

- Make it illegal to permanently replace strikers.
- Provide final and binding interest arbitration for first contracts.

Make information and access more equal

- Allow union access to employer premises (nonworking areas).
- Allow union supporters to speak at any "captive audience" meetings held by the employer.
- Allow union access to the public parts of shopping centers.

Expand coverage of the law and its protection of workers

- Update the definitions of supervisor and manager to insure that only those with full supervisory or managerial authority and responsibility are excluded from coverage.
- Insure that no one is excluded because of participation in group decision processes, like work teams.
- Grant supervisors the right to remain neutral in organizing campaigns.
- Reaffirm and extend protections of individuals against discrimination for participating in employee involvement processes or for drawing on the services of an outside labor organization. **—PV**

In a system of minority representation, individual employees would be empowered to join any independent labor, professional, civil rights, or other employee organization and designate it as their representative at the workplace. Whenever a significant number of employees designated the same organization, employers would be required to consult with that organization on their employees' behalf; that is, they would have to "meet and confer" but not necessarily bargain.[24] Collective bargaining by the employer would be required only when a majority of employees designated the same organization as their representative. This process could be integrated into the current system by conferring exclusive bargaining status on an employee organization only when that organization had won a representation election. Alternatively, such exclusivity could be granted when a clear majority of employees were dues-paying members of one labor organization.

Such a system would give employees the ability to initiate employee involvement in decision making, consultation over workplace practices, involvement in improving health and safety, or anything else they desire short of bargaining. It would be a marked departure from our current system in which only employers can initiate employee involvement in these activities. Equally importantly, minority representation would facilitate organizing in a competitive economic environment (particularly in the growing service sector), because employers would become organized automatically whenever a majority of their employees made the choice for representation. This would facilitate rapid, market-wide organization.[25]

Another issue is whether public policy should continue to support "exclusive representation" by a single labor organization, as opposed to "members only" representation by multiple employee organizations in a single enterprise. Currently, American management as well as organized labor strongly oppose moving away from exclusive representation.[26] This preference can be integrated with systems of minority representation, as demonstrated here. A system in which individuals join a labor organization of their choice, pay dues, and obtain some representation services short of full collective bargaining offers enormous promise for expanding employee representation. This is particularly true since a large number of nonunion employees desire union representation now, but they are not now working in environments where they constitute a majority. What is needed is a set of legal obligations—that labor organizations must be allowed on worksites to meet with represented individuals, that they may be present at disciplinary proceedings as a representative of employees, that employers must meet and confer with employee representatives, and so forth.

Other legal changes related to increased employer and employee fluidity are also needed. The Commission on the Future of Worker-Management Relationships made a number of suggestions in this area.[27] One priority is to insure that employees cannot lose legal protections by being falsely classified as owner-operators or independent consultants. Another is to constrain employer use of variations in corporate form to evade labor law. In particular, we must prohibit the use of sham subsidiaries to evade bargaining responsibilities, a tactic popularly known as "double-breasting." Similarly, where employee leasing or subcontracting restricts the ability of employees to organize, expanded use of the "joint employer" doctrine should be used to restore their rights.[28] For instance, when a janitorial service contractor's employees organize, it should be considered an unfair labor practice for a client to cancel the janitorial service contract in order to avoid having union employees on the premises. Or, when a leasing service provides nurses to a hospital, the service and the hospital should become joint employers of the nurses in question. These are complex issues, but more encompassing definitions of the employer-employee relationship are of great practical importance for union representation in situations of fluid employment.

It is comfortable to retreat to proposals for conventional labor law reform when talking about needed legal changes; the issues posed by fluid employer and employee relationships and competitive labor markets are daunting in comparison. Yet the next generation of labor law reform efforts will have to consider these issues if we are to provide the option of union representation in the emerging economic environment.

Conclusion

In a world of intense economic competition, independent labor organizations that reach beyond the individual firm are needed for ensuring effective economic and political voice for workers. Employee involvement, participatory democracy within the firm, and employer discussions of the need to empower workers are all hopeful, positive developments in nonunion as well as union workplaces, but they are not likely to be a sufficient basis for voice in a world of increasingly small companies, transient employees, and competitive pressures that keep employers from committing to a permanent relationship with employees. Only independent employee organizations that reach beyond the individual firm can provide effective employee representation in the next century. The public policy challenge is providing an appropriate legal basis for the development of those organizations.

NOTES

1. Freeman and Rogers 1995.

2. Stevens 1995; Freeman and Medoff 1984.

3. Freeman 1992 surveys relevant research.

4. Belman 1992.

5. Belman 1992; for this reason some claim unions reduce investment in the long run (Hirsch and Link 1987; Hirsch and Connolly 1987), although again the empirical evidence is murky at best (Freeman 1992).

6. Freeman 1992, 1993.

7. Among them, Freeman 1993.

8. See Voos 1994 for a fuller discussion of these issues.

9. Appelbaum and Batt 1994.

10. Fox 1966 discusses academic expressions of this view in management theory.

11. Quoted in Gunn 1995.

12. For example, Weiler 1993.

13. The Commission on the Future of Worker-Management Relations recommended that speech protections for nonunion employees engaging in participation be reaffirmed and extended for this very reason (*Report and Recommendations* 1994, p. xvii and pp. 8-9). However, it seems doubtful that the National Labor Relations Board could effectively handle an avalanche of unfair labor practice charges related to discharge or discrimination for free speech by nonunion employers.

14. For this reason, the Occupational Safety and Health Administration Reform Act introduced into the last Congress, and most proposals for mandated participation or works councils, include the right of employees to elect their representatives (e.g., Freeman and Rogers 1993). However, the U.S. employer community is now strongly opposed to any legal requirement that employee representatives be elected by employees, even for limited arenas like safety and health.

15. As Freeman and Medoff have pointed out, this is an important aspect of voice, and it is one that is related to an altered balance of power within the firm:

> As a voice institution, unions also fundamentally alter the social relations of the workplace. Perhaps most importantly, a union constitutes a source of worker power in the firm, diluting managerial authority and offering members a measure of due process, in particular through the union innovation of a grievance and arbitration system....As a result, in unionized firms workers are more willing and able to express discontent and object to managerial decisions. (1979, p. 73)

Grievance arbitration systems are now being imitated in some nonunion workplaces through a variety of alternative dispute resolution systems, but they rarely, if ever, change the balance of power within the firm and protect worker voice to the same extent as do union grievance arbitration systems.

16. Greenfield and Pleasure 1993.

17. Rogers and Streeck 1994a, 1994b.

18. Eaton and Voos 1994.

19. Delaney and Schwochau 1993; Kerr 1964.

20. Delaney and Schwochau 1993.

21. Commission on the Future of Worker-Management Relations 1994a.

22. See its *Report and Recommendations,* 1994b.

23. Cobble 1991, 1994.

24. If significant numbers of employees chose different organizations, all organizations would be required to meet and confer at the same time, reducing the burden on the employer and encouraging compromise between diverse groups of employees.

25. Under such a system of minority representation, it probably would be necessary to enhance protections against hiring discrimination by employers against individual union members. There are other possible problems. One is that a workforce that is divided by race, gender, ethnicity, and occupation might choose representation by different organizations, working against effective economic representation. The history of the American labor movement is one in which ethnically divided workers discovered the need for common representation and cooperation in order to make economic gains. Hence, a system of minority representation might not result in excessive fragmentation of labor organization in the United States.

26. For example, Adams 1994.

27. For a more extensive list see Gold 1994 and Hiatt 1994.

28. With these changes in the definition of the employer, some economic pressure tactics that are now considered secondary appropriately would be viewed as primary because they do pertain to what is effectively a single economic unit. If organized employees with closely related economic interests could aid individuals seeking to organize, unionization would be greatly facilitated.

REFERENCES

Adams, Rex (Vice President, Administration, Mobil Corp.). 1994. Testimony to the Commission on the Future of Worker-Management Relations, September 8.

Appelbaum, Eileen and Rosemary Batt. 1994. *The New American Workplace: Transforming Work Systems in the United States.* Ithaca, N.Y.: ILR Press.

Belman, Dale. 1992. "Unions, the Quality of Labor Relations, and Firm Performance." In Lawrence Mishel and Paula B. Voos, eds., *Unions and Economic Competitiveness.* Economic Policy Institute Series. Armonk, N.Y.: M.E. Sharpe.

Cobble, Dorothy Sue. 1991. "Organizing the Post-Industrial Work Force: Lessons From the History of Waitress Unionism." *Industrial and Labor Relations Review,* Vol. 44, No. 3, pp. 419-36.

Cobble, Dorothy Sue. 1994. "Making Postindustrial Unionism Possible." In Sheldon Friedman et al., eds., *Restoring the Promise of American Labor Law.* Ithaca, N.Y.: ILR Press.

Commission on the Future of Worker-Management Relations. 1994. *Report and Recommendations.* Washington, D.C.: U.S. Departments of Labor and Commerce.

Commission on the Future of Worker-Management Relations. 1994. *Fact Finding Report.* Washington, D.C.: U.S. Departments of Labor and Commerce.

Delaney, John and Susan Schwochau. 1993. "Employee Representation Through the Political Process." In Bruce E. Kaufman and Morris M. Kleiner, eds., *Employee Representation: Alternatives and Future Directions.* Madison, Wis.: Industrial Relations Research Association.

Eaton, Adrienne E. and Paula B. Voos. 1992. "Unions and Contemporary Innovations in Work Organization, Compensation, and Employee Participation." In Lawrence Mishel and Paula B. Voos, eds., *Unions and Economic Competitiveness.* Economic Policy Institute Series. Armonk, N.Y.: M.E. Sharpe.

Freeman, Richard B. 1993. "How Much Has De-Unionization Contributed to the Rise in Male Earnings Inequality?" In Sheldon Danziger and Peter Gottschalk, eds., *Uneven Tides: Rising Inequality in America.* New York: Russell Sage Foundation.

Freeman, Richard B. 1992. "Is Declining Unionization of the U.S. Good, Bad, or Irrelevant?" In Lawrence Mishel and Paula B. Voos, eds., *Unions and Economic Competitiveness.* Economic Policy Institute Series. Armonk, N.Y.: M.E. Sharpe.

Freeman, Richard B. and James L. Medoff. 1979. "The Two Faces of Unionism." *Public Interest,* Vol. 57 (Fall), pp. 69-94.

Freeman, Richard B. and James L. Medoff. 1984. *What Do Unions Do?* New York: Basic Books.

Freeman, Richard B. and Joel Rogers. 1993. "Who Speaks for Us? Employee Representation in a Nonunion Labor Market." In Bruce E. Kaufman and Morris M. Kleiner, eds., *Employee Representation: Alternatives and Future Directions*. Madison, Wis.: Industrial Relations Research Association.

Freeman, Richard B. and Joel Rogers. 1994. "Worker Representation and Participation Survey: First Report of Findings." Unpublished Paper.

Freeman, Richard B. and Joel Rogers. 1995. "Worker Representation and Participation Survey: Wave Two." Unpublished Paper.

Fox, Alan. 1966. "Managerial Ideology and Labour Relations." *British Journal of Industrial Relations*, Vol. 4, No. 3, pp. 366-78.

Gold, Laurence (General Counsel, AFL-CIO). 1994. Testimony to the Commission on the Future of Worker-Management Relations, July 25.

Greenfield Patricia A. and Robert J. Pleasure. 1993. "Representatives of Their Own Choosing: Finding Workers' Voice in the Legitimacy and Power of Their Unions." In Bruce E. Kaufman and Morris M. Kleiner, eds., *Employee Representation: Alternatives and Future Directions*. Madison, Wis.: Industrial Relations Research Association.

Gunn, Erik. 1995. "Labor's New Day Now Seems a False Dawn." *Milwaukee Journal*, January 15.

Hiatt, Jonathan P. (General Counsel, Service Employees International Union). 1994. Testimony to the Commission on the Future of Worker-Management Relations, July 25.

Hirsch, Barry T. and R. A. Connolly. 1987. "Do Unions Capture Monopoly Profits?" *Industrial and Labor Relations Review*, Vol. 41, No. 1.

Hirsch, Barry T. and Albert N. Link. 1987. "Unions, Productivity, and Productivity Growth." *Journal of Labor Research*, Vol. 8 (Fall), pp. 323-32.

Kaufman, Bruce. 1995. "The Challenge for Labor Law: Protecting the Right to Organize Without Giving Away the Store." Unpublished paper presented at the John M. Olin Institute's Symposium on *The Dunlop Commission Report on the Future of Worker-Management Relations*, Washington, D.C., April 25.

Kerr, Clark. 1964. "Unions and Union Leaders of Their Own Choosing." In *Labor and Management in Industrial Society*. New York: Anchor.

Kochan, Thomas A. 1995. Personal communication to Paula Voos.

Rogers, Joel and Wolfgang Streeck. 1994a. "Workplace Representation Overseas: The Works Council Story." In Richard Freeman, ed., *Working and Earning Under Different Rules*. Chicago: University of Chicago Press.

Rogers, Joel and Wolfgang Streeck. 1994b. "Works Councils: Concepts and Problems." In Joel Rogers and Wolfgang Streeck, eds., *Works Councils: Consultation, Representation and Cooperation.* Chicago: University of Chicago Press.

Stevens, Carl M. 1995. "The Social Cost of Rent Seeking by Labor Unions in the United States." *Industrial Relations*, Vol. 34, No. 2, pp. 190-202.

Swoboda, Frank. 1995. "The Return of Robert Reich." *Washington Post National Weekly Edition,* May 15-21.

Voos, Paula B. 1994. "An Economic Perspective on Contemporary Trends in Collective Bargaining." *Contemporary Collective Bargaining: In the Private Sector.* Madison, Wis.: Industrial Relations Research Association.

Weiler, Paul C. 1993. "Governing the Workplace: Employee Representation in the Eyes of the Law." In Bruce E. Kaufman and Morris M. Kleiner, eds., *Employee Representation: Alternatives and Future Directions.* Madison, Wis.: Industrial Relations Research Association.

CHAPTER 8

TRAINING
A Plan for All Workers

by Peter Berg

BECAUSE A NATION'S PRODUCTIVITY AND ABILITY TO INNOVATE DEPENDS in large part on worker skills, training policy is a key area of national competitiveness. Currently, national policy focuses on two broad areas: public-sector training to help people find jobs or to provide skills to disadvantaged youth and adults, and private-sector training that concentrates on increasing the skills of people currently working or on increasing training standards across occupations. While both of these types of training are important to the skill base of the nation, training of current, incumbent workers is most critical in increasing productivity and raising the productive capacity of the U.S. economy. Such training means more rapid wage growth and promotion opportunities, and it provides the nation with a productive workforce that is better able to adapt to new technologies and new forms of work organization.

As in many other areas that affect productivity, the United States has allowed its industrial competitors to take the lead in creating the institutions and systems that promote continual worker training. But our desire to develop a high-wage, high-skill economy will require support of innovative work systems and broad general skills training not just for the unemployed and underemployed but for millions of currently employed workers. Successful efforts by specific industries, the states, and other countries offer insight into how the federal government can foster initiatives nationwide.

Numerous studies document the positive effects of company-provided training.[1] Despite the benefits to firms and individuals of invest-

---

Peter Berg is an economist specializing in workplace organization at the Economic Policy Institute.

ing in training, the percentage of workers receiving firm-provided training is generally lower in the United States than in other industrialized countries. One recent study estimated that 16.8% of employed workers received some formal training during their current jobs; another placed participation in formal training at 25%.[2] Both figures are well below the training rates of 32% in France in 1990 and 36.7% in Japan in 1989.

In addition, what formal training there is in the United States tends to focus on college-educated technical and managerial employees.[3] According to one study, only 4% of young workers without college degrees receive formal training at work;[4] instead, these workers learn their skills informally through unstructured on-the-job training.[5] Thus, U.S. firms provide less training to their employees than other industrialized countries, and the training they do provide is concentrated on managerial and technical employees.

Factors Determining the Amount and Type of Employer-Provided Training

Using public policy to increase training of incumbent workers requires an understanding of what factors drive training at the workplace. Too often policies geared toward increasing training focus exclusively on defining skills or on broad subsidies to boost training without any consideration of the context in which training takes place. Company-provided training is closely linked with several factors: the technology at the workplace, the organization of work, and education and labor-market institutions.

Technology. Technology can increase or decrease the skills required of workers. On the one hand, the use of micro-electronic technology in manufacturing has, in many cases, required high levels of training for workers to meet increased skill requirements. The ability of these machines to more precisely measure output and gather data has increased the need for workers with knowledge of the production process and the ability to analyze and adjust to it. On the other hand, tasks previously performed by the worker or operator can now be performed by the machine's software, thereby lowering the skills required of workers. Thus, whether technology is "upskilling" or "deskilling" depends on the occupation or industry in which it is put to use.[6]

Work organization. Work organization defines the tasks workers perform and the training required to perform those tasks. In Taylorist, mass production forms of work organization, jobs are narrowly defined and tasks are limited to a few operations. Assembly-line workers are not expected to think about or understand the entire production process. Not surprisingly under this form of work organization, blue-collar workers receive little formal training. However, under new forms of work organization there is less tolerance for mistakes; more is being required of front-line workers, and this demand is influencing the composition of training. For example, if workers are organized in teams and engage in continuous improvement activities, they need training in problem solving and communication in addition to technical skills.

This close relationship between work organization and training has been documented by several studies. Based on an international study of 57 automobile assembly plants, MacDuffie and Kochan (1995) found that whether a plant was high-tech or low-tech bore little relationship to the amount of training offered employees. Rather, the availability of training had more to do with the plant's production strategy. Flexible production, in contrast to mass production, requires assembly workers to have a high level of competency in reading, math, reasoning, and communication skills. The training is primarily structured, on-the-job training that allows workers to gain first-hand knowledge about their jobs and the production process as a whole.

Education and labor-market institutions. While the organization of work influences the demand for incumbent worker training, education and labor-market institutions can affect the overall supply of skilled workers and the business strategies of companies. The U.S. vocational training system remains a primarily school-based system with no formal involvement of business or labor representatives in the training. While the federal government recommends minimum occupational training standards, each state sets its own. Training tends to be narrow and specific, and the quality of training varies greatly across states. Many vocational programs and community colleges tend to customize training to the specific needs of local industry rather than train students in broad occupational skills.

Other countries approach the training of non-college-bound students differently. The German apprenticeship system, for example, provides young vocational students with workplace-based training in general and firm-specific skills. National certification of the training as well as employer and union participation in the training process ensures the training is recognized and rewarded by employers. A study of the U.S. and German automobile industries found that the German apprenticeship training system generates a broad set of skills that firms build on with their own training.[7] The involvement of German employer associations and labor unions in the vocational training process (they monitor the training and establish occupational training standards) encourages active employer participation in the apprenticeship system. The widespread participation of employers and the national certification process combine to produce a supply of broadly skilled workers who are able to respond to unforeseen problems.

Labor-market structure also has consequences for worker training. The relatively flexible structure in the United States—characterized by high mobility of labor and the lack of collective or coordinated bargaining discourages company investments in worker training. The lack of coordinated employer training strategies leaves individual firms to bear the costs of training; moreover, the lack of centralized labor-management relations and the low level of unionization reduce the means to raise training investments or to coordinate skill standards within an industry.

New Work Systems and the Need for Training

During the 1970s and 1980s, the intensification of international competition and the increased use of micro-electronic technology weakened the traditional mass production system. In this system, production costs decline with increases in the volume produced of a standardized product; unit costs also decline with an increase in the size of the market for the product. As volume increases, firms learn the most efficient method for mass producing an item. Deviating from this approach, either by increasing product variety or by improving product quality, brings an end to these types of productivity gains and increases costs.[8]

Competition from newly industrialized countries, slower economic growth, and more volatile demand have made achieving productivity gains from economies of scale and mass production less likely. In addition, new technologies have made it possible to produce higher-quality products meeting more precise specifications and to produce a wider range of products. These developments have raised quality standards in mass-consumption markets and encouraged competition on a variety of features such as service and design. In this competitive environment, companies in industrialized countries are forced to reevaluate their production strategies and move to forms of work organization that are based in different forms of organizational learning. Simply cutting costs and reducing wages will not be a successful competitive strategy against companies in low-wage, less-developed countries.

For companies in industrialized countries, economic success depends more on effective use of human resources, labor and management participation, a broadly trained workforce, and flexible production systems that allow companies to make continuous improvements in products and processes and that reward workers for their effort. Innovative work systems that organize work in teams, increase the participation of frontline workers in decisions about work, build mechanisms to increase the flow of information within the organization, and allow workers to share in the company gains have been shown to have positive effects.[9]

Thus, the adoption of new work systems provides a means for nations to maintain domestic production, increase productivity, and raise wages. Economic success and higher wages, however, are not guaranteed: achieving results for employers and employees depends on how the work system is organized and who is involved in decisions establishing the organization and in decisions around continuous improvements to the production process.

In the United States, there was extensive experimentation with new work systems throughout the 1970s and 1980s. While the pace of implementation appears to have increased in the last 10 years, different surveys obtain different rates of adoption of key elements of new work systems. Osterman (1992) found that 35% of establishments in manufacturing have 50% or more of their core employees involved in new work systems. A recent national survey found that 54% of establishments involve their nonmanagerial and nonsupervisory workers in meetings to discuss work-related problems; in addition, these workers are involved in a total quality management program at 37% of establishments. However, this survey also discovered that nonmanagerial and nonsupervisory workers are involved in job rotation at only 18% of establishments and involved in self-managed work teams at only 13% of establishments.[10] While no single model of production dominates the work systems being established in the U.S. economy, the trend toward leaner, more flexible systems is clearly discernible. In manufacturing, price competition and the example of Japanese car manufacturers, who were able to reduce costs and increase quality through work reorganization, have spurred companies to adopt new work systems. Their implementation in services is a more recent phenomenon, and their dissemination is not as widespread as in manufacturing. It remains unclear what the impact will be in this sector on cost and improvements in quality and productivity.

Global competition and new production strategies are directly affecting the factors that influence training. Micro-electronic technology continues to develop and affect the skill requirements of workers. It is no longer a question of whether changes in work organization will occur, but rather how work will be structured and what actors will determine that structure. Experimentation is taking place within labor–management relations. Many union contracts in traditional manufacturing industries are negotiating more employee voice and security in exchange for greater flexibility on the shopfloor. In addition, educational institutions are attempting to work more closely with employers to raise vocational training standards and make education more relevant to the workplace.

Federal Training Policy

Confronted with a changing competitive environment and the need to boost the skills of U.S. workers, the federal government has taken some steps to affect private-sector training. Federal policy has concentrated on shaping the direction of skill building across occupations and industries. The School-to-Work Opportunities Act of 1994 was devised to restructure occupational education through the introduction of a work-based component to the education process and through employer involvement. This policy, geared toward educational institutions, is designed to increase the quality of young labor available to companies rather than increase the skills of incumbent workers. In addition, the federal government has established the National Skills Standards Board to develop skill standards across occupations in different industries. It is designed to influence the training goals and content of company-provided training, and is currently the most direct policy to influence private-sector training. Both of these initiatives offer benefits for improving job skills, but each has serious drawbacks that weaken their ability to help create a high-wage, high-skilled workforce.

School-to-Work Opportunities Act (STWOA). Because education and occupational training are matters of local control, the federal government generally uses financial incentives to encourage states to adopt certain education or training reforms. The STWOA is designed to foster in-school education and training programs and external work experience opportunities to smooth the transition from school to career-oriented work or to further education. States, localities, and private organizations are eligible to receive grants for establishing partnerships between schools, government, employers, and labor organizations to design curricula, train teachers, conduct or obtain an analysis of local labor-market demand, develop skill certification criteria, and integrate work into school programs. Examples of programs that are being supported include the Protech program in Boston, which has built a youth apprenticeship program for high school students that offers paid work experience and a new curriculum, and Oregon's use of skill certificates in areas such as health care, finance, manufacturing, and commercial fishing.

While the STWOA has encouraged school and work training initiatives, many of which were underway before the Act was passed, it has not brought about a new national training system and provides little incentive for employers to get involved. There are primarily two reasons employers might participate in work-based education programs: to obtain well-trained future employees or to have an immediate source of low-cost labor.[11] Two recent studies found that most employers participating in some form of work-based education saw these programs as a source of labor.[12] However, many work-based education programs are designed to allow students to pursue postsecondary and higher education, thus reducing the likelihood of firms retaining trainees after an apprenticeship. The low cost of apprentice labor may be attractive to employers in such areas as construction and teaching hospitals, but generally

U.S. employers are not prevented from paying low wages to workers as long as they are as high as the legislated minimum wage.[13] Moreover, the cost of establishing an infrastructure within the firm to supervise apprentices and trainees is quite high. Employers are likely to see these costs as a greater barrier to participation than trainee wages.[14]

One study suggests that collective motivation may play a role in encouraging employer participation in work-based education programs. Employers might be interested in strengthening their industry's labor pool if they believed that enough other employers were willing to participate as well. Concerted effort is the key, because firms that did not participate would have the free ride of an improved labor pool without any of the training costs.[15]

While the STWOA provides funds to help states and localities build work-based education programs, it provides little concrete guidance for or incentive to involve employers in taking on apprentices and providing training. Without such involvement, the work-based programs will remain a marginal piece of vocational education in the United States. Bringing employer and labor representatives together to reach collective agreements about participation and training seems the best way to have an impact on the quality of labor supply in particular industries. Achieving this will require more direct action by the federal government with employer associations and labor unions. One area where this is occurring with employer associations is in skill standards.

Skill standards. The establishment of industry skill standards is currently the primary private-sector training initiative of the federal government. In 1994, Congress established the National Skills Standards Board, which has been directed to identify broad clusters of major occupations across one or more industrial sectors, to encourage and fund voluntary industry-led partnerships for the purpose of developing skill standards systems for each of these clusters, to endorse the standards developed by these partnerships, and to develop a comprehensive national system of voluntary skills standards. The board is composed of eight representatives from business; eight representatives from organized labor; two neutral human resource professionals; six representatives of education and other constituencies; the secretaries of Education, Labor, and Commerce; and the chairperson of the National Education Standards and Improvement Council. The board relies heavily on the work of 22 industry-led skills standards partnerships funded by the Departments of Education and Labor in 1992 and 1993.[16]

Establishing industry skill standards is an important way to raise the quality of training across companies and to provide consensus and uniformity to the training practices of firms within an industry. If the standards reflect broad skills and increased responsibility and decision making for traditional blue-collar occupations, they can be a positive force for innovative work systems. Another positive benefit of establishing skill standards is that it brings together the parties directly involved in training and in the production of a product or delivery of a service and forces them to define training content in the context of a work system. Moreover, if widely accepted by firms and educational institutions, skill standards could provide workers with portable credentials and enhance their career mobility.

Relying on employer and trade associations to develop skill standards, however, has proven to be an arduous process. The array of trade associations, some industry-based and others occupationally based, has made it difficult to build coalitions and reach consensus on standards. Some of the 22 partnership grantees have not reached consensus on a single standard, while others have developed skill standards on just one job, despite the directive of the Departments of Labor and Education to generate a progression of standards based on a progression of jobs.[17] The vast majority of partnership grantees view skill standards as a way to improve the information available to students about prospective jobs rather than as part of a strategy to reform both work and education and move workplaces toward high-performance work systems.[18]

Even more problematic, however, has been the lack of involvement of workers or unions in the development of skill standards. Many of the 22 partnership grants were given to trade associations with no requirement that they involve workers or unions. While the formal participation of labor representatives on the national board is important, the cooperation and participation of workers and unions at the state and local levels are essential. Training is a two-party process; the skill standards established around a particular occupation have economic consequences for both the employer and the employee. The involvement of workers and unions in establishing skill standards should be a requirement of any federal support for their development.

Moreover, the standards being written tend to compartmentalize or list the skills for particular jobs rather than link the skills to a context or the work process as a whole.[19] As competition encourages firms to adopt new work systems, jobs are becoming more professionalized, requiring that employees understand a body of knowledge relating to their work and be able to apply different approaches to solving problems as they arise in the course of their jobs. However, the compartmentalized approach to setting skill standards works against the development of innovative and high-performance work systems.

While skill standards can be important in defining training content and the direction in which employer training should be headed, they do nothing to actually increase the training employers provide. Without incentives to increase training within firms, the policy efforts in the area of skill standards will have little positive impact. Thus, other policies that could more directly affect company-provided training need to be explored.

During the 1992 presidential election, Clinton advocated a training levy that would tax firms a certain percentage of their payroll. If that particular amount were invested in workforce training by the firm, the tax would be refunded. The intent of the levy was to increase the amount of training offered by employers and spread the costs of training across firms. The funds generated from the tax would also support government training initiatives. The training levy, however, was not without its problems. First, there was a concern that a tax on worker payroll acts against job creation. Second, experiences in France with such a levy indicate that small firms bear more of the tax burden because they do not have the same resources to increase training as do large firms. Also, small firms are less likely to receive training grants from the government because they lack the managerial resources to apply for grants. Third, since most firm-based training is provided to managerial and professional workers, the training levy would probably just increase training for these groups. While the training eligible for the tax break could be restricted to nonmanagerial or frontline workers, enforcing this limitation would be difficult. Fourth, any training levy scheme would most likely count only formal training expenditures against the tax. Because the costs of on-the-job training would be difficult to monitor, it would most likely be excluded from the plan. Unfortunately, it is structured on-the-job training that new work systems are finding most valuable. As the Japanese production model has shown, the continual learning that takes place on the job is of critical importance to the productivity of workers.[20] Given these problems and strong opposition from business, Clinton's training levy was never proposed.

A more comprehensive approach to enhancing private-sector training by the federal government was the High Skills, Competitive Workforce Act of 1991. This bill was considered in the Senate Committee on Labor and Human Resources but never made it to a vote on the Senate floor. It addressed training issues on a number of different levels by proposing:

- a voluntary system of national occupational standards and grants to organizations to develop school-to-work programs.
- grants to industry, education, and labor organizations to disseminate information and provide technical assistance to firms and labor unions in developing high-performance forms of work organization. These grants were also to assist in the development of joint labor/management training programs, to provide services to coordinate employment training with the introduction of new technology, and to disseminate employee training materials.
- grants to companies or trade associations that formed consortia that emphasized training for participation in high-performance work organization and that included employees and their representatives in the design and implementation of the training programs.[21]

The bill sought to influence the context or work system in which training takes place and the procedure by which training decisions are made. This type of training policy, which focuses directly on employers and labor representatives, is likely to have the greatest impact on the skills of incumbent workers. The comprehensive nature of the bill was perhaps its downfall, since no consensus could be reached on its proposals.

The aspects of the bill for which there was broad support have appeared in STWOA and the skill standards initiative. The training strategy of the Clinton Administration has been to support these measures to affect education and training institutions and solicit industry involvement in occupational skills standards; in addition, the administration has put a lot of emphasis on training for the economically disadvantaged through adult and youth training grants and through the creation of One-Stop Career Centers. But rhetoric about creating a high-skilled workforce that can command high wages does not fit with this focus.

Creating a high-skill, high-wage workforce requires more of a direct focus on incumbent worker training at the workplace. Moreover, achieving sustainable effects from training policy requires policies that support innovative work systems that structure jobs broadly and involve employees in decisions surrounding their work, as well as policies that create an atmosphere of trust and participation in labor–management relations. Leaving training decisions solely in the hands of employers leads to more company-specific skills and a less-than-optimal amount of training. As research from other countries shows, the involvement of employees and their representatives at various stages of the training process can affect the mix and distribution of training, the organization of work, and the amount of training offered to workers.[22]

New Directions for National Training Policy

U.S. employees want involvement in training decisions. A recent national survey of U.S. employees found that only 29% felt they had a lot of direct involvement in deciding what training was needed for people in their work group or department. However, 62% felt it was very important for them to have a lot of influence in training decisions.[23] Tapping into this desire for participation could lead to not only more training but creative solutions to overcoming skill deficiencies as well as new ways of learning. Moreover, employees would have more control over skills that affect their long-term career interests. Some large companies and industries have established joint training committees, and these programs have made positive impacts on employee training. Federal incentives for further training contingent on joint participation by management and employees could help spread these programs to smaller firms.

One possible way to introduce employee decision making about training is through the establishment of joint employer/employee training councils linked to some type of training grant or tax incentive. Credit could be given for formal classroom and on-the-job training, although the latter poses special problems. Structured on-the-job training is a key component of continuous improvement activities and high-performance work systems. Yet, in many small firms on-the-job training is simply learning-by-doing without any progression of tasks or systematic skill building. Because of the difficulties in monitoring on-the-job training, firms are unable to receive support for their efforts to conduct systematic on-the-job training programs. Establishing a joint training council to certify the nature and extent of on-the-job training would encourage small firms to train more systematically and would encourage training within the context of a high-performance work system. Such councils would consist of management and elected employee or union representatives and have a clear and enforceable set of training-related rights and responsibilities. In order to ensure that federal dollars are not being used to support training that would have been conducted anyway, skills training with a high general skills component or specific forms of technical training could be supported.

The extent to which this approach would increase training and diffuse training across large and small firms would depend on the amount of the incentive. Creating a high-skilled workforce with the capacity to adjust to and solve unforeseen problems does not come cheaply: an effective incumbent worker training policy requires a commitment by federal leaders. However, perhaps the impact of the federal training grant or incentive could be enhanced by requiring the state, the firm, and the employees to commit an equal amount to the training process.

This cost-sharing strategy is part of another approach to increase training that is currently under way in Canada. The Canadian government is supporting a strategy to boost private-sector training. It has established national boards of labor, business, and government leaders that support labor- and business-training initiatives within different industrial sectors. After a needs assessment of the industry labor market, public funds are matched with private to create a sectoral training council that directly provides training funds to companies.[24] Each sectoral council consists of employers and employee representatives. In the steel industry, a sectoral council was formed with several objectives: to encourage employers to increase their investment in the skills of their active workforces, to ensure that the programs are designed to meet the needs of workers and employers, to assist the steel industry in establishing a training procedure for its workforce, and to promote co-management of training programs by employers and union representatives. Companies and unions contribute dues to be steel council members. In order to receive funds, joint training committees, with an equal number of management and labor representatives, must be established at the plant and at the corporate level. These committees create the training plans for the programs that will receive council funds.

The types of training funded by the steel council must be generic and portable, and they must enhance the opportunities for those employed in the steel industry. These include foundation skills such as literacy, problem solving, group and communication skills; general skills such as the economics of the steel industry, work reorganization, and facilitator and supervisor training; and industry-specific skills, such as metallurgy, casting, melting, rolling, and programmable logic controllers. In addition, the steel council funds on-the-job training if it is part of a training plan that includes other methods of formal instruction.[25]

Through this sectoral training strategy, the federal government in Canada is empowering industries to devise training strategies that will meet the future skill needs of both employers and employees. Requiring that this strategy be devised jointly respects the desire of workers for participation in training decisions and is consistent with emerging innovative work systems.

A similar strategy can be found in some state efforts in this country to promote regional training consortia. The Wisconsin Regional Training Partnership is a good example. The partnership serves as a labor-market board for the Milwaukee metropolitan area, providing one-stop shopping for labor-market services. It also serves as an umbrella organization for regional and sectoral training initiatives. One of its key initiatives is the Wisconsin Manufacturing Training Consortium. The governing boards of both the partnership and the manufacturing consortium consist of employer and labor representatives. The goals of the consortium include: jointly administering workplace education and training programs, benchmarking investment in incumbent worker training as a percentage of payroll, expanding future workforce programs for unemployed adults and youth, incorporating sectoral skills standards into incumbent and future workforce training, and developing a partnership approach to manufacturing extension programs for supplier upgrading.[26] Thus, the consortium brings together those companies interested in workplace-based vocational training, high-performance work systems, skill standards, and a broadly trained workforce and allows them to collectively enhance the work process and the skills of industry employees.

The Wisconsin training consortium was formed out of the need of employers for a broadly trained supply of labor in the manufacturing sector in southeastern Wisconsin and out of a recognition that merely poaching each other's skilled workers would not build up the industry workforce. Unions were an integral force in pushing for joint decision making around training issues, and they were willing to allow for greater shopfloor flexibility in exchange for management investment in training according to broad skill standards. The consortia proved an effective way to recruit employers to help formulate occupational standards for youth apprenticeships and for sector-wide training. In conjunction with technical colleges, the consortium created a certification program for training that matches job skills with different jobs and responsibilities. Manufacturing certificates progress from basic skills to applied occupational skills to advanced occupational skills. Each certificate is associated with a higher-paid and more highly skilied job. The progression of manufacturing certificates enables workers to accept more responsibility and obtain promotions and pay increases through training.[27]

More analysis is needed to evaluate the success of training consortia like the Wisconsin program. However, training consortia appear to hold great promise for increasing the amount and quality of skills training over the long term. They provide a way to involve a critical mass of employers and unions in work-based vocational training schemes, and they are able to monitor the quality of training in member firms and provide a force for encouraging firms to hire trainees. In addition, the joint decision making procedures encourage trust within the industry between labor and management, and they promote cooperative efforts on issues such as work organization and job structure. Thus, the Wisconsin Regional Training Partnership and the Wisconsin Manufacturing Training Consortium bring together the key elements that affect incumbent worker training.

Conclusion

National policy for private-sector training should concentrate on fostering regional or sectoral training consortia that directly involve employers and employee representatives in decisions about training. Moreover, training policy should match training rhetoric. Building a high-wage, high-skill economy requires direct support of innovative work systems and broad general skills training at the workplace. Limiting federal procurement to companies moving in the direction of high-performance work systems or providing large amounts of employee training would have a significant impact on encouraging firms to adopt new work practices and increase training. At a time when cutting the federal budget deficit is generally seen as a cure for all economic ills, we must be careful not to undermine the potential of the federal government to significantly raise the productive potential of the U.S. workforce through a well-targeted training policy.

Notes

1. Bartel (1994) finds that formal training programs have a positive and significant effect on labor productivity growth. Holzer et al. (1993) conclude that public-sector funding of company training leads to an increase in training and a lasting effect on product quality. Using data on individuals, Brown (1989), Lillard and Tan (1986), and Bishop (1990) find that on-the-job training has a positive and significant effect on wages. In her study of young workers, Lynch (1992) concludes that private-sector training plays an important role in the determination of wages. Specifically, she finds that off-the-job training significantly raises wage growth, and that schooling raises the probability of receiving off-the-job training.

2. Lynch (1994, p. 11) used the Current Population Survey to arrive at the first figure for 1991. Olson (1994), using the National Household Education Survey, found the latter figure for 1990.

3. Society for Human Resource Management 1989.

4. Lynch 1991, 1992.

5. Lynch 1993, pp. 71-2.

6. Cappelli 1993; Kelley 1989.

7. Berg 1994.

8. See Abernathy and Wayne 1974; Hayes and Wheelwright 1984.

9. Mishel and Voos 1992; Levine and Tyson 1990; Berg, Appelbaum, Bailey, and Kalleberg, forthcoming.

10. EQW Issues 1995.

11. Bailey 1995.

12. Lynn and Wills 1994; Pauley, Kopp, and Haimson 1994.

13. Bailey 1995, p. 7.

14. Hershey and Silverberg 1993.

15. Bailey 1995.

16. Hilton 1995a.

17. Hilton 1995a.

18. Bailey 1996.

19. Bailey 1996.

20. Brown and Reich 1995.

21. U.S. Congress 1995.

22. Wever and Berg 1993; Lynch 1993a; Wever, Berg, and Kochan 1994.

23. Freeman and Rogers 1994.

24. Hilton 1995b.

25. Canadian Steel and Employment Congress 1993.

26. Parker and Rogers 1995.

27. Parker and Rogers 1995.

References

Abernathy, William J. and Kenneth Wayne. 1974. "Limits of the Learning Curve." *Harvard Business Review*, September-October.

Bailey, Thomas. 1995. "Incentives for Employer Participation in School-to-Work Programs." In *Learning to Work: Employer Participation in School-to-Work Transition Programs.* Washington, D.C.: Brookings Institution.

Bailey, Thomas and Donna Merritt. Forthcoming. "Making Sense of Industry Skill Standards." National Center for Research in Vocational Education, Berkeley, Calif.

Bartel, Ann P. 1994. "Productivity Gains from the Implementation of Employee Training Programs." *Industrial Relations*, October.

Berg, Peter, Eileen Appelbaum, Thomas Bailey, and Arne Kalleberg. Forthcoming. "The Performance Effects of Modular Production in the Apparel Industry." *Industrial Relations*.

Berg, Peter. 1994. "Strategic Adjustments in Training: A Comparative Analysis of the German and U.S. Automobile Industries." In Lisa Lynch, ed., *Training and the Private Sector*. Chicago: University of Chicago Press.

Bishop, John. 1990. "Job Performance, Turnover, and Wage Growth." *Journal of Labor Economics*, Vol. 8, No. 3.

Brown, Clair and Michael Reich. 1995. "Employee Voice and Training and Career Development." Paper presented at Industrial Relations Research Association Meetings, Washington, D.C.

Brown, James. 1989. "Why Do Wages Increase With Tenure?" *American Economic Review*, December.

Cappelli, Peter. 1993. "Are Skill Requirements Rising? Evidence From Production and Clerical Jobs." *Industrial and Labor Relations Review*, April.

Canadian Steel and Employment Congress. 1993. *Skills Training Program*. Toronto: CSTEC.

EQW Issues. 1995. *A Reality Check: First Findings From the EQW National Employer Survey*, No. 10.

Freeman, Richard and Joel Rogers. 1994. *Worker Representation and Participation Survey, Top-Line Results*. Princeton Survey Research Associates. Manuscript.

Hayes, Robert H. and Steven C. Wheelwright. 1984. *Restoring Our Competitive Edge: Competing through Manufacturing*. New York: Wiley.

Hershey, Alan M. and Marsh K. Silverberg. 1993. "Employer Involvement in School-to-Work Transition Programs: What Can We Really Expect?" Paper presented at the Association for Public Policy and Management meeting, Washington, D.C.

Hilton, Margaret. 1995a. Draft Issue Paper. Workshop on Policies to Improve Productivity and Job Quality in the Service Sector, Silver Spring, Md.

Hilton, Margaret. 1995b. Memorandum. Margaret Hilton Inc., Silver Spring, Md.

Holzer, Harry J., Richard N. Block, Marcus Cheatham, and Jack H. Knott. 1993. "Are Training Subsidies for Firms Effective? The Michigan Experience." *Industrial and Labor Relations Review*, July.

Kelley, Mary-Ellen. 1989. "Unionization and Job Design Under Programmable Automation." *Industrial Relations*, Spring.

Levine, David and Laura D'Andrea Tyson. 1990. "Participation, Productivity, and the Firm's Environment." In Alan Blinder, ed., *Paying for Productivity*. Washington D.C.: Brookings Institution.

Lillard, Lee, and Hong Tan. 1986. "Private Sector Training: Who Gets It and What Are Its Effects?" Rand monograph R-3331-DOL/RC, Santa Barbara, Calif.

Lynch, Lisa. 1994. "Introduction." In Lisa Lynch, ed., *Training and the Private Sector.* Chicago: University of Chicago Press.

Lynch, Lisa. 1993a. "Payoffs to Alternative Training Strategies at Work." In Richard Freeman, ed., *Working Under Different Rules.* New York: Russel Sage Foundation.

Lynch Lisa. 1993b. *Strategies for Workplace Training.* Washington, D.C.: Economic Policy Institute.

Lynch, Lisa. 1992. "Private-Sector Training and the Earnings of Young Workers." *American Economic Review,* March.

Lynch, Lisa. 1991. "The Role of Off-the-Job vs. On-the-Job Training for the Mobility of Women Workers." *American Economic Review,* May.

Lynn, Irene and Joan Wills. 1994. *School-to-Work Transition: Lessons on Recruiting and Sustaining Employer Involvement.* Washington, D.C.: Institute on Educational Leadership.

MacDuffie, John Paul and Thomas Kochan. 1995. "Do U.S. Firms Invest Less in Human Resources? Training in the World Auto Industry." *Industrial Relations,* April.

Mishel, Lawrence and Paula B. Voos. 1992. *Unions and Economic Competitiveness.* Economic Policy Institute Series. Armonk N.Y.: M.E. Sharpe.

Olson, Craig. 1994. "Who Receives Formal Firm Sponsored Training in the U.S.?" University of Wisconsin School of Business. Manuscript.

Osterman, Paul. 1992. "How Common Is Workplace Transformation and How Can We Explain Who Adopts It? Results from a National Survey." Sloan School, MIT. Manuscript.

Osterman, Paul. 1995. "Skill, Training, and Work Organization in American Establishments." *Industrial Relations,* April.

Parker, Eric and Joel Rogers. 1995. *The Wisconsin Regional Training Partnership: Lessons for National Policy.* Manuscript.

Pauley, Edward, Hillary Kopp, and Joshua Haimson. 1994. *Home-Grown Lessons: Innovative Programs Linking Work and High School.* New York: Manpower Demonstration Research Corporation.

Society for Human Resource Management. 1989. *1989 Training/Retraining Survey.* Minneapolis, Minn.: SHRM.

U.S. Congress. 1991. "High Skills, Competitive Workforce Act of 1991." S 1790. Washington, D.C.: U.S. Government Printing Office.

Wever, Kirsten and Peter Berg. 1993. "Human Resource Development in the United States and Germany." *International Contributions to Labour Studies.* Vol. 3.

Wever, Kirsten, Peter Berg, and Thomas Kochan. 1994. *The Role of Labor Market Institutions in Employee Training: Comparing the United States and Germany.* Washington, D.C.: Economic Policy Institute.

CHAPTER 9

THE MINIMUM WAGE
Blocking the Low-Wage Path

by William Spriggs & John Schmitt

HISTORICALLY, AT ANY GIVEN TIME ABOUT 10% OF THE WORKFORCE IS earning the federal minimum wage, and one estimate suggests that more than 60% of all workers have earned it at some time in their lives.[1] Perhaps most importantly, the minimum wage also acts as a reference point for millions of workers whose pay is somehow tied to it by their companies' personnel policies or the workings of local job markets.

It is not surprising, then, that the long erosion since 1980 in the after-inflation value of the minimum wage has made a substantial contribution to the steep increase in inequality during the last 15 years. One study, for example, estimates that between one-fourth and one-third of the rise in wage inequality between 1979 and 1989 can be attributed to the decline in the real value of the minimum wage.[2] More recent research indicates that the link between a decaying minimum wage and overall inequality has continued in the five years since the last increase went into effect in early 1991.[3]

The minimum wage has always enjoyed broad popular support. Until recently, it could also count on solid backing in Congress, even from Republicans.[4] Nevertheless, the Republican victory in the 1994 congressional elections appears to have emboldened the measure's traditional opponents. Low-wage employers and conservative idealogues have taken aim at the minimum wage. Their immediate goal is to block further increases in the rate, thus allowing its real value to erode with time. The longer-term goal is outright abolition, as part of a more sweeping move

William Spriggs is senior economist of the Democratic staff at the Joint Economic Committee of the U.S. Congress. (The views expressed are the author's and do not necessarily reflect those of the JEC.) John Schmitt is a labor economist at the Economic Policy Institute.

to roll back labor rights in the United States to their 1930s level.

We advocate an increase in the federal minimum wage from its current level of $4.25 per hour to $5.75, its average level, in today's dollars, during the 1970s. To make our case, we document the long slide in the after-inflation value of the minimum, then review how an increase would affect different groups of workers, and address one of the principal objections—that it will cost jobs. The message is clear: if the United States is to travel a high-wage path, we must first block the low-wage route.

The Declining Value of the Minimum Wage

The Fair Labor Standards Act (FLSA) established the minimum wage at $0.25 per hour in 1938 and required that it rise to $0.40 by 1945. Increases in the minimum wage since then have required separate Congressional approval. In the four decades following passage of the FLSA, Congress voted regular raises in the minimum wage that generally kept it at about half the average wage for private, nonsupervisory workers.

Since 1980, however, the increases have lagged behind inflation. As **Figure A** shows, the 1990 and 1991 increases (the only ones in the last

FIGURE A
Real Value of the Minimum Wage, 1960-95

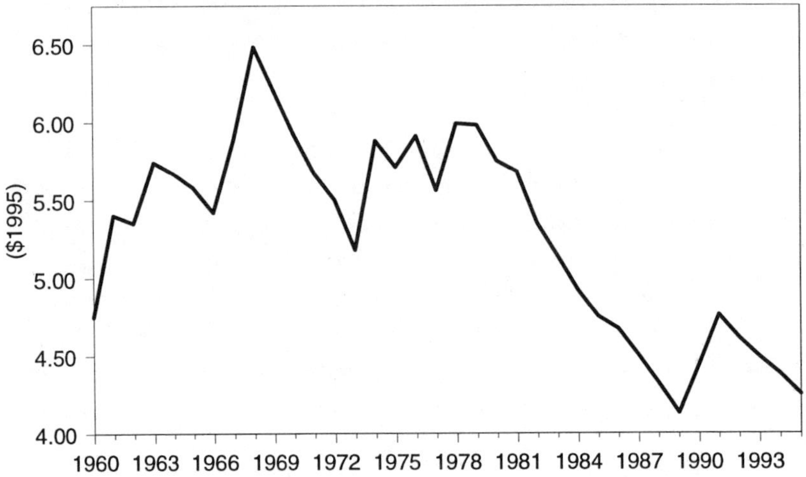

Source: Economic Policy Institute.

15 years), did not compensate for the erosion in the buying power of the minimum wage during the 1980s. The $4.25 rate in 1995 stood far below the $5.74 average rate (in 1995 dollars) for the 1970s. Without an increase soon, the real value of the minimum will, sometime during 1996, reach its lowest point since 1955.

This erosion in buying power has dramatic implications for the working poor. In 1979, a minimum-wage earner working year-round, full time could support a family of three above the federal poverty line. By 1994, the same family would find itself $2,503 below the poverty level.

DIRECT BENEFITS: REDUCING INEQUALITY BY HELPING THE WORKING POOR

Contrary to the stereotype—that minimum-wage workers are primarily well-off teenagers working part-time for pocket money—workers at or near the minimum wage[5] generally make a crucial contribution to their families' economic well-being. An analysis of government data for 1993 (the most recent available at the time of writing), conducted by Lawrence Mishel, Jared Bernstein, and Edith Rasell (1995), identified key characteristics of these workers:

- A substantial share (38%) are the only earners in their families.
- On average, they contribute almost half (45%) of their families' total earnings.
- Just under half (47%) work full time; another third work between 20 and 35 hours per week.
- They are disproportionately women (58%), blacks (15%), and Hispanics (14%).
- Only a small fraction (12%) are teenagers in families with above-average incomes.

The study concluded that 76% of the benefits from an increase in the minimum to $5.15, the level proposed by President Clinton in early 1995, would go to families with below-average incomes.

Given this profile of low-wage workers, the minimum wage has historically had a strong, direct, and measurable impact on inequality. By

TABLE 1
Characteristics of Minimum Wage and Other Wage Earners, 1993

Characteristic	Workers Directly Affected by Clinton Proposal* ($4.25-$5.14)	Other Low-Wage Workers ($5.15-$6.14)	Workers Above Minimum Wage ($6.15+)	All Workers
Average Wage	$4.67	$5.71	$13.73	$11.66
Employment (000)	12,260	8,933	80,320	104,681
Share of Total	11.7%	8.5%	76.7%	100.0%
Demographics**				
Male	42.1%	42.5%	55.2%	52.1%
Female	57.9	57.5	44.8	47.9
White	68.2%	70.0%	80.0%	77.6%
Male	27.3	27.8	44.2	40.3
Female	40.9	42.2	35.8	37.3
Black	15.0	14.6	9.9	11.0
Male	6.3	6.4	5.0	5.3
Female	8.7	8.2	4.9	5.7
Hispanic	13.8	12.1	6.8	8.1
Male	7.3	6.9	4.2	4.8
Female	6.5	5.2	2.6	3.3
Total	100.0%	100.0%	100.0%	100.0%
Teens (16-19)	25.6	9.7	1.0	5.1
Work Hours				
Full-Time (35+)	47.2%	67.6%	89.1%	81.2%
Part-Time				
20-34 hours	33.3	22.7	7.8	12.8
1-19 hours	19.4	9.6	3.1	6.0
Total	100.0%	100.0%	100.0%	100.0%
Avg. Weekly Hours	30.0 hrs.	35.1 hrs.	40.3 hrs.	38.5 hrs.
Industry				
Manufacturing	9.8%	14.3%	20.0%	17.9%
Retail Trade	44.3	31.1	10.5	17.0

* Increase to $5.15 per hour.

** Numbers presented do not sum to 100 because some ethnic minorities are excluded.

Source: Mishel, Bernstein, and Rasell (1995).

shoring up the earnings of the working poor, even modest increases can contribute significantly toward reducing wage disparities. Princeton economists David Card and Alan Krueger estimate that the increases in the federal minimum enacted in 1990 and 1991 (a total of $0.90 per hour in two, equal increments) "rolled back some 30% of the previous decade's accumulated increase" in wage inequality.[6]

Indirect Benefits: The "Contour" Effect

Former Secretary of Labor John Dunlop coined the phrase "wage contour" in 1957 to describe groups of jobs with "common wage-making characteristics." While workers on the same contour don't necessarily make the same wage, their pay tends to move together over time, generally in response to the human resources policies of firms and to local labor market conditions. Research by Spriggs and Klein (1994) has linked millions of jobs in the U.S. economy to the "minimum-wage contour." Most of these jobs pay more than the minimum wage, but their pay rates, nevertheless, move up or down with changes in its value.

The existence of wage contours means that the federal minimum can have a powerful, if indirect, impact on the wage distribution, one that reaches far beyond the 5% or so of workers currently earning the minimum wage. Spriggs and Klein found that the minimum-wage contour includes many of the jobs in the retail trade, personal services, and business and other services industries, as well as many in the sales, administrative, and other service occupations across nearly all industries. As we might expect, those workers on the minimum-wage contour tend to be from groups that have traditionally been victims of labor-market discrimination or who have suffered most from declining wages in the last 15 years: women, blacks, Hispanics, and workers with only a high school education or less. Spriggs and Klein calculated that the average hourly wage of workers on the minimum-wage contour fell 19% between 1979 and 1992 (from $7.69 to $6.22 in 1995 dollars).

Opponents of the minimum wage have argued that wage floors lead to unemployment as employers eliminate unprofitable, low-productivity jobs. We will argue below that there is little evidence to believe that modest increases in the minimum wage will destroy jobs, but we are intrigued by a different aspect of employment dynamics that flows from such thinking. Might not the abolition of wage floors encourage firms to create low-productivity jobs *instead* of higher-productivity, better-paying jobs? We believe that the dramatic decline in the real value of the minimum wage did not lead firms to expand *total* job opportunities as much as it induced them to alter the *composition* of employment by substituting low-wage, low-productivity jobs for what used to be higher-productivity, better-paying ones. Spriggs and Klein, for example, have shown that the share of high-school-educated workers on the minimum-wage contour increased from 48% to 61% between 1979 and 1990. In this sense, a decline in the real value of the minimum wage hits low-wage workers from two directions: first, it lowers their starting wages; and, second, by biasing the composition of work toward low-paying jobs, it reduces their future job choices.

The Minimum Wage and Jobs

Opponents of the minimum wage argue that it destroys jobs, thus hurting low-wage workers more than it helps. A large and growing body of recent research, however, finds that moderate increases from today's low level would have little or no impact on low-wage employment.

Most of these new studies have looked at what actually happened in particular labor markets when a state or the federal government raised the minimum wage. David Card (1992b), for example, analyzed the impact of the 1988 increase in the California state minimum from $3.35 to $4.25. He calculated that the minimum wage boosted the earnings of low-wage workers by between 5% and 10%, but found no reduction in employment among teens or in the retail trade industry. Card (1992a) also conducted a separate analysis of the April 1990 increase in the federal minimum, using state data on teenage employment from before and after the increase. He uncovered "no evidence of ... losses in teenage employment."

Lawrence Katz and Alan Krueger (1992) analyzed a sample of fast-food restaurants in Texas before and after the April 1991 increase in the federal minimum. Contrary to conventional theory, Katz and Krueger discovered that employment actually *grew* in restaurants that were forced to increase their wages the most after the 1991 increase.[7] Their data also suggested that the higher minimum may have induced firms to upgrade from part-time to full-time employees. William Spriggs and Bruce Klein (1994) applied Katz and Krueger's methodology to a sample of food-service establishments (including fast-food and other restaurants) in Jackson, Miss., and Greensboro, N.C. They found that the federal increase had no measurable impact on employment in restaurants in the two cities.

Card and Krueger (1994) collaborated on a study of New Jersey's 1992 increase in the state minimum wage. They analyzed a sample of 410 fast-food restaurants in that state and a "control" group from neighboring Pennsylvania, where the minimum wage did not change. They found that employment increased slightly *more*, on average, in the New Jersey restaurants than in the Pennsylvania control group, although the difference was not statistically significant.[8] David Neumark and William Wascher (1995) criticized Card and Krueger's survey technique and attempted to gather more accurate data from payroll records for a subsample of Card and Krueger's original group of restaurants.[9] However, Neumark and Wascher asked owners only about total hours worked per week, not total employment, and therefore the two sets of results are not directly comparable. Neumark and Wascher's findings suggest that New Jersey's 18.8% increase in the minimum wage reduced hours worked by 4.6%, but their data did not determine whether there were fewer jobs or fewer hours per worker. Taken together, the two studies indicate that, after the increase: (1) total employment was unchanged and (2) total hours worked fell slightly, but by less than the increase in wages. The bottom line, then, is that the average weekly pay for a worker at the old minimum rose by about 14% after the hike (4.6% fewer hours, but each paid at an 18.8% higher rate).[10]

Other recent studies have taken a different approach, focusing on national employment data for teenagers or low-wage industries, sectors that should be most sensitive to changes in the value of the minimum wage. Like the state and local research, these studies indicate that the minimum wage has little or no impact on low-wage employment. Alison Wellington (1991) explored the employment impact on young workers over the period 1954-86. She found that a 10% increase in the minimum would reduce teen employment by less than 1%; her research could not identify any impact on young adults aged 20-24. Card and Krueger

(1995) further updated Wellington's work. They detected small, statistically significant effects of the minimum wage on teen workers for the period 1954-79 and an even smaller—and statistically insignificant—impact for 1954-93, suggesting that the experience of the last 14 years broke the historic relationship. Dale Belman and Paul Wolfson (1995) looked at the effect of the 11 minimum-wage increases between 1968 and 1991 on employment in 35 "low-wage and youth industries." Their findings were "consistent with recent studies that find that legislated increases in the minimum wage have not influenced employment." In fact, their data show that, historically, minimum-wage hikes have been just as likely to be associated with an increase in industry employment as a decrease.

Minimum-wage workers are conspicuously absent from the coalition of low-wage employers and conservative politicians who are raising concerns about the employment effects of raising the minimum wage. The overwhelming weight of recent evidence supports the view that low-wage workers will benefit overwhelmingly from a higher federal minimum.

Conclusion

The value of the minimum wage has declined enormously from its level in the 1970s. The consequences for the distribution of earnings are significant; the implications for the future are even more so. An increase in the minimum wage to $5.75 would have a substantial and immediate impact on wage inequality and little or no impact on low-wage employment. Even more importantly, it would send a clear message that as a society we value work and are committed to economic growth along a high-wage path.

NOTES

1. The 60% figure is from Card and Krueger 1995, p. 5. With the real value of the minimum wage approaching a 40-year low, current coverage is down from 10% to about 5%.

2. Dinardo, Fortin, and Lemieux 1994.

3. Mishel, Bernstein, and Rasell 1995.

4. George Bush, Bob Dole, and Newt Gingrich supported the 1989 legislation that authorized minimum-wage increases in 1990 and 1991. House Republicans backed hikes in 1989 (79% voted in favor), 1974 (86%), 1966 (61%), 1955 (87%), and 1949 (91%). They opposed increases only in 1977 (88% voted against) and 1961 (81%).

5. Following Mishel, Bernstein, and Rasell 1995, we define workers "at or near the minimum wage" as those earning between $4.25 per hour (the current federal minimum wage) and $5.14 per hour (one cent below the new level proposed by President Clinton in early 1995).

6. Card and Krueger 1995, p. 297.

7. While a rise in employment contradicts standard economic theory, there are many reasons that increasing the minimum wage could leave employment higher or unchanged. Raising the minimum, for example, could help fill vacancies faster and help retain workers longer.

8. The most accurate interpretation of the results is not that the minimum wage increased employment, but rather that the 18.8% increase in the minimum wage had no measurable effect on fast-food employment.

9. The Neumark and Wascher sample is not directly comparable with Card and Krueger's. Neumark and Wascher's sample is smaller and includes restaurants that did not appear in the original sample.

10. Neumark and Wascher report their results in terms of full-time equivalent (FTE) employees, not hours. However, they have simply taken their hours data and divided by 35 to arrive at an FTE employment count. They did not collect separate data on the number of employees. Card and Krueger asked managers or assistant managers specifically how many full-time and part-time employees worked at each restaurant.

REFERENCES

Belman, Dale and Paul Wolfson. 1995. "An Intervention Analysis of Employment and the Minimum Wage." University of Wisconsin, Milwaukee. Photocopy.

Card, David. 1992a. "Using Regional Variation in Wages to Measure the Effects of the Federal Minimum Wage." *Industrial and Labor Relations Review*, Vol. 46, No. 1, pp. 22-37.

Card, David. 1992b. "Do Minimum Wages Reduce Employment? A Case Study of California, 1987-1989." *Industrial and Labor Relations Review*, Vol. 46, No. 1, pp. 38-54.

Card, David and Alan B. Krueger. 1994. "Minimum Wages and Employment: A Case Study of the Fast-Food Industry in New Jersey and Pennsylvania." *American Economic Review*, Vol. 84, No. 4, pp. 772-93.

Card, David and Alan B. Krueger. 1995. *Myth and Measurement: The New Economics of the Minimum Wage*. Princeton, N.J.: Princeton University Press.

Dinardo, John, Nicole M. Fortin, and Thomas Lemieux. 1994. "Labor Market Institutions and the Distribution of Wages, 1973-1992: A Semiparametric Approach." C.E.D.R. University of Montreal. Photocopy.

Katz, Lawrence and Alan Krueger. 1992. "The Effect of the Minimum Wage on the Fast Food Industry." *Industrial and Labor Relations Review*, Vol. 46, No. 1, pp. 6-21.

Mishel, Lawrence, Jared Bernstein, and Edith Rasell. 1995. *Who Wins With a Higher Minimum Wage.* Briefing Paper. Washington, D.C.: Economic Policy Institute.

Neumark, David and William Wascher. 1995. "The Effects of New Jersey's Minimum Wage Increase on Fast Food Employment: A Re-evaluation Using Payroll Records." National Bureau of Economic Research Working Paper No. 5224.

Spriggs, William E. and Bruce W. Klein. 1994. *Raising the Floor: The Effects of the Minimum Wage on Low-Wage Workers*. Washington, D.C.: Economic Policy Institute.

Wellington, Alison. 1991. "Effects of the Minimum Wage on the Employment Status of Youths: An Update." *Journal of Human Resources*, Vol. 26, No. 1, pp. 27-46.

CHAPTER 10

WELFARE REFORM

Fixing the System Inside and Out

by Jared Bernstein & Irwin Garfinkel[1]

WELFARE—PUBLIC AID TO THE POOR—COMES WITH CAPITALISM. THE market forces that create economic growth and a tide of winners also create recessions and the occasional losers who need assistance. But since the creation of the English poor laws in the 14th century, welfare programs have been controversial. While they reduce insecurity, they also cost taxpayers money and reduce reliance on work and the family as sources of economic support. This inherent tension has, at different points in U.S. history, fueled intense debates. Welfare policy inevitably forces a choice between our values of compassion and community on the one hand and self-reliance and self-interest on the other. As a result, the generosity of welfare programs fluctuates with the resolution of each round of reform.

With Bill Clinton's campaign promise to "end welfare as we know it," welfare reform is once again at the center of national debate. The Clinton Administration's plan would limit cash assistance for those able to work to two years and provide work relief after that. Tougher plans put forth by congressional Republicans would eliminate eligibility for any aid after a five-year period (with no provision for those who do not find work), eliminate eligibility for children born to unmarried teenage mothers, and even end federal financing.

These reforms address a number of concerns about welfare that, even though they are continually invoked by policy makers and widely held by the American public, are for the most part not true. Chief among

Jared Bernstein is deputy chief economist of the U.S. Department of Labor. (The views expressed are the author's and do not necessarily reflect those of the Department of Labor.) Irwin Garfinkel is a professor of social work at Columbia University.

these myths are the following:

- few people on welfare are truly needy; rather, government handouts entice able-bodied people away from the workforce and into the system. Once there the living is easy, and dependence becomes long-term.
- subsidies for children have created an explosion of out-of-wedlock births, seriously threatening the stability of American society.
- runaway welfare spending is one of the chief culprits behind ballooning federal deficits.

Yet myths can be powerful, and in the case of welfare reform their tenacity is leading us down a path in which we risk exacerbating some of our most serious social problems without solving any of them. This result, however, is far from inevitable, particularly if we take this opportunity to broaden the focus of welfare reform.

The key to reforming welfare lies not within the system but outside it—in the labor market and social institutions that are creating economic insecurity and fostering dependence on welfare. If we ignore these needed institutional reforms and only reform welfare from within, we will once again be faced with the impossible tradeoff that has bedeviled every round of welfare reform. If we simply make welfare more generous, thus reducing economic insecurity, we run the risk of increasing dependence. Yet, if we reduce access to welfare, or further reduce benefits, we reduce economic security, increase poverty, and, as we shall see, do little to reduce births to unmarried teenagers.

This is not to say that there is nothing that needs to be done about the welfare program. In conjunction with progressive reforms outside welfare, the Aid to Families With Dependent Children (AFDC) program should be converted to a time-limited cash-relief program culminating in eligibility for work relief. Long-term cash relief is an inappropriate tool for aiding those capable of work; a work-relief program, which provided eligibility to intact as well as split families, would reinforce both work and family.

The Modern History of Welfare in the United States

Although AFDC gets a tremendous amount of attention from policy makers and the media, it is a small part of the modern American welfare state, representing just 9% of total social welfare expenditures and 1% of the federal budget.[2]

AFDC was created in 1935, as a minor part of the landmark Social Security Act, to aid the children of widows and other single mothers.[3] President Roosevelt and the other architects of the Act believed government should both provide relief to people who needed it and prevent as many people as possible from needing it. Assistance programs like AFDC were intended to provide a safety net to relieve the poverty of single mothers and to temporarily support victims of market failures in times of severe economic stress. At the same time, public education and social insurance programs were expected to *prevent* poverty and recourse to the safety net.

Work relief versus cash relief. The creators of the Social Security Act considered work relief to be more appropriate than cash relief for those expected to work—that is, able-bodied men. Thus, in the depths of the Great Depression the federal government launched the Works Progress Administration, providing 3.33 million work-relief jobs.[4] AFDC provided cash assistance because poor single mothers were not expected to work; it was designed to help these mothers imitate the child-rearing practices of the middle class—that is, to refrain from market work and stay home to raise their children.

Although AFDC was expected to shrink in importance once Survivor's Insurance was enacted (1938) and matured, its caseloads instead grew as divorce, separation, and out-of-wedlock births increased. Criticism of welfare grew as well. By the early 1960s, AFDC was criticized for providing inadequate benefits, discouraging work and independence (since benefits were reduced by a dollar for each dollar earned), and, by failing to cover two-parent families, encouraging marital dissolution. These critiques have driven every round of welfare reform since.

The Kennedy Administration agreed that AFDC discouraged work and marriage, and it proposed the provision of social services to promote work and independence and the extension of eligibility to unemployed workers.[5] Congress enacted legislation first to encourage and then (under Nixon) to force AFDC mothers to work and become independent. Under Reagan, access to the welfare rolls was tightened through the imposition of more stringent eligibility standards, and stiffer work requirements were imposed.[6]

Despite stronger laws, the compulsion to work has been weak, for a number of reasons. State governments have been unwilling to spend the necessary job and training funds to implement a work requirement. Demand in the labor market for workers with the skills of the average welfare recipient has been weak. The difficulty and expense of child care have precluded the option for many parents willing to work. And, since time limits have never been a requirement, lack of employment has never been used to force recipients to leave the welfare rolls.

Yet despite the lack of enforcement, the emphasis on work represents an important shift in AFDC policy. In retrospect, this new emphasis is not surprising. By the 1960s, the child-rearing practices of middle-class mothers were in the midst of a revolution. At the beginning of the century less than 10% of married mothers with children worked. This percentage has grown consistently since then, reaching 68% by 1993.[7] Hence, the model for motherhood on which the AFDC program is based is no longer that of a parent staying home to raise the children. When the overwhelming majority of mothers work, it becomes politically indefensible to argue that poor single mothers should not have to. Furthermore, there are both economic and psychological reasons for encouraging work among recipients: abstaining from work increases the isolation of welfare mothers and their children from mainstream society and reduces their opportunity to improve their economic and social status.

Similarly, in light of the shift in AFDC caseloads from widowed mothers to divorced, separated, and never-married mothers, it is not surprising that welfare policy has increasingly emphasized child-support enforcement.

Trends in welfare benefits. Between 1960 and 1970, the average AFDC cash benefit grew about 35%. Medicaid was added in 1965 and food stamps in 1972-74 to the welfare benefit package. Starting in the mid-1960s, the efforts of welfare rights organizations and progressive lawyers helped make AFDC more accessible than ever before. By the mid-1970s, close to 90% of eligible families sought assistance; the share of female-headed families on welfare grew from 30% in 1960 to 54% in

1975.[8] All of these effects, combined with the growth in single motherhood, resulted in a dramatic growth in AFDC caseloads from 0.8 million in 1960 to 3.5 million in 1975.

During the last two decades, the value of welfare benefits has declined. AFDC plus food stamps fell 27% between 1972 and 1992 (almost all of this decline is due to the fall in the real value of AFDC benefits). At first, real benefits declined because state legislators failed to increase them to keep pace with inflation. Lately, however, many states have actually cut benefits. As the real value of benefits has declined, so too has the proportion of families headed by single mothers that received welfare. Indeed, by 1992 the proportion on the welfare rolls had fallen from 54% in 1975 to 42%.

Finally, both the increase in welfare benefits during the 1960s and early 1970s and the subsequent decrease since then were, given the benefit of hindsight, predictable. The average standard of living in the United States is the best single predictor of the need for welfare benefits. The 1960s were prosperous years, but since 1973 the real wages of most Americans have fallen, and families have been able to maintain their living standards only by increasing their hours of work. Welfare, then, takes a double hit: not only does the need for it rise, but, with most families struggling to keep from falling behind, public support for it falls.

The Limits of Reform From Within

The related goals of welfare reform are to reduce both poverty and dependency on public support. But reform that seeks only to change the incentives within the existing welfare system, while lowering caseloads, will not significantly slow the increase in single-parent families and will increase the poverty and deprivation of our most vulnerable families. Time limits, in the absence of low-wage labor market reform, will also increase economic insecurity.

Welfare benefits and female-headed families. The growth in welfare caseloads has been driven by the growth in families headed by females. Some conservatives claim that welfare caused this growth, and that eliminating welfare will reverse it. Both economic theory and common sense suggest that welfare benefits increase the ability of a poor single woman with a child to live independently and to be selective about a new partner. Neither theory nor common sense, however, suggests how large the effect will be.

Compared with other factors—increases in employment opportunities for women, decreases in employment opportunities for men, and changing social values—government benefits account for a small portion of the growth of mother-only families. (Improvements in employment opportunities for women appear to be the single most important factor.) A review of the literature reveals that government transfers have reduced remarriage, but have had only a minor effect on divorce and out-of-wedlock births.[9] The increase in benefits that occurred between 1960 and 1975 accounts for at most 15% of the overall growth in families headed by women. Furthermore, although welfare benefits have declined since 1975, the share of families headed by a single mother has continued to grow.[10] Finally, while Canada, France, Germany, the Netherlands, Sweden, and the United Kingdom provide more generous government benefits to all families (including those headed by single mothers) than does the United States, the proportions of single-mother families in all these countries is considerably lower than in the United States.[11] In short, the evidence indicates that even a substantial reduction in welfare benefits will result in only a small reduction in the number of families headed by single mothers.

Reducing welfare dependency. It is true that a substantial reduction in welfare benefits would lead to a notable reduction in dependence on welfare. In the extreme case, eliminating welfare eliminates welfare dependence. But substantial reductions in benefits also lead to increases in poverty. We've already performed the experiment, and the historical evidence is clear: from 1960 to 1975, as the welfare benefit package increased, the proportion of single-mother families on welfare rose—from 30% to 54%—and poverty rates for female-headed families fell. From 1975 to 1993, as the value of the benefit package fell, the proportion of single mothers on welfare shrank to 43%, and poverty rates rose slightly.[12]

What is the extent of welfare dependency? This fundamental issue has been the subject of much research, but the central finding is that a minority of welfare recipients are "long-termers." A classic study by Mary Jo Bane and David Ellwood in 1983 revealed that 30% of families were on welfare for eight years or more, including multiple spells. More recent research by LaDonna Pavetti, using monthly rather than annual data, shows a significantly smaller share—15%—of long-term welfare dependents.[13] Nevertheless, these families account for the largest share of recipients at a point in time and are the most costly to the welfare system. Not surprisingly, those most likely to be welfare-dependent are young, never-married, minority women who are high school dropouts.

Work and training programs are one way within welfare to simultaneously reduce poverty and promote independence. Controlled experiments conducted by the Manpower Development Research Corporation show that many of these programs are a good investment: within a few years the benefits exceed the costs for both recipients and taxpayers. Despite this success, the reductions in poverty and AFDC caseloads are small to modest—usually well under 10%.[14]

Placing a time limit on cash assistance and providing work relief thereafter are likely to reinforce the positive effects of work and training programs, although at this point we do not know how significant the effect might be. Moreover, there are costs to substituting work relief for cash assistance.

To begin with, work relief is more expensive per recipient than cash relief. The work must be organized and supervised, and child care must be provided to single mothers with young children. Unless caseloads decrease substantially, time limited cash assistance followed by work relief will be more expensive than pure cash relief. Also, work relief will reduce the standard of living of current beneficiaries. Cash relief allows mothers to spend their time in child rearing and other productive activities. Recent research indicates that most welfare mothers now supplement their welfare checks with part time, off-the-books earnings.[15] Because a person cannot be in two places at once, work relief limits such opportunities. Work relief may also displace other public sector jobs and thereby lower wages (since work relief will pay less than public sector jobs) and increase unemployment. Displacement effects are a particularly valid concern in the public sector, where "workfare" employment has the potential to displace good, public sector jobs. This possibility calls for the involvement of local public sector unions which can help organize local work projects that do not jeopardize their members' employment.[16]

Finally, any positive impact of time limits will be constrained by the condition of low-wage labor markets. Given her labor-market profile, any

The Lorelei of Block Grants

A number of recent welfare reform proposals put forth by House Republicans and a group of Republican governors call for providing block grants to states so that they can take responsibility for AFDC and food stamps. Under a block grant system, the federal government would provide states with a fixed level of funding for their welfare caseloads, and this level would not be adjusted for changes in economic conditions. Thus, when demand for AFDC benefits expanded due to a recession, states would not have federal resources to provide the needed assistance. This would be a major step backward in U.S. welfare policy.

One of the most useful features of entitlement programs is that they automatically expand and contract as the economy goes through its ups and downs. One study[17] has shown that, had the food stamp program been inflexibly "capped" by a block grant since 1989, funding for states would have been 29% lower in 1994 than was actually the case.

As a recent Urban Institute report states,[18] moving to a block grant system of welfare provision "is likely to set off a competitive scramble [among states] to cut benefits and limit eligibility." Each state fears that if it approaches adequate benefit levels, its costs will include taking care of the poor from other states who are induced to migrate. The incentive, then, is to provide fewer benefits than neighboring states to promote out-migration of the poor.

We interpret states' desire to control welfare as resulting from failed attempts at national reform. In the context of our inside/outside approach to reform, however, state control is far less likely to generate the results we seek. The structural problems of the low-wage labor market and the gaps in social policy we discuss here are national problems that are unlikely to be ameliorated at the state or local levels. In fact, many of the remedies we suggest would be undermined if implemented anywhere but at the national level. Also, under a block grant structure, states have incentives to under-provide the very social protections that are integral to effective reform. **—JB & IG**

unsubsidized employment a former welfare recipient can find will invariably place her in the low-wage sector, which is currently characterized by weak demand. Among entry-level high school graduates, pre-tax hourly wages fell 29% for males and 18% for females from 1979 to 1993. Unemployment for young, female dropouts—a group disproportionately represented on welfare—was 18% for whites in 1993 and 42% for blacks (the national average was 6.8%). Another symptom of weak demand in low-wage labor markets is the steep decline in the proportion of young workers with a high school education or less who are employed (the employment/population rate). For young black male dropouts (age 25-34), this rate fell from 83.0% in 1973 to 52.4% in 1993. These figures, taken together, portray a very weak labor market that is unlikely to provide a useful foothold for welfare recipients.

Because substituting work relief for cash relief would reduce the economic well-being of an already vulnerable population, such a policy shift should not be undertaken without other changes that increase the economic well-being of poor single mothers and their children. As part of a broader set of labor market and social policy reforms that make work pay, however, instituting time limits on cash assistance followed by work relief is a policy we ought to adopt. For those expected to and capable of work, welfare should be a temporary safety net, not a permanent source of income.[19]

Outside Welfare: Reducing Economic Insecurity, Poverty, and Dependence

Policy makers are clearly responding to the American public's demand to lower welfare caseloads. As noted above, reducing the value of welfare is one way to accomplish the goal, but reducing welfare will increase poverty. The objectives of reform should be to lower welfare expenditures by reducing poverty and economic insecurity. This goal can be reached only by reforms outside welfare, specifically by reforming low-wage labor markets and the relevant social policies.

This broader approach to welfare reform is necessary because the problem of dependency is a poverty problem, a connection conspicuously missing from the welfare debate. And poverty has begun to do a strange thing. Up until the early 1980s, if the economy performed well and employment was healthy, poverty, as one might expect, declined. Since about 1983, however, this relationship disappeared: in bad times as well as good, poverty has increased. One explanation for this new phenomenon can be found in the growth of wage inequality,[20] through which the distribution of economic rewards has been skewed to the point where less advantaged families are unable to benefit from overall growth. As a result, fewer are able to avoid the clutches of poverty.

The impact on poverty and welfare caseloads of the decline in male wages and labor force participation has also received too little attention. Bernstein's (1994) study of the determinants of welfare caseloads in 17 states from 1960 to 1990 found that the wage trends of low-wage males had a larger impact than those of low-wage females. A branch of poverty analysis associated with William Julius Wilson has examined this relationship. Wilson's hypothesis is that, as males become less-eligible marriage prospects from an economic perspective, the incentive among women to marry falls and more welfare-eligible families are formed. In a sense, the welfare benefit becomes a replacement for the contribution of male earnings to the household. Thus, taxpayers from higher up the wage scale, who fund this replacement, pay part of the price of the failure of low-wage labor markets to sustain a family wage.

If nothing else had changed, the decline in welfare benefits after 1975 would have led to a decline in welfare caseloads. But the number of families headed by single females continued to increase as the wage rates of those at the bottom plummeted. Thus, strengthening low-wage labor markets is integral to true welfare reform.

Labor-market policy. There are four primary reasons for the expansion of low-wage sectors of the labor market: the increased returns to education and experience (which place young, less-educated workers at a relative disadvantage); the decline in the real value of the minimum wage; declining unionization rates; and the shift from manufacturing to service employment (which reflects, in part, increased trade). If we are serious about "making work pay," these are the proper areas of intervention.

In this context, worker training should be seen as raising the human capital of welfare recipients so that they might benefit from the increase in education returns. This goal is at least rhetorically part of welfare reform already, but it has historically been underfunded.

Increasing the minimum wage to its 1979 value in real terms would have particularly strong effects for female workers, 58% of whom earned hourly wages at or below this level in 1993. (The current minimum wage is $4.25; to make it worth as much in 1994 as it was in 1979 would require raising it to $5.81.) In fact, correcting the decline in the real value of the minimum would fully reverse the hourly wage loss experienced by high-school-educated women.[21] (For a fuller discussion of the minimum wage, see the chapter in this section by William Spriggs and John Schmitt.)

Since unions are historically associated with higher wages for non-college-educated workers, particularly women,[22] labor law reform that facilitates organizing will help turn around wage decline. Trade policies (like NAFTA) that pit our low-wage workers against labor forces with much lower wages both contribute to wage decline and hasten the shift from manufacturing to low-wage services. Such policies should be avoided. (The impact of trade on wages is discussed more fully in the chapters by Robert Scott and Jerome Levinson.)

Finally, serious welfare reform should force us to rethink the concept of full employment. The labor-market policies of the Federal Reserve Board, as discussed in the chapters by Robert Eisner and James Galbraith, have reflected the belief that overall unemployment rates below around 6% will lead to hyperinflation. As noted above, the unemployment rate for young, female high school dropouts in 1993 was 18% for whites and 42% for blacks (when the overall rate was 6.8%). Thus, a monetary policy that enforces this level of employment is unlikely to reduce the need for welfare assistance.

Social policy. Public opinion polls consistently show that large majorities of Americans favor spending more on the poor but less on welfare. Together, these opinions suggest strong public support for aiding the poor outside the welfare system. Public opinion is consistent with the traditional social democratic view: welfare is a necessary last resort, but large caseloads are undesirable and suggest that something is amiss in the broader society.

Welfare reform becomes the occasion for addressing these broader social ills through social policy reforms. Of great importance in this regard are the earned income tax credit (EITC), universal health care, child care, child support, and child allowances.

Outside of public education and social insurance, the transfer system in this country as it affects children is split in two, with welfare benefits going to families at the very bottom of the income distribution and tax subsidies going primarily to families in the upper-middle and upper segments. Furthermore, the bulk of welfare benefits are targeted at the poorest of the poor because the payments are limited to single-parent families. The near-poor, the lower middle class, and even the middle class pay the price, and many are resentful. This system is not only inequitable; it also undermines work and marriage at the bottom of the income distribution.

The Clinton Administration has said that the first objective of welfare reform must be to "make work pay." To this end President Clinton proposed and persuaded Congress to adopt as part of the 1993 budget agreement a substantial increase in the EITC. By 1996 the maximum annual EITC benefit for a family with one child will equal $2,094; it will equal $3,560 for a family with two or more children. President Clinton argued at the time that universal health care coverage had to precede welfare reform because, while welfare mothers are able to receive health care coverage from Medicaid, the working poor are forced to make do without health insurance.

Most Americans now believe that one objective of social policy should be equal access to health care. The benefits of such a policy extend far beyond improvements in health: some estimates indicate that a universal health care system would reduce child poverty by 20-30%, reduce welfare caseloads by up to 20%, and increase the probability of marriage by up to 2.6%.[23]

To insist that poor single mothers work is to strengthen the case for public subsidization of child care, and not just for single-parent families but also for two-parent families among the working poor. Mothers cannot work and care for their children at the same time, and few will maintain that poor single mothers can afford to pay for adequate child care.[24] Child care has the added advantage in that it reduces poverty and insecurity at the same time that it rewards work and independence. France and Sweden have the most universal systems of child care in the world, practically no child poverty, and lower rates of welfare dependence than does the United States.[25]

Ultimately, the case for subsidizing universal child care should be made on the most general level. Nothing is more vital to future productivity than child rearing. The traditional method of providing child care—full-time care by the mother—is high quality but very expensive, since the foregone market earnings of the mothers are enormous. As a consequence, most mothers of pre-school-age children now work. It is in the national interest to make certain that modern forms of substitute child care are as high in quality as the traditional form.

Public subsidization of child care is also essential for achieving gender equity. In modern industrial societies, the responsibility for child rearing falls principally on the mother, and the foregone labor-market experience stunts her human capital growth. Such an arrangement is not only inequitable but also inefficient. A nation that relies only on its men for market work squanders half its human potential.

Another social issue that is having a burdensome impact on welfare caseloads is the failure of our system of public enforcement of private child support. Only 60% of mothers with children potentially eligible for child support obtain legal entitlement to support. Of those, only half obtain the full amount to which they are legally entitled; a quarter receives nothing. If child support were perfectly enforced, payments in 1990 would have been about $50 billion instead of $13 billion, poverty among children potentially eligible for child support would have been reduced by about one-fourth, and AFDC caseloads would have been about 20% lower.

The Clinton Administration is correct in trying to strengthen child support enforcement, but it doesn't go far enough. To redress the failings of our current system, we should add a Child Support Assurance System (CSAS) to our menu of Social Security programs. Under CSAS, child support awards would be set by a legislated formula—based on a percentage of the nonresident parent's income—and payments deducted from the absent parent's earnings, just like Social Security deductions. The government would guarantee a minimum level of support—the assured benefit—just as it guarantees minimum benefits in old age and unemployment insurance. The assured benefit would be financed from welfare savings and from a very small addition to the Social Security payroll tax.

The Child Support Assurance System would increase the economic security of all children who live apart from a parent, rich and poor alike. Withholding a fixed percentage—17%, for example—from the paychecks of all nonresident parents would increase the amount and regularity of private payments. Even so, private support payments for many poor children would continue to be low and irregular, as are the incomes of their absent parents. The assured benefit would compensate by providing a steady, secure source of income for these children. It would more than double the reduction in poverty and welfare dependence achieved by private support alone.[26]

In 1984 and 1988 Congress took steps toward implementing a CSAS on the collection side by requiring states to adopt numerical guidelines for determining child support awards and to withhold child support from the paychecks of obligors. Tentative steps in the direction of an assured benefit were also taken in the form of waiver authority for Wisconsin and New York to experiment with variants of the concept. Wisconsin did not proceed with the test, but New York has been experimenting since 1988 with an assured benefit limited to families with incomes low enough to qualify for welfare. As part of his welfare reform proposal, President Clinton would strengthen enforcement of private support and provide federal funds for state experiments with an assured benefit.

Finally, the United States is the only Western industrialized country without a children's allowance. During the 1992 presidential campaign, Bill Clinton proposed a middle-class tax cut that had as its centerpiece a refundable tax credit of $1,000 per child. After assuming office he backed off the proposal because of its cost, but has since revived it as a nonrefundable credit of $500 per child. A nonrefundable credit is of little help to those who owe no taxes, but a credit is more progressive than the current child exemption in the income tax, and it will therefore be of help to the working poor and lower middle class.

Conclusion

Welfare can relieve, but not prevent, poverty. When welfare caseloads grow large, something in broader society is amiss. Poverty and welfare dependence are now high because of a disastrous deterioration in the low-wage labor market and the inadequate development of social policies in the areas of health insurance, child care, child support, and tax treatment for families with children.

Reforming welfare from within can do little to reduce poverty. At best, work and training programs will make a small positive contribution. Cutting or eliminating benefits will reduce dependence on welfare, but only at the cost of increasing poverty.

To prevent both poverty and dependence on welfare requires solutions outside the system. Increasing the minimum wage, strengthening unions, promoting full employment, and providing universal child care, national health insurance, child support assurance, and child allowances are the essential ingredients of real welfare reform.

NOTES

1. The authors acknowledge the helpful comments of Sheldon Danziger, Heidi Hartmann, and Christopher Jencks.

2. Eliminating the program *entirely* would shave $17 billion, or about 10%, from the projected FY 1995 deficit of $170 billion, and would trim the national debt by less than 0.5%. Proponents of reducing federal spending may consider such savings worthwhile, but they should not be deluded into thinking that these savings will eradicate deficits.

3. The program was originally called Aid to Dependent Children. The name was changed in 1950 to Aid to Families With Dependent Children when the program was amended to add benefits for the child's caretaker as well as the child.

4. Because of congressional opposition, FDR proposed neither a permanent work relief program nor national health insurance.

5. In 1961 Congress gave states the option of extending eligibility for AFDC to families with an unemployed parent—AFDC-UP. Only about half the states adopted AFDC-UP programs, and eligibility was severely restricted.

6. By tightening eligibility standards, the Reagan changes cut the welfare caseload by as much as 500,000 (Levitan 1990).

7. Bergman 1986; U.S. House of Representatives 1994.

8. Our participation rate levels differ from those in Moffitt 1992, Table 3, apparently due to different data sources; however, the trends are similar. Our data for these rates come from the following sources: data on family cases headed by single parents are from various issues of *Characteristics and Financial Circumstances of AFDC Recipients*, U.S. Dept. of Health and Human Services, Administration for Children and Families, Office of Family Assistance; female heads-of-household with children is from Bureau of the Census, Series P-60-185, p. 6.

9. See Garfinkel and McLanahan's 1986 review of empirical research in the United States.

10. The most recent comprehensive review of the literature by Robert Moffitt in 1992 comes to the same conclusion: welfare has had very little effect on female headship.

11. Smeeding and Rainwater 1991. That Sweden has a lower proportion of single-parent families than the United States may come as a surprise. This is because of the confusion between marital status and residence patterns. Children who live with unmarried mothers are frequently included in the Swedish count of single-mother families. About half of these children, however, are living with their natural fathers and therefore should be counted as two-parent families (Gustafson 1991).

12. There are many other important determinants of the poverty rates for mother-only families. Our point is simply that cutting welfare benefits has never made these families better off, while increasing them has done so.

13. Bane and Ellwood 1983; Pavetti 1992.

14. Geuron 1991.

15. Jencks and Edin 1990; Spalter-Roth, Burr, Hartmann, and Shaw 1995.

16. Meiklejohn 1995.

17. Greenstein 1995.

18. Peterson 1995.

19. In the Clinton welfare reform plan, recipients who cannot find private-sector employment essentially work off their welfare grant. We would rather see recipients paid a wage (no lower than the minimum), like any other worker in the labor market. If their wages and hours were such that they did not earn their former benefit level, the wage would need to be subsidized.

20. The ratio of the wage at the 90th to the 10th percentile grew for both males and females between 1979 and 1993—from 3.6 to 4.6 and from 2.7 to 3.8.

21. Mishel and Bernstein 1994.

22. Hartmann, Spalter-Roth, and Collins 1994.

23. For the effects on child poverty, see Kim 1993; for welfare caseloads, Moffitt and Wolfe 1992; for likelihood of marriage, Yelowitz 1994.

24. Larry Mead, professor of politics at New York University, argues that the lack of child care is not a barrier to work for poor single mothers because they can get adequate care by relatives. If he is correct, the cost of public subsidization will be slight because there will be few takers.

25. Garfinkel and McLanahan 1994.

26. We acknowledge that a CSAS could lead to an increase in divorce, though we suspect this effect would be small (see Garfinkel 1992). At any rate, with CSAS these newly divorced families are less likely to need public support.

References

Bane, Mary Jo and David Ellwood. 1983. "The Dynamics of Dependence: The Routes to Self-Sufficiency." Prepared for the U.S. Department of Health and Human Services, Washington, D.C.

Bergman, Barbara R. 1986. *The Economic Emergence of Women.* New York: Basic Books.

Garfinkel, Irwin. 1992. *Assuring Child Support: An Extension of Social Security.* New York: Russell Sage Foundation.

Garfinkel, Irwin and Sara McLanahan. 1994. "Single Mother Families, Economic Insecurity, and Government Policy." In Sheldon Danziger, Gary Sandefur, and Daniel Weinberg, eds., *Confronting Poverty*. Cambridge, Mass.: Harvard University Press.

Garfinkel, Irwin and Sara McLanahan. 1986. *Single Mothers and Their Children*. Washington, D.C.: Urban Institute Press.

Greenstein, Robert. 1995. Testimony to the Subcommittee on Human Resources of the House Ways and Means Committee, January 13.

Geuron, Judith. 1991. *From Welfare to Work*. New York: Russell Sage Foundation.

Gustafsson, Siv. 1995. "Single Mothers in Sweden: Why Is Poverty Less Severe?" In Katherine McFate, Roger Lawson, and William Julius Wilson, eds., *Poverty, Inequality and the Future of Social Policy*. New York: Russell Sage Foundation.

Hartmann, Heidi, Roberta Spalter-Roth, and Nancy Collins. 1994. "What Do Unions Do for Women?" *Challenge*, July/August.

Jencks, Christopher and Kathryn Edin. 1990. "The Real Welfare Problem." *The American Prospect*, No. 1, Spring.

Kim, Y.H. 1993. "The Economic Effects of the Combined Non-Income-Tested Transfers for Families With Children: Child Support Assurance, Children's Allowance, and National Health Insurance." University of Wisconsin, Madison. Ph.D. Dissertation.

Levitan, Sar. 1990. *Programs in Aid of the Poor*. Baltimore, Md.: Johns Hopkins University Press.

Meiklejohn, Nanine. 1995. *Work and Training Opportunities for Welfare Recipients*. Washington, D.C.: American Federation of State, County, and Municipal Employees.

Mishel, Lawrence and Jared Bernstein. 1994. *The State of Working America 1994-95*. Economic Policy Institute Series. Armonk, N.Y.: M.E. Sharpe.

Moffitt, Robert. 1992. "Incentive Effects of the U.S. Welfare System: A Review." *Journal of Economic Literature*, 30, pp. 1-61.

Moffitt, Robert and Barbara L. Wolfe. 1992. "The Effect of the Medicaid Program on Welfare Participation and Labor Supply." *Review of Economics and Statistics*, Vol. 74, December.

Pavetti, LaDonna. 1992. "The Dynamics of Welfare and Work: Exploring the Process By Which Young Women Work Their Way Off Welfare." JFK School of Government, Harvard University.

Peterson, George. 1995. "A Block Grant Approach to Welfare Reform." Urban Institute Welfare Reform Brief, No. 1.

Smeeding, Timothy and Lee Rainwater. 1991. "Cross National Trends in Income Poverty and Dependency: The Evidence for Young Adults in the Eighties." Paper presented at the Joint Center for Political and Economic Studies, Washington, D.C., September 20-21.

Spalter-Roth, Roberta, Heidi Hartmann, and Beverly Burr. 1994. *Income Insecurity: The Failure of UI to Reach Working AFDC Mothers.* Washington, D.C.: Institute for Women's Policy Research.

Spalter-Roth, Roberta, Beverly Burr, Heidi Hartmann, and Lois Shaw. 1995. *Welfare That Works: The Working Lives of AFDC Recipients.* Washington, D.C.: Institute for Women's Policy Research.

U.S. Department of Health and Human Services, Office of Family Assistance. Various Issues. *Characteristics and Financial Circumstances of AFDC Recipients.* Washington, D.C.: U.S. Government Printing Office.

U.S. House of Representatives. 1994. *Green Book: Background Material and Data on Programs Within the Jurisdiction of the Committee on Ways and Means.* Washington, D.C.: U.S. Government Printing Office.

Yelowitz, Aaron S. 1994. "Will Extending Medicaid to Two Parent Families Encourage Marriage?" UCLA Department of Economics. Mimeo.

SECTION III

Money and Finance

Overview

Money and Finance

by Eileen Appelbaum

There is perhaps no area of economic policy that is more important in people's daily lives than monetary policy and the regulation of financial markets. Policies pursued by government regulatory agencies will largely determine the availability of mortgages for new home buyers, the availability of loans for people wanting to start a new business, and even the availability of jobs in the economy. Despite its importance to the public, however, the news media pay scant attention to monetary and financial policy, and most people remain largely ignorant of important decisions that will affect their lives.

Discussion of monetary and financial issues are usually relegated to the financial pages of newspapers or to special television or radio shows devoted to business. In these forums, policies tend to be addressed from the standpoint of their impact on profits and stock prices, and usually in technical terms that can make the discussion impenetrable to a nonexpert. This has the effect of limiting, if not actually eliminating, democratic input into matters that are essential to the public's well-being. The government's monetary and financial policies then end up being decided primarily by those who stand to gain the most—the financial industry.

A first step to achieving any reform in the area of monetary and financial regulation is to increase awareness of the ways in which government policy affects outcomes in these areas. The last two decades have been a period of rapidly increasing concentration in the financial industry, as large banks and other financial institutions have swallowed up thousands of smaller institutions. This consolidation was an outcome of a

Eileen Appelbaum is associate research director at the Economic Policy Institute.

conscious government policy that allowed, if it did not actually encourage, large banks to buy out smaller competitors. This contrasts with an earlier policy, dating from the New Deal, that attempted to protect the market position of smaller banks.

Has the public been well served by financial concentration? Are banks with headquarters in downtown Manhattan or San Francisco as likely to make loans in poor inner-city neighborhoods and depressed rural areas as were the local banks they displaced? Do people today have better and cheaper access to checking accounts, savings accounts, and other financial services than they would have without this movement toward concentration? Is the government able to effectively regulate the massive financial institutions that have resulted from the wave of consolidation, or are we likely to see more S&L-type bailouts, requiring billions of dollars of public funding? These are the sorts of questions that need to be asked if the public's interest in regulatory policy is to be served. And the discussion can't be buried in the financial pages alongside the stock market listings: it belongs on the front page of newspapers and at the top of the news shows, since it is so vital to people's well-being.

The articles in this section address very different areas of monetary and financial policy. The first piece, by James Galbraith, discusses the recent conduct of monetary policy by the Federal Reserve Board. Between February 1994 and February 1995, the Federal Reserve Board raised interest rates six different times, for a total increase of three percentage points. These increases slowed the economy, weakened job growth, and cost consumers tens of billions of dollars in higher interest charges on mortgages and car loans. The justification for these increases was the need to slow inflation, but Galbraith argues that inflation never posed any serious threat during this period. He argues instead that the Federal Reserve was primarily motivated by a desire to serve its banker constituency. Since five of the 12 members of the Federal Reserve Board's Open Market Committee (the body that determines monetary policy) are actually appointed by bankers, this charge is certainly plausible.

Galbraith argues the need for a more expansive monetary policy in order to try to achieve high levels of employment even as deficit reduction is contracting the economy. He also argues for a sunset review process to evaluate whether the Federal Reserve Board, in its current structure, is fulfilling its intended purpose. More generally, he argues the need for more public oversight of the Federal Reserve Board's actions to ensure that it serves the public's interest, and not just the interest of the banking community.

The chapter by Jane D'Arista and Tom Schlesinger discusses some of the changes that have taken place in the financial system in recent years. They note that, in addition to a trend toward concentration, there has been a change in the structure of the banking system so that nonbank institutions, such as finance and insurance companies, now perform many of the functions formerly performed by banks. By failing to keep pace with these changes, the federal regulatory structure often places regulated institutions at a disadvantage compared to their nonregulated competitors. The current regulatory structure also leaves large areas, such as the rapidly growing derivative market, outside of the regulatory sphere altogether.

The fact that the current regulatory system is not well suited to regulate the modern financial system has been widely noted. Most discussion has focused on deregulating the system, abandoning public ends such as community reinvestment (the requirement that banks actively lend money in the communities in which they take deposits). D'Arista and Schlesinger go in the opposite direction, laying out a series of measures aimed at setting up a uniform regulatory structure, where institutions will be regulated by function. This means, for example, that all institutions that take deposits will have their deposits regulated in the same way as banks are regulated. D'Arista and Schlesinger argue that, by leveling the financial playing field *up*, the twin public purposes—wide access to credit and a sound financial system—will be best served.

The last chapter, by Gary Dymski and John Veitch, begins by describing the difficulties inner-city neighborhoods experience in meeting their needs for credit. While the financial system serves the wealthy quite well and meets the basic needs of most middle-income people, it has virtually abandoned large segments of America's cities. These areas are largely cut off from access to the mortgage and small business loans that are essential for a community to prosper.

Dymski and Veitch have developed a creative market-oriented proposal to address this problem. They propose a government-sponsored Community Development Mortgage Association—Cindy Mae—to create a secondary market in loans to depressed inner-city areas. A secondary market would allow banks and other financial institutions to issue loans to businesses and homeowners in inner-city areas, and then resell them in broader financial markets. This mechanism could drastically increase the amount of capital available to inner-city communities. The model for this institution is the Federal National Mortgage Association (Fannie Mae), which the federal government created to foster a secondary market in home mortgages. Fannie Mae has been enormously successful in this purpose and now operates largely as an independent private corporation. A well-managed Cindy Mae could be equally successful.

The proposals presented in these chapters hardly exhaust the range of progressive policy reforms in monetary and financial policy. They are suggestive of the directions that such reform could take, and they provide some specific and well-thought-out measures that will make the financial system more responsive to the needs of the majority, and not just the wealthy few.

CHAPTER 11

The Federal Reserve

Give It Till Sunset

by James K. Galbraith

On October 27, 1915, the Antarctic explorer Sir Ernest Shackleton gathered his men. They were on an ice floe, adrift on the Weddell Sea. Their ship *Endurance* had just been crushed; they had three lifeboats and some dogs. Shackleton's words were simple and direct: "Ship and stores are lost; so now we'll go home."[1]

On November 8, 1994, those who would reform the Federal Reserve found themselves in similar trouble. The election brought the turnover of both congressional banking committees to Republicans, the defeat of Senator Jim Sasser, one of the leading voices in the Senate for monetary reform, and the destruction of many Democratic staffs in Congress. Ship and stores are lost, the Fed remains untouched, and its hold on interest rates and on the well-being of American families remains as strong as ever.

At least Shackleton got close to where he wanted to be. As for our small band of monetary reformers—a handful of members of Congress, a tiny cognoscenti among the staff, and a few professional economists and agitators—we held back, husbanding our resources for that moment when tight money policies would finally incline Congress toward action. Our not-so-daring strategy had as its goal a not-so-bold program: structural reform of the Federal Reserve, wherein its system of appointments and decision making would be opened up to more democratic scrutiny and accountability.

But this approach has failed and cannot be revived in the present constellation of President and Congress. Circumstances have changed radi-

James K. Galbraith is professor of economics at the LBJ School of Public Affairs and the Department of Government at the University of Texas/Austin.

cally, and so must we. No more reform around the edges. If we truly want a monetary system that provides reasonable incomes and access to credit for working people, isn't it time to build a new one from the ground up?

The Failed Campaign for Low Interest Rates

In 1993 and 1994, monetary reformers sought low and stable interest rates. We hoped to achieve this goal by demanding a monetary policy consistent with a fiscal policy that had become, by the middle of 1993, focused solely on deficit reduction. We campaigned through the press, through efforts to engage the President's attention, through congressional hearings.

This seemed a reasonable way to proceed at the time. We did not miss any grand opportunities. We transmitted our views, internally and in the press. We hoped that the Administration would realize that economic performance was not good enough, that the middle class was hurting too badly, that there would be a fearful price to pay if it did not act.

Clinton had not started badly. Deficit reduction was sold to Congress on the explicit promise of low and stable interest rates. The President underlined the point by seating Federal Reserve Chairman Alan Greenspan next to Mrs. Clinton at the first presidential speech to Congress. And short rates were stable, while long rates actually fell, through the enactment of the deficit program in the fall of 1993. As late as the publication of the *Economic Report of the President* on February 4, 1994—the very date of the first rise in short-term rates—the Administration appeared committed to the policy, and to the hope, of low and stable interest rates.

But the impression of monetary/fiscal coordination is not the same thing as the substance of it. And when Chairman Greenspan pulled his bait-and-switch (by raising short-term rates after promising, in effect, to hold them down), the President and his minions refused to admit they'd been had. Instead, they bit their tongues, repeating pieties about "respect for the independence of the Fed" through a year of falling markets, upward income redistribution, and slow economic growth (constantly advertised as the contrary). In effect, they made themselves accessories after the fact. Meanwhile, costs rose, while incomes largely did not, for the millions of middle-class Americans with adjustable-rate mortgages and car loans who had hoped that "change" and "growth" and "recovery" would mean a little more disposable income in their pockets and a little more security in their investments, rather than the reverse.

The effects on Clinton's presidency were corrosive. Having been elected in 1992 by attacking the economic status quo, he found himself two years later defending an economic situation that was actually worse for many millions of people whose interest costs were up and whose investment assets were down. "Denial: it's not just a river in Egypt," a Clinton phrase from the 1992 campaign, became a hallmark of his own policy in 1994 and on into the early months of 1995 as rates continued to rise.

Worse still from a political standpoint, the rise in interest rates highlighted the President's weakness. He was turned into an ineffectual figure before people's eyes—not just on interest rates, a relatively abstract matter, but on the economy itself. Plainly, his bold policy of deficit reduction and low interest rates had been made a mockery. The new party line—that everything was going well so why worry?—was a cover for an unwillingness and inability to confront the Federal Reserve and the hugely powerful forces it represents. But the people remembered his earlier promises.

Politically, the 1993 promises of low interest rates were a stealth version of George Bush's pledge of "read my lips, no new taxes": a litmus test of spine. They were a stealth version because, unlike the situation with Bush, the political community (as distinct from the public) didn't take notice. The press and pollsters did not ask about interest rates, the Republicans were not in any position to mention the issue, and all of us who could have played the Patrick Buchanan role stood by our leader. The middle class took the hit, and voted in 1994 according to its sense of economic improvement or—more often—lack of it, as polls afterward revealed.

The cause of the political failure therefore lies mainly with the Clinton Administration. It failed to secure coordination between monetary and fiscal policy at the outset. And it failed again to confront and protest the ruinous shift in monetary policy toward rising interest rates at the moment it occurred. It thereby threw away the one political-economic issue that just might have saved the Democratic party in 1994.

The 1994 elections were not, in the direct sense, a referendum on monetary policy. But the President's policy on interest rates actually captured quite well his larger problem with the public. Suppose the President had defied the interests, the markets, and the press, and had picked a fight with Alan Greenspan and the Republican Federal Reserve Board from February 4 onward. Suppose he had allied himself with the angry middle classes on this issue. Would he not then have both passed a test of "character" and, at the same time, given himself an issue of real importance to the "forgotten middle class?"

The Economy in Mid-1995

As a regular commentator on monetary policy, I have been extremely reluctant to forecast the effects on the economy as a whole of higher interest rates. In 1994, indeed, economic growth was higher than predicted, despite higher interest rates, and those who emphasized recession risks in that period did so prematurely. But there is evidence now that the situation is changing.

The economic situation as of about the middle of 1995 is as follows.

- Growth in the first quarter of 1995 began to fall below the predicted range of 3-4%, unemployment began to rise, and signs of a general growth slowdown (a "growth recession," as it was once called) are now widespread. The slowdown is being led by housing, so the causal role of higher interest rates is unmistakable. So far, the recessionary forces remain weak. But those who confidently predicted a "soft landing" are reexamining their metaphors.

- Inflation remains indistinguishable for any practical or social purpose from zero, especially if one accepts Greenspan's recent claim that our estimates of increases in the consumer price index are too high. But there is no evidence that rising interest rates deserve any credit for the nonacceleration of inflation. Inflation is low because of pressure on wages from trade, from high unemployment, and from immigrant labor. Inflation will probably fall further as tariffs are lowered under GATT. Inflation is structurally low, will remain so, and would have remained low had interest rates been kept at 1993 levels.

- In other words, the best evidence is that rising interest rates have now started to hurt growth and employment without being able to claim credit for any measurable anti-inflation benefit. There is thus no evidence that the authors of the policy of rising rates in 1994—who promised "stable, noninflationary growth"—were right, and every evidence that the worst fears of the critics were correct.

How these conditions will play out remains uncertain, not least because the direction of monetary policy as of this writing remains unclear. Stable, high interest rates through the first half of the year and resulting signs of slowdown caused nervousness even at the Federal Reserve, which cut rates by one-quarter point in July. Sharply lower interest rates might actually help ward off decelerationist forces—if the Federal Reserve does not delay too long.

What would be a proper strategy for the short term? Before, we held that fiscal responsibility should be maintained: no tax cuts, no big spending programs. Low interest rates were promised in return. That strategy is now crushed in the ice.

The second-best strategy is a matter of choosing a direction in which to haul our lifeboats. Some longer-range suggestions for monetary policy proper are made below. But the immediate issue is: where should we stand on the one question of deficits and tax cuts?

How about: no more deficit reduction without lower interest rates first. Members of Congress should drop their absurd fixation with the books of the government and suspend their fetishism of the number zero as it regards the budget. New social programs, public investment, and even a modest tax cut (targeted to the middle class) should properly be fair game all around. It is, after all, the books of the public, not those of the government, that matter for economic welfare. And if the Federal Reserve cannot keep a bargain, why should members of Congress?

If, as a result of congressional action to help the middle class, the deficit widens and interest rates are driven up—well, let the issue be joined. The Federal Reserve has already added back over $200 billion to the five-year deficit in higher interest costs alone. This is where the finger of responsibility needs to be pointed. Congressional allies may yet be found to champion a firm directive against rising interest rates. (Let conservatives vote against it!) A future administration can re-learn the lesson, if need be, that deficit reduction doesn't work without the low and stable interest rates that were promised last time around.

For a brief period it seemed the Clinton Administration had partly learned this lesson. The President's original FY 1996 budget, which held the deficit at $190 billion and dumped responsibility for further cuts onto the Congress, was a correct plan on economic grounds. Too bad the Administration later caved in to the mindless drumbeat for budget balance. The Administration's refusal to defend the dollar at the G-7 meetings in Halifax in April 1995 dumped that problem into the hands of the Europeans and Japanese, who could solve it by lowering their own interest rates if they really wanted to (it cannot be solved any other way). And the balance of power may be shifting, just a bit, at the Federal Reserve, where the endgame of Alan Greenspan's tenure may be playing out. If the Administration can play that game correctly—so that interest rates fall and then hold steady through the elections—then it could conceivably both save the economy and itself and remake the case for stable and low interest rates in its second term.

Monetary Policy and the Banking System

Unfortunately for us all, this macroeconomic dimension to monetary policy is far from being the whole of the story. In 1994 the Federal Reserve tightened money and yet growth accelerated. Growth accelerated, and yet the largest group of working Americans—middle class, continuously employed homeowners—were materially worse off and much angrier than they had been before. The very wealthy, who earn interest on liquid assets, did just fine. And the banking sector picked up ground that it had been losing to the stock and bond mutual funds.

This structural lesson for monetary politics can scarcely be put in stronger terms.

Why do rising interest rates matter? Because they depress the wealth and squeeze the disposable incomes of middle-class Americans, to the benefit of financial creditors like the very wealthy and the commercial banks. Adjustable-rate mortgages and auto loan rates are up and stock and bond mutual funds are down, to the benefit of bank market share and bank profits. The issue is distributive, it is a matter of fairness and equity, and it is political to its core.

Even in the absence of an economic slowdown or recession, these issues of distribution, fairness, and equity should be the main basis for a renewed campaign against the direction of monetary policy. The question is: can America tolerate a Federal Reserve policy that sacrifices the living standards of working Americans to the benefit of the rich and the profits of the banks, and that does so for no higher purpose?

The monetary system of the United States has always relied on the commercial banking industry to create liquidity for enterprise, and it has effectively vested in that industry the sovereign right to "coin money"—through the creation of new bank deposits—reserving for itself only the authority to "regulate the value thereof."

This creation of new money is a major basis of bank profitability. Banks make money from the difference between what they receive in interest on loans and what they pay out in interest on deposits. So long as this difference is greater than the cost of opening and maintaining each loan and deposit, they make more money when loans and deposits are expanding than when they are stagnant or contracting. The modern form of seignorage is the commercial bank profit on a newly created deposit and loan, made possible by an increase in central bank reserves.

But this system has in large measure broken down. The private commercial banking sector is no longer fulfilling its function of expanding loans to the private sector. It has not done so for over a decade. Indeed, private bank loans for industrial and commercial purposes have been falling throughout the past three years of economic growth, reflecting a declining willingness by banks to take ordinary commercial risks. And, as a result, the money supply has been stagnant or even declining—the monetary counterpart of low income and wage growth for the middle class.

What happened is a complicated story with a simple theme. Perhaps as long as 20 years ago, bank profit expectations came to be driven not by the average of what the economy could deliver over the medium or long term but by some examples of selectively high performance within the banking industry itself. Flying high became the standard against which the average was to be judged. But as the average expected returns rose to unrealistic levels, there followed an increasingly wild pursuit of speculative investments—herd movements into and out of assets, from real estate investment trusts in the 1970s to Third World debt to real estate development again in the 1980s. The result by the late 1980s was an exhausted financial sector, with several large institutions that might have been bankrupt had they been forced to mark their asset values to market price.

To the rescue rode Alan Greenspan, the Federal Reserve, and the unwitting American middle class. The instrument of the rescue was a driving down of short-term interest rates to which banks tied their deposit rates, while at the same time loan rates remained exceptionally high. Thus, large commercial banks were treated to a period of high profitability based on doing nothing at all. With loans at 7% and deposits at 2%, an institution with 3% costs could make good money even while deposits and loans to the private industrial and commercial sectors declined.

How was the spread maintained? This too is a complicated story, but one essential element was this: the Federal Reserve repeatedly reinforced private market beliefs that the low level of short-term interest rates was only temporary. Sooner or later, they told us, short rates would have to rise. Since long markets reflect the balance of current and expected future short-term interest rates, arbitrage between short and long markets helped assure that long rates stayed high.

Thus, the Clinton program of cutting deficits in order to reduce long-term interest rates ran at clear cross-purposes to the maintenance of the spread and the hidden politics of the banking system. And indeed, by the end of 1993, there was tension in the bond market, based on speculation that long rates would have to fall if short rates continued low for much longer. Many investors, notably exemplified by Orange County, California, made heavy commitments based on an expected fall in long rates. Yet it was precisely to prevent a fall in long rates—and not to encourage one as many said at the time—that the Federal Reserve acted to raise short-term rates in February 1994.

There was a second problem with the Federal Reserve's high-spread rescue strategy: disintermediation, that is, the withdrawal of funds from bank accounts so that they can be invested at higher rates elsewhere. Maintaining very low short-term interest rates radically reduced the attractiveness of holding bank deposits relative to direct investment in stocks and bonds. And mutual funds were creating a means whereby the vast American middle class could move out of bank savings accounts or certificates of deposit and into long-term assets at reasonably low costs.

But the threat of disintermediation could be dealt with—by destabilizing the markets for stocks and bonds. In an amazing statement to the Senate in May 1994, Greenspan testified that this was, in effect, part of Federal Reserve thinking. The middle-class investor, he said, had become accustomed to an "unsustainable combination" of high returns and low volatility and had failed to appreciate the "inherent risks" of holding long-term assets. He did not quite acknowledge, though it is perfectly apparent, that the main risk in question was the instability of monetary policy itself. But the implication was clear: while savings is the epitome of virtue, it should not be done by ordinary mortals at rates of return close to those enjoyed by the rich.

It is impossible to justify the monetary policy of 1994 on economic or political grounds. But it makes fair sense to understand the Federal Reserve's motivations as an exercise in corporate welfare for the benefit of beleaguered private commercial banks, or as an Endangered Species Act for the dinosaurs of the financial sector. When long-term rates went up, banks along with other bondholders took paper losses on their bonds. But they gained much more than they lost, by the forceful reminder to everyone else that there's no deposit like cash, and no capital like that insured by the Federal Deposit Insurance Corporation.

The question for us, the small furry mammals, is: what do we propose to do about it?

The Return of Monetary Politics

The creation of the Federal Reserve System in 1913 removed monetary policy from American politics. In the absence of battles over money, fiscal Keynesianism waxed and waned. But now, with fiscal Keynesianism dead and buried, progressive forces have no alternative but to return to the alignments and issues of the pre-Federal Reserve era.

Our ultimate goal is to redesign an economic system where working Americans have reasonable incomes in relation to their needs and reasonable access to credit—at reasonable and stable interest rates. If a moribund banking sector and a bank-captive Federal Reserve cannot provide this, then the political process must be called back into action.

In the last Democratic Congress before the Republican takeover, the idea of a congressional mandate on monetary policy foundered on the opposition of leading Democrats and the pro-Fed position of the Administration. These constraints are now, paradoxically, greatly relaxed. The Democrats now need a working-class issue. This is it.

The first step toward our goal, of course, is to get interest rates back down. Congress can do this, under the Constitution: through a mandatory resolution, ordering further cuts in rates along the lines begun in July. If Congress cannot be moved to take this step now, the concept can still form the basis of a public campaign—and there will be more opportunities later. But as we have seen, a larger agenda of financial sector and regulatory reform will still remain before us.

The Failed Program of Reforming the Structure of the Federal Reserve

Over the longer run, our program sought to reform the structure of the Federal Reserve System. It can be said without fear of contradiction that the Federal Reserve is the most ridiculous of all government agencies, the platypus of institutions, a bureaucracy designed by a committee, governed by an odd hybrid of public governors and private presidents, the latter spread out along the lines of economic and political power (four on the East Coast, three in the Upper Midwest, two in Missouri, and one each in the South, Southwest, and West) prevailing in 1913 at the climax of the Railroad Age.

The Federal Open Market Committee, in particular, is flagrantly unconstitutional in that it allows voting participation by regional Federal Reserve Bank presidents who are formally beholden to their private bank directors and not "appointed by the President with the advice and consent of the Senate," as the Constitution requires. The entire system is also an insular white male club, equally unencumbered by the budget process and the Freedom of Information Act, responsive to no constituency below the top 1% of the income distribution.

Faced with this, our proposals were modest. We sought to abolish the Open Market Committee and proposed instead either that the Federal Reserve Bank presidents form a nonvoting Open Market Advisory Committee (the Hamilton-Sarbanes proposal), or that the bank presidents be made presidential appointees (the Gonzalez proposal). We sought to place the system under the budget, to broaden its base of appointees, and to expose its internal debates to external review.

These were sensible efforts in an inside strategy of watching and waiting, in games of legislative position-taking and subtle pressure. But like the too-square *Endurance* trapped in the ice, our ship had a design flaw. There was no clear, demonstrable link between a reform strategy addressed to, say, the constitutionality of the Open Market Committee and the desired policy of stable interest rates. By May 1994, President Clinton's own appointees, Alan Blinder and Janet Yellen, were joining unanimous votes to raise rates and signing on to statements of justification for them. What difference would rearranging the chairs or the votes have made?

As a result, while in 1994 House Banking Committee staff made progress, through the splendid efforts of Dr. Robert Auerbach, in building a case for more rapid and complete disclosure of the minutes and transcripts of Open Market Committee hearings, and while at the end of the Senate session Senator Paul Simon circulated a resolution calling for no further increases in interest rates, and while Senators Jim Sasser and Paul Sarbanes subjected Chairman Greenspan to some of the most elegant grilling in years, none of this really counted for much in the end. In contrast to the summer of 1982, when congressional restiveness truly did disturb the institutional slumber on Constitution Avenue, what happened in 1994 evidently did not. Indeed, all agreed that the moment for a real test would come later, in the 104th Congress, when reformer Sarbanes in the Senate and reformer Henry Gonzalez in the House would both chair their respective banking committees. But the 104th turned out to be less promising than previously expected.

A New Structural Program: Sunset the Federal Reserve

What then to do with the Federal Reserve and indeed with the banking system? One cannot will Congress into action on this issue. And, as previous episodes of credit control have shown, notably in 1980, the Federal Reserve cannot be forced to administer a policy that runs counter to the heart of its political and bureaucratic culture.

An answer to this dilemma may lie in the concept of sunset review.

Many states have a process in which the enabling statutes for government agencies undergo periodic review, with open public input, and must be reenacted if the agency is to survive. This process provides a powerful lever for agency modernization and for consolidation and elimination of redundant functions. Also, it can operate with some independence from the gridlock of interests that settles in on a legislative committee structure.

Was there ever an agency more in need of this process than the Federal Reserve and its associated bank regulatory systems?

A New Political Strategy: Tell the People

In sum, we should favor:

- An end to rising interest rates, and indeed lower interest rates, enforced if necessary by intervention of the Congress. And a suspension of budget disciplines so long as the reward of lower interest rates is not forthcoming.
- A full sunset review of the Federal Reserve and the banking regulatory system, conducted in full independence of the agency and its allies by a board of outsiders not dominated by private commercial banks, through an open process with full public input.

A final point concerns the focus of our efforts. We have, for the most part, been playing an insider's game focused on a largely indifferent press and a tiny group of friends and allies in prominent positions. The weakness of this strategy is now plain. And so is the potential behind the alternative, long practiced by the Republican right, of building links to the public through a myriad of devices from C-SPAN to talk radio.

Something quite remarkable happened on November 15, 1994, just a week following the election. A small demonstration, organized mainly by the AFL-CIO, was held outside the Federal Reserve. It was the first public demonstration in front of that building in perhaps 12 years. A few hundred people attended. And, surprise of surprises, it got more attention from the press and public than all of the inside arguments of the past decade put together. This should tell us something about tactics.

A public campaign of direct pressure for lower interest rates might get somewhere. Such a campaign could have many angles: public demonstrations outside Federal Reserve banks in Washington and in the district bank cities, teach-ins at universities, union campaigns, and other grass-roots political measures.

A few years ago, William Greider put the essential question in the form of a title, "Who Will Tell the People?" Plainly, we should. Ship and stores are lost; so now it's time to carry this battle home.

Note

1. From Roland Huntford, *Shackleton,* New York: Atheneum, 1986.

CHAPTER 12

FINANCIAL MARKETS
Restructuring and the U.S. Regulatory Framework

by Jane D'Arista & Tom Schlesinger

DURING THE PAST TWO DECADES, A SERIES OF PROFOUND CHANGES HAS transformed financial markets. These include the decline of traditional intermediary institutions, such as banks, as lenders and repositories of savings; a concomitant growth of institutional savings and nonbank lenders; the erosion of barriers that previously divided the financial sector into distinct institutional segments; and an explosive increase in capital-market transactions based upon the packaging, unpackaging, or hedging of financial instruments.

As a result of these structural shifts, current laws and regulations no longer correspond to the reality of the financial marketplace. Furthermore, the growing overlap of different financial activities and products—a process referred to as institutional homogenization—has exacerbated regulatory gaps and inequalities. As a result, banks, insurers, securities firms, finance companies, and other financial firms that now offer similar or identical loan and investment products operate under starkly different regulatory regimes. This pattern has led to the development of transactions and products driven by regulatory arbitrage—efforts to exploit or compensate for competitive and cost advantages and disadvantages resulting from differences in regulation.

The public policy implications of these developments cannot be ignored. The real-world consequences of regulatory arbitrage undermine the financial system's essential role as a catalyst in promoting economic activity. Despite many philosophical and strategic differences, all market countries have made the preservation of that role the paramount objec-

Jane D'Arista is lecturer of law at the Boston University School of Law. Tom Schlesinger is director of the Southern Finance Project.

tive of their regulatory systems. For, unless the underlying economy prospers, returns to investors fall and financial intermediaries fail.

This chapter provides a brief overview of financial restructuring. It focuses on the key institutional changes that have eroded the effectiveness of the existing regulatory framework, producing a financial system that is more fragile and crisis-prone as well as less responsive to monetary policy and the needs of the real economy. The chapter also offers reform proposals that stress the need to view the U.S. financial system as a whole, to focus on the products offered rather than the types of institution (bank, mutual fund, insurance company) that are offering them, and to ensure a more even application of regulatory costs and protections across the system.

The Changing Face of Financial Intermediation

The factors reshaping U.S. financial markets have included inflation and disinflation as well as wide swings in interest rates and exchange rates. They also include improvements in information and communications technologies that enable large amounts of capital to flow across national boundaries and that integrate financial markets on a global scale. The instability produced by more volatile, globally integrated financial markets has forced financial institutions to restructure their operating procedures and products. While much has been written about these factors themselves, the structural changes to which they have contributed are only now beginning to receive attention.

What has drawn the attention of regulators, economists, and other financial observers to the usually ignored subject of financial structure is the changing role of banks. As a result of significant changes in the composition of household financial assets and business borrowing patterns, depository institutions have declined in importance as lenders and repositories of savings at the same time that institutional investors, such as pension funds, and nonbank lenders have expanded dramatically. Between 1978 and 1993, the deposit-taking industry's share of U.S. financial-sector assets fell from 57% to 34%. During the same period, the portion of assets held by mutual funds and pension funds more than doubled, rising from 20% to 42% (see **Table 1**).

TABLE 1
Assets Held by Leading Financial Sectors*

Sector	1978 (Billion Dollars)	1978 (Percent Shares)	1993 (Billion Dollars)	1993 (Percent Shares)	Percentage Change, 1993-90
Commercial Banking[1]	$1,222.0	35.7%	$3,868.9	25.1%	-10.6
Thrifts & Other Savings Institutions[2]	731.0	21.3	1,313.9	8.5	-12.8
Insurance Companies (Excl. Pension Reserves)	396.5	11.6	1,385.2	9.0	+2.6
Insured Pension Reserves[3]	121.6	3.6	1,043.5	6.8	+3.2
Private Pension Funds	351.3	10.3	2,336.1	15.2	+4.9
State & Local Government Retirement Funds	152.0	4.4	1,065.2	6.9	+2.5
Mutual Funds[4]	64.8	1.9	2,082.3	13.5	+11.6
Finance Companies	159.6	4.7	658.2	4.3	-0.4
Security Brokers & Dealers	32.5	1.0	465.6	3.0	+2.0
Bank Personal Trusts	176.7	5.2	658.6	4.3	-0.9
Other	19.3	0.6	509.2	3.3	+2.7
Totals	3,427.3	100.0	15,386.7	100.0	

* Includes only assets held by financial institutions. Financial assets held by households, government units, and others are excluded. Totals may not add to 100% due to rounding.

1 U.S.-chartered banks, foreign banking offices in the United States, bank holding companies and banks in U.S. territories and possessions.
2 S&Ls, mutual savings banks, federal savings banks, and credit unions.
3 Pension reserves of life insurance companies.
4 Mutual funds, closed-end funds, and money mutual funds.

Source: Federal Reserve System, *Flow of Funds Accounts*, various editions.

As household savings migrated into pension funds and mutual funds (see **Table 2**), depository institutions saw their role in credit markets diminish. Between 1983 and 1993, depository institutions' holdings of mortgages, consumer credit, corporate bonds, state and local government securities, and total domestic credit market debt all dropped relative to holdings by nonbanks. Even short-term business credit—once the banking industry's mainstay product—is increasingly supplied by nonbank sources. Between 1950 and 1993, bank loans declined from 91% to 55% of total short-term credit market debt owed by nonfinancial corporate business in the United States. In the decade leading up to year end 1993, the deposit-taking industry's share of total credit market debt dropped

TABLE 2
Net Flows of Household Financial Assets*
(Billions of Dollars)

Type of Asset	1983	1989	1993
Deposits	$197.2	$64.8	$-14.2
Life Insurance Reserves	8.0	28.8	55.6
Pension Fund Reserves	168.2	309.7	241.9
Mutual Fund Shares	-3.1	122.1	274.8
Credit Market Instruments	93.3	78.6	-84.6
Open-Market Paper	21.7	-0.6	-24.4
Corporate Equities	-22.5	-131.4	-43.5
Equity in Noncorporate Business	-90.7	-31.1	-24.9
Investments in Bank Personal Trusts	1.4	23.1	10.9
Net Acquisition of Financial Assets	370.0	491.6	464.6
Net Flows to Pension & Mutual Funds as Pct. Net Acquisition of Assets	44.6%	87.8%	111.2%
Net Flows to Depository Institutions and Insurers as Percent of Net Acquisition of Assets	55.5%	19.0%	8.9%

* Includes financial assets held by nonprofit organizations.

Note: Security credit and miscellaneous assets not listed in the table. However, net flows of security credit and miscellaneous assets are included in the row displaying "Net Acquisition of Financial Assets."

Source: Federal Reserve System, *Flow of Funds Accounts*, Fourth Quarter 1993.

from 41% to 27%, while the share held by private nonbank financial institutions rose from 36% to 51%.[1]

The banking industry's hold on short-term business credit has been usurped in large measure by the growth of the unregulated commercial paper market. Commercial paper, a type of noncollateralized corporate IOU, serves as an important source of unintermediated short-term credit for large nonfinancial businesses with good credit ratings. It also constitutes the principal means of funding for finance companies, enabling those firms to seize their own growing share of the market for business credit.

In 1993, finance companies issued more than three-fifths of all outstanding commercial paper. Most of that paper was purchased by money market mutual funds. Thus, the commercial paper market links two halves of a parallel banking system, with money funds functioning as the funding side and finance companies as the lending side. This parallel system has become an increasingly important force in the business loan market. Although their assets equalled barely one-quarter of commercial bank assets, finance companies claimed more than two-thirds of the business loans held by banks at the end of 1993. The success of the parallel system can be traced to the cost advantages that finance companies enjoy from their unregulated status and to the indirect promise of Federal Reserve liquidity supplied through an extensive system of commercial bank guarantees.

The restructuring of loan origination markets has developed in tandem with lenders' growing tendency to pool loans and sell participations in the loans as securities. This process of securitization has been spurred by the emergence of a government-sponsored secondary mortgage market and institutional appetites for large-scale, tradable investments. In response to these developments, lenders have securitized a growing volume and variety of assets. Between 1980 and 1993, the value of mortgage-backed securities outstanding rose from $110.8 billion to $1.5 trillion. During that time, the growth in volume of these securities outpaced the growth in total mortgage debt by almost six to one.[2] Securitization rates also rose dramatically for consumer credit, short-term commercial debt, and even commercial real estate. Indeed, between 1983 and 1993, the total volume of assets held by all issuers of asset-backed securities multiplied more than 100 times over.[3]

The institutionalization of the savings side of the financial system and the growth of securitization and indexing on its investment side helped "marketize" finance, boost trading activity, and elevate the role of asset management. As a consequence, the operating outlook of traditional intermediaries changed along with their market shares. In recent years, commercial banks have shifted considerable portions of their business to fee-generating, off-balance-sheet activities ranging from the pedestrian to the exotic (see **Table 3**). The industry also has adjusted to financial change by undergoing significant consolidation (see **Table 4**). By transforming themselves, banks have contributed to institutional homogenization in the financial system—they have become more like everyone else at the same time that everyone else was becoming more like them. As depository institutions, insurers, securities firms, and other financial companies compete to sell similar products and services to the same customers, they are blurring or eliminating the bright lines that previously segmented the financial system into distinct sectors performing specialized tasks. Multifunctional financial conglomerates, many of which are controlled by commercial or industrial corporations, have captured growing shares in a variety of increasingly interconnected financial markets. Yet, despite these integrative forces, statutory segmentation has endured. The continuation of sector-by-sector regulation despite increasing institutional homogenization has created regulatory gaps and inequalities. The result has been the growth of regulatory arbitrage as a primary form of competition in financial markets.

This competition has contributed to growing levels of financial instability and the declining effectiveness of traditional policy tools. The most important evidence of this decline can be found in the increasing difficulty the Federal Reserve System has in transmitting monetary policy initiatives to the economy. Federal Reserve Chairman Alan Greenspan has acknowledged that, "as banks and other intermediaries have become less special, many of the targets and indicators traditionally used by policymakers have become less useful."[4] In fact, the problem runs deeper.

Open market operations serve as the primary tool of monetary policy. By changing the volume of bank reserves, open market operations directly affect the price of bank credit and the volume of bank lending. Through this channel, monetary policy creates and extinguishes money and influences the expansion and contraction of credit. However, open market operations also include a second channel that has grown increas-

TABLE 3
Growth Rates of Banking Assets and "Nonbank" Activities for Banks and BHCS, 1983-93
(Billions of Dollars)

	1983	1989	1993	Growth Rate 1983-93
Assets of FDIC-Insured Commercial Banks and Trust Companies	$2,342.0	$3,299.4	$3,705.9	58.2%
"Nonbank" Activities				
Assets of Bank Holding Companies' Nonbank Subsidiaries (1986-1993)	n.a.	194.5	249.4	70.1%
As a % of Commercial Banking Assets	n.a.	5.9%	6.7%	
Bank Commitments to Purchase Foreign Currency & U.S. Dollar Exchange (1984-1993)	n.a.	2,250.6	3,689.4	531.9%
As a % of Commercial Banking Assets	n.a.	68.2%	99.6%	
Assets Held in Bank Trading Accounts	17.1	42.8	122.4	615.8%
As a % of Commercial Banking Assets	0.7%	1.3%	3.3%	
Bank-Managed Mutual Fund Assets	15.0	60.0	219.0	1,360.0%
As a % of Commercial Banking Assets	0.6%	1.8%	5.9%	
Assets of Bank Trust Depts. & Trust Companies	741.2	6,458.9	9,928.7	1,239.5%
As % of Commercial Banking Assets	31.7%	195.8%	267.9%	

Sources: FDIC *Statistics on Banking* (1983-93 annual eds.); Federal Reserve System *Flow of Funds Accounts* (1993 fourth quarter); FFIEC Trust *Assets of Financial Institutions* (1983-93 annual eds.); Lipper Analytical Services.

TABLE 4
Selected Commercial Banking Consolidation Data
($ Million)

	Banks by Peer Group[1]						10-Bank Concentration Ratio U.S.[3]		No. of States With 3-Bank Concentration Ratio[4]					
	Less Than $50M		Less Than $100M[2]		More Than $1B				More Than 50%[5]		More Than 67%		Less Than 34%	
Year	Number	Assets	Number	Assets	Number	Assets	Assets	Deps.	Assets	Deps.	Assets	Deps.	Assets	Deps.
1993	5,012	$137,587	7,788	$334,965	382	$2,694,102	26.9%	25.0%	14	13	12	10	7	8
% of All U.S. Banks	45.7%	3.7%	71.1%	9.0%	3.5%	72.7%								
1989	6,983	174,231	9,728	365,601	378	2,308,211	20.3%	18.0%	12	11	9	7	8	10
% of All U.S. Banks	54.9%	5.3%	76.5%	11.1%	3.0%	70.0%								
1983	9,893	216,965	12,521	398,273	257	1,467,190	20.9%	17.2%	11	9	7	7	15	18
% of All U.S. Banks	66.8%	9.2%	84.6%	17.0%	1.7%	62.5%								

1 Includes District of Columbia and U.S. territories and possessions.
2 Includes banks with less than $50 million in assets.
3 Percentage of total assets and deposits held by the 10 largest banking organizations. Data for 50 states and D.C.
4 Percentage of total assets and deposits held by the three largest banking organizations. Data for 50 states and D.C.
5 Includes only states with three-bank concentration ratios between 50% and 67%.

Sources: *FDIC Statistics on Banking*: 1981-93 Editions; *Federal Reserve System Annual Statistical Digest,* 1990-93 editions and 1980-89 compilation.

ingly dominant with the decline in banks' lending functions and the expansion of nonbank financial firms.

The principal assets the Fed buys and sells in open market transactions are treasury bills. By directly affecting the price and volume of T-bills, the central bank induces changes in the composition of portfolios in the nonbank financial sector. Relatively small changes in the price of T-bills can reshape these sectors' allocation of credit. However, to alter borrowers' demand for credit, the Fed must produce larger shifts in the price (or interest rate) of T-bills. This imperative slows the transmission of monetary policy. Because it affects credit expansion and contraction in a less immediate fashion, the sale and purchase of T-bills has proved a weaker tool than changes in bank reserves. As the impact of open market operations on total credit has diminished, the effectiveness of monetary policy has eroded. Because the Fed must hammer asset markets with larger and larger changes in interest rates to achieve its policy goals, financial instability has increased.

A decline in banks' lending functions may also inhibit the Federal Reserve's ability to stabilize markets, provide liquidity in times of crisis, and act as lender-of-last-resort to financial institutions and markets outside the banking sector. The rapid growth of mutual funds and pension funds evokes special concern. Although the Federal Reserve has emergency powers to make direct loans to nonbanks, this channel is untested as a tool of crisis management and may be circumscribed by the inability of pension funds and many mutual funds to borrow, given the nature of their structure and regulation. Additionally, banks' reduced role in lending may compromise their capacity to act as a conduit for central bank assistance during a major crisis outside the banking system that, left unattended, could spread throughout the financial markets.

Financial restructuring has produced another troubling paradox as well. Despite a proliferation of financial service providers, the nation's financial markets are not meeting the needs of significant numbers of households, enterprises, and communities. Serious investment problems afflict the corporate sector. It is in the entrepreneurial economy, however, where changes in the financial system play out most damagingly.

New, young, and small enterprises have experienced persistent problems in gaining access to capital and credit. So, too, have households in economically distressed communities. Because they are nonstandard, most borrowing needs of these households and businesses can be answered only by a lending process that involves patience and judgment and results in illiquid loan agreements that must be held to maturity. Yet the mutual funds and pension funds that constitute the fastest-growing outlets for household savings have no direct lending capacity and generally bypass large areas of the entrepreneurial economy. Nonbank lenders who use savings aggregated by those funds rarely originate nonstandard credits, negotiate flexible terms, or structure unique deals. (In another chapter, Gary Dymski and John Veitch address the growing inability of inner-city residents to find and qualify for mortgage financing.)

Thus, portfolio lending to many businesses and households remains a market primarily served by banks. However, as commercial banking diminishes relative to other segments of the financial industry, consolidation is rapidly thinning the ranks of small institutions that have been the most active and patient small business lenders. At the same time, larger banks have resorted to more nonbanking activities and jettisoned offices that once served as the focal point for lending in hard-pressed communities. As a result, the Community Reinvestment Act—a federal law that requires regulated depository institutions to serve all areas of their defined markets—covers a numerically shrinking industry that is cutting back traditional lending and deposit-taking activities. Business and household borrowers who depend on community-based lending increasingly find themselves stranded in an ocean of global finance.

The Shift Away From Open, Public Markets

While U.S. financial markets were reshaped in the 1980s by a shift from banks to capital markets for business financing, by the rise of securitization, and by a substantial increase in trading activity, the end of the decade witnessed a new phenomenon. Market participants dramatically increased their use of nontradable instruments that are not counted as assets or liabilities on their balance sheets by the institutions that originate and hold them.

Banks have traditionally offered financial guaranties such as letters of credit. But this kind of contingency financing expanded in the 1970s and 1980s as banks increased their commitments to backstop the commercial paper issued by major corporations (including finance companies). Moreover, the rapid growth in foreign exchange markets that began in the mid-1960s had already greatly enlarged banks' exposure to off-balance-sheet assets and liabilities. In the 1980s, large banks (and some U.S. broker-dealers and insurance companies) augmented the supply of off-balance sheet instruments by introducing interest rate and currency swaps, currency options, forward rate agreements, and equity swaps. These and other customized financial derivatives—instruments that derive their value from the performance of an underlying asset, rate, or index—have become the fastest-growing segment of the national and international financial system.

Policy makers' concern about the growth of derivatives transactions is reflected in numerous studies and reports that analyze the risks involved in their use. Since the largest banks are the principal dealers in this market, concern has focused on the extent of their exposure[5] and the need for sound management practices and internal controls.[6] The broader issue, however, is whether derivatives increase the potential for systemic risk.

The concentration of market-making activities in a very small number of institutions—10 large banks, four securities firms, and two insurance companies in the United States alone[7]—could heighten the risk of a domino effect should one of the major dealers default on its obligations. Moreover, new forms and concentrations of risk are created as derivative positions cross and recross markets and national borders, interacting with more than one underlying market—equity, fixed-income, foreign exchange, and commodities—in more than one country (U.S. House Banking Committee Minority Staff 1993). Additionally, the growth in derivatives transactions compounds the difficulties faced by central banks in implementing monetary policy.

The derivatives boom is only the most recent example of an extraordinary expansion of unstructured markets over the last two decades. Some of these markets involve tradable instruments like commercial paper, private placements, and asset-backed securities. Others transform instruments that are traded on commodity exchanges (futures and options on foreign currencies and financial instruments) into nontradable assets or liabilities held in off-balance-sheet portfolios.

The over-the-counter (OTC) foreign exchange market is the most significant example of an unstructured, nonpublic market. Banks and other large financial institutions conduct this market over the telephone rather than on the floors of organized exchanges. The OTC foreign exchange market is probably the largest single market in the world (and the most globally integrated), with an estimated daily turnover of $880 billion in 1992.[8] But unlike other unstructured markets, it provides no ongoing information about volume, price, the size of individual contracts, or the identity of buyers and sellers. Indeed, what little information is available comes from periodic surveys by the major central banks—a one-time snapshot on a particular date, usually at three-year intervals.

This OTC foreign exchange market is only one component of the burgeoning trade in OTC derivatives. It might appear that the growth in derivatives transactions by U.S. banks reflects an adaptive response to events in the 1980s: the loss of business borrowers to the securities markets and unregulated lenders, competition from foreign banks, and the introduction of capital adequacy standards that enhanced the attractiveness of off-balance-sheet activities. But the rise in OTC derivatives activity actually began with the then-remarkable growth of foreign exchange transactions in the 1970s. It reflects the imposition of a dominant financial sector's culture on other market sectors. In the cases of foreign exchange and derivatives transactions, banks imposed their culture on trading markets, making the markets less liquid than they would have been had they developed as structured, public securities markets.

Disclosure has remained the keystone of market regulation in the United States because it ensures that participants have the facts needed to make informed decisions. But transactions in opaque, nonpublic, over-the-counter markets now dwarf the volume of transactions in structured markets. In addition to jeopardizing public confidence in the market system, this development is loaded with ironies. For the growth of unstructured markets—like the emergence of a parallel banking system—rests upon the explicit existence of public sector safety nets and the implicit promise of far-ranging, ad hoc public sector crisis interventions.

Proposals for Reform

The implications of a growing derivatives market has convinced many observers that derivatives transactions should be regulated on a functional basis, regardless of which category of institution performs the activity.[9] The same prescription fits many other activities and products offered by different segments of the broader financial services industry. In short, the United States needs a regulatory framework that can respond effectively to changes in financial structure, minimize regulatory inequalities, and enhance the financial system's stability and responsiveness.

To achieve this objective, we propose that all U.S. financial institutions be licensed and be required to comply with the same major regulations with respect to soundness, diversification, and other important goals of financial regulation.[10] To reduce the potential for unregulated, marginal participants to precipitate systemic crises, uniform licensing requirements must be applied to any entity that:

- directly accepts funds from the public for investment;
- makes loans to the public or buys loans or securities using funds other than its own equity capital and retained earnings; or
- sells loans or third-party securities to financial institutions or investors.

Ensuring that all licensed entities are subject to the same or equivalent regulatory standards will require the following major elements:

- uniform application of comparable reserve, capital, and liquidity requirements; comparable risk diversification standards and risk weighting techniques; and limits on concentration and prohibitions against conflicts of interest and self-dealing;
- greater system-wide transparency through the regular public disclosure of Uniform Performance Reports;
- greater harmonization of the methods and costs of supervision and examination on a domestic and international basis;
- enhanced self-regulation and consolidation of duplicative regulatory functions;
- licensing of financial intermediaries on a renewable basis;
- system-wide compliance with community reinvestment standards and fair lending laws; and
- comprehensive insurance coverage for individuals' savings up to a cer-

tain amount and for transaction balances to replace the current coverage of financial institutions.

The two elements in this proposal dealing with financial guaranties and community reinvestment follow the key concepts involved in extending consistent prudential supervision throughout the financial system as a whole. Several major components of the system already participate in financial guaranty funds: banks and thrifts have deposit insurance funds; insurers have state guaranty associations; securities firms have the Securities Investor Protection Corporation; and defined-benefit pension plans have the Pension Benefit Guaranty Corporation. But these various public guaranty programs provide different (and, in some cases, uncertain) degrees of protection to customers and extend only partial or indirect coverage to some sectors such as mutual funds.

Our answer to the need for a more even and equitable distribution of public guaranties is to stop insuring institutions altogether. Instead, we should provide guaranties directly to individual savers on the basis of their Social Security numbers rather than types of accounts, and provide 100% coverage for all transaction balances held in the form of non-interest-bearing demand deposits in federally regulated depository institutions.

To systematically apply community reinvestment standards, we recommend the establishment of a National Reinvestment Fund. Financed with investments by all private nonbank financial institutions and administered by the 12 Federal Reserve Banks, the fund would undertake a twofold mission: help capitalize the growth of community development financial institutions (CDFIs), and provide credit enhancements, financial guaranties, and policy coordination for federal loan guaranty programs. Key features of the reinvestment fund system would expand the central bank's leverage, enhance its accountability, and renew the reserve banks' regional development mission.

By supporting the growth of CDFIs, the fund would boost long-term reinvestment in sectors served poorly by conventional capital markets and enable one of the emerging strengths of the existing financial system—CDFIs' success in local intermediation—to remedy one of its emerging weaknesses — the diminution of patient, labor-intensive direct lending. By rationalizing federal credit programs and paring taxpayers' exposure to them, the fund would strengthen a major component of reinvestment policy.[11]

In summary, within the framework we propose, it will be possible to apply uniform regulations to all institutions engaged in a given financial activity regardless of their institutional classification. Such a framework should encourage ongoing evolution, innovation, and experimentation in institutional structures and products. It will also eliminate the regulatory distortions that have made the credit markets less responsive to monetary policy and less capable of promoting sustainable growth.

Notes

1. Board of Governors of the Federal Reserve System 1994.
2. *Mortgage Market Statistical Annual for 1994.*
3. Board of Governors of the Federal Reserve System 1994.
4. Federal Reserve Bank of Kansas City 1993.
5. Bank for International Settlements 1986, 1992.
6. Group of Thirty 1993.
7. Becketti 1993.
8. Bank for International Settlements 1993.
9. U.S. House Banking Committee Minority Staff 1993, and U.S. General Accounting Office 1994.
10. D'Arista and Schlesinger 1993.
11. Southern Finance Project 1995.

References

Bank for International Settlements. 1993. *Annual Report.* Basle: BIS.

Bank for International Settlements. 1986. *Recent Innovations in International Banking.* Basle: BIS.

Bank for International Settlements. 1992. *Recent Developments in International Interbank Relations.* Basle: BIS.

Barth, James R., R. Dan Brumbaugh Jr., and Robert E. Litan. 1992. *The Future of American Banking.* Armonk, N.Y.: M.E. Sharpe.

Becketti, Sean. 1993. "Are Derivatives Too Risky for Banks?" *Economic Review* (Federal Reserve Bank of Kansas City), Third Quarter.

Board of Governors of the Federal Reserve System. 1994. *Flow of Funds Accounts.* Washington, D.C.: U.S. Government Printing Office.

Boyd, John H. and Mark Gertler. 1994. "Are Banks Dead? Or Are the Reports Greatly Exaggerated?" *Quarterly Review* (Federal Reserve Bank of Minneapolis), Summer.

Crockett, Andrew D. 1993. "Monetary Implications of Increased Capital Flows." In *Changing Capital Markets: Implications for Monetary Policy.* Proceedings of a symposium sponsored by the Federal Reserve Bank of Kansas City, Jackson Hole, Wyo., August.

D'Arista, Jane W. 1994. *The Evolution of U.S. Finance, Vol. II: Restructuring Institutions and Markets.* Armonk, N.Y.: M.E. Sharpe.

D'Arista, Jane W. 1991. *No More Bank Bailouts: A Proposal for Deposit Insurance Reform.* Briefing Paper Series. Washington, D.C.: Economic Policy Institute.

D'Arista, Jane W. and Tom Schlesinger. 1993. *The Parallel Banking System.* Washington, D.C.: Economic Policy Institute.

Federal Reserve Bank of Chicago. 1994. Proceedings of a Conference on the Declining Role of Banking, Chicago, May.

Federal Reserve Bank of Kansas City. 1993. *Changing Capital Markets: Implications for Monetary Policy.* Proceedings of a symposium, Jackson Hole, Wyo., August.

Group of Thirty. 1993. *Derivatives Practices and Principles.* Washington, D.C.: Group of Thirty.

Inside Mortgage Finance Publications Inc. 1994. *The Mortgage Market Statistical Annual for 1994.* Washington, D.C.: Inside Mortgage Finance Publications Inc.

International Monetary Fund. 1993. *International Capital Markets, Part II: Systemic Issues in International Finance.* Washington, D.C.: IMF.

Kaufman, George G. and Larry R. Mote. 1994. "Is Banking a Declining Industry? A Historical Perspective." *Economic Perspectives* (Federal Reserve Bank of Chicago), May/June.

Southern Finance Project. 1995. *Reinvestment Reform in an Era of Financial Change.* Philomont, Va.: Southern Finance Project.

U.S. General Accounting Office. 1994. *Financial Derivatives: Actions Needed to Protect the Financial System.* Washington, D.C.: U.S. Government Printing Office.

U.S. House Banking Committee Minority Staff. 1993. *Financial Derivatives.* Washington, D.C.: U.S. Congress.

CHAPTER 13

CREDIT FLOWS TO CITIES
Introducing Cindy Mae

by Gary Dymski & John Veitch

HEALTHY CITIES ARE ESSENTIAL FOR SOUND LONG-TERM U.S. ECONOMIC growth, and revitalizing cities means arresting the economic decline of the inner cities. Elliott Sclar's essay in this volume suggests some broad policy measures for urban revitalization. This essay suggests a financial mechanism for turning around inner-city economies.

Many lower-income communities in American cities suffer from the same problems as less-developed countries: their residents lack the human, physical, and social capital needed to achieve higher incomes and living standards. Financial structures, as they have evolved to date, have amplified growth or decay in urban neighborhoods, thus making lower-income, high-minority communities increasingly isolated from more prosperous ones. Furthermore, deregulation since 1980 has placed competitive pressures on the financial sector, leading financial firms to move toward upscale customers and neighborhoods while leaving lower-income—and less profitable—customers behind.

In this new financial environment, low current levels of income, wealth, or human capital within a neighborhood inevitably reinforce continued poverty in the future. A lack of capital, in turn, restricts the future access to capital necessary for the economic growth that can overcome today's poverty. Race continues to play a role: despite increased public attention to discrimination in credit markets, available evidence suggests that the pernicious effects of past discrimination continue to compromise, both individually and collectively, the economic dynamics of communities of color.

Gary Dymski is associate professor of economics at the University of California at Riverside. John Veitch is associate professor of economics at the University of San Francisco.

This need not be the end of the story. If it is not profitable now to lend to low-income, inner-city areas, there are ways to make it so. If lending to these areas is made profitable enough, new market participants will find ways to raise the necessary financing. Government may not have the resources to meet the credit needs of underserved areas, but it can change the structure of incentives and subsidies underlying activities in these markets. If it does this correctly, it can induce changes in credit supply by private-sector firms.

Financial System Restructuring in the 1990s

The restructuring of the U.S. financial system has largely erased the geographic and product-line restrictions imposed in the past. Whereas the customer base of a financial firm once included all households and businesses within its market area—with the exception of certain minority areas—customer bases today have been carved into at least three distinct market segments: the well-off, the middle class, and low-income groups.

The most desirable segment, obviously, comprises wealthy households that largely occupy the top 20% income areas within cities. These communities are well served by the formal banking sector. Indeed, despite an overall pattern of downsizing and branch closures, financial institutions continue to seek market share among these customers by locating new branches in these areas. Customers there have a wide range of options for conducting their financial transactions, meeting their payments obligations, and investing their wealth. Personal service and personalized products through brokers and account representatives are the norm. The intense competition for these highly profitable customers mandates this type of service.

Next are the middle-income households who tend to live in the middle 40% income areas within cities. They too retain access to a wide range of financial services. They readily maintain bank accounts, accumulate personal savings, acquire houses and mortgages, and so on. They differ from wealthy areas, however, because they do not receive personalized financial service. Their needs are met only because their financial characteristics are easily measured, standardized, and serviced. Financial services are provided as commodities, that is, impersonally and at low cost, via ATM networks and computerized loan decisions made on the basis of arm's length credit scoring.

At the bottom are the low-income households who live in areas with the 40% lowest incomes. In the past, many of these households would have established relationships with banks, and they would have used these relationships to overcome barriers posed by the difficulty of evaluating economic prospects in these areas or by weaknesses in household (or business) balance sheets. However, in the 1980s, formal financial institutions all but withdrew from the areas in which these households live. Firms have also priced their financial services in such a way that these households typically cannot afford to maintain accounts.

Discarded by the formal sector, households in low-income areas must turn to a growing second-tier financial sector to meet their financial needs. Check-cashing outlets and money orders—widely available to even the poorest households, for a price—are used for cash transactions and payments. Generally, the cost of these informal transactions varies inversely with the household's economic status. For obtaining credit, the options are fewer. Pawnbrokers have been described as the short-term credit market for the poor, but this characterization is overly generous. Pawnbrokers act as the lender of last resort for low-income households. They offer credit on terms more onerous than those of the formal sector. And whereas bank credit facilitates the accumulation of new human or physical assets that enhance future income, pawnbroker credit requires a household to liquidate its stock of assets to meet current income crises.

Studies of informal credit markets have focused on the cost of financial services as the key problem, but cost is not invariably a problem in underserved areas. For example, check cashing facilities often charge modest fees for steady customers. In addition, mortgage brokers originate much of the mortgage credit flows in underserved areas at market rates and terms.

While monopoly pricing by mortgage brokers in some underserved areas is a problem, another problem is more important in these communities: the lack of sufficient savings to sustain the level of investment needed to reignite growth. To some extent this is the result of discrimination and of unequal access in labor markets. It is also, however, the legacy of the urban growth process itself. Urban growth tends to occur at uneven rates in different urban communities, even within the same metropolis. Prior to banking deregulation, traditional banks dampened this tendency toward community boom and bust because they were located evenly throughout urban areas—at least they would be found in these areas' upper- and middle-income neighborhoods. But as banks and thrifts have increasingly sought out desirable, upper-end customers, they have reduced their presence in middle- and lower-income neighborhoods.

In consequence, lower-income communities cannot rely on traditional banks that pool local savings to meet local business and homeowner needs. The resulting financing gap must be closed through "greenlining"—that is, by attracting funds from outside the area.[1]

The South Shore Bank of Chicago, the most acclaimed community development bank in the United States, demonstrated the importance of greenlining in the 1970s. It attracted capital pledges from religious organizations and social-investment funds, and used these to turn around a minority Chicago neighborhood. But the sources tapped by South Shore are unlikely to yield sufficient funds for underserved communities in the United States as a whole, since many of these communities face worse problems today than did the South Shore community two decades ago.

Other sources of greenlining must be found. One possibility is public financing. President Clinton's community development banking program, if fully funded, would provide approximately $500 million of capital for community development banks over five years. But even if this initiative is implemented successfully, it will suffice for only selected underserved communities across the country.

This leaves profit-oriented firms and funds in the private sector. The chronic lending binges over the last two decades—for less-developed countries, merger deals, and commercial real estate ventures—show that loanable funds are plentiful within the U.S. economy. But here is where the boom/bust aspect of urban growth comes into play. The withdrawal of most banks and thrifts from lower- and even middle-income communities further reduces economic activity there, and it reduces credit-market opportunities even for lenders that remain committed to these areas. It should give us pause that the only people who want to become bankers in the cities in the 1990s are community activists.

One can bemoan the end of the New Deal banking regulation, whose restrictions on competition encouraged integrated savings and lending processes, localized loan decision-making, and cross-subsidies to lower-income groups, but this regulatory structure is gone. The financial system has moved from the traditional model of integrated financing by banks and thrifts into the era of "particle finance," wherein mortgage brokers originate loans, banks bundle these loans and sell them as securities, and pension funds are (indirectly) the largest source of mortgage finance.

But this is not to say that nothing can be done. In many other important credit markets, such as those for mortgage finance, small business lending, and student loans, the federal government enhances rates of return through mechanisms that collect, standardize, and guarantee pools of loans made by existing market-driven financial institutions. It can play this same role to revitalize growth in the inner city.

Community Development Mortgage Association (Cindy Mae)

In thinking about credit enhancements for underserved urban areas, it is useful to conceptualize the saving and lending process as involving several discrete parts: originating new loans; funding these loans in the short term; bundling small loans into a diversified pool; warranting the risk of the loan pool through guarantees or sinking funds; selling the loan pool to long-term investors; and servicing the loans in the pool. In the past, all these functions were performed by a single bank or thrift, which made a loan and held it on its books to maturity. In modern finance, different functions are performed by different market participants.

The goal is to attract private-sector interest in originating credit for low-income individuals and communities. Today, a large percentage of loans are originated by brokers who act as a bridge between borrowers and lenders; the brokers hold the instruments they originate only momentarily. Origination thus occurs only if placement—the identification of an investor to hold the resulting loan—is ensured in advance. Solving the apparent problem, origination, thus depends on solving a different problem: encouraging investors to accept the resulting loan.

Attracting private-sector savings pools—such as mutual funds or pension and retirement funds—into holding loans from underserved inner-city areas requires mechanisms for securing these loans. Small loans must be bundled together into securities that are attractive to investors, and this process requires standardization of terms that stabilizes the pool's risk and return. In this way, a set of individually risky loans becomes a pooled financial commodity that can be offered to investors. Providing liquidity by establishing a secondary market enhances investors' ability to sell, and thus expands the investor pool even more.

Currently, in mortgage markets the role of the Federal National Mortgage Association (FNMA, popularly known as Fannie Mae) is to facilitate this process. FNMA defines characteristics such as loan-to-value ratios, interest coverage ratios, and sales price caps with which any mortgage contract it accepts for backing must conform. FNMA then stabilizes the return on the bundled mortgages by guaranteeing them.

Unfortunately, underserved areas are excluded from this process by many financial institutions because of the cost in assessing the risk of the individual seeking credit or of the area in which the investment is to be made. By structuring its guaranties and requirements correctly, the government can use its creditworthiness to enhance the creditworthiness of individuals in lower-income and high minority communities. By pooling large numbers of loans, the government can reduce much of the individual default risk through diversification.

A Community Development Mortgage Association (CDMA, or Cindy Mae) might differ from FNMA by accepting mortgages that carry higher-than-normal risk on one of their defining characteristics. If indeed higher degrees of risk attach to these instruments, a loan-loss equalization fund—equal to the difference in risk times the security's face value—might be set aside in advance to insure their ready acceptability in the market. (Indeed, if loan-loss equalization is accomplished at 100%, then the market might be willing to buy and sell CDMA securities on equal terms with FNMA securities in the FNMA secondary market. Otherwise, it would be necessary to establish a separate CDMA secondary market.)

The government could limit its risk exposure by requiring originators to put up sinking funds linked to the loans they originate. This is standard financial market practice for secured assets, and it avoids a potential hazard associated with originating but not holding loans. By establishing a sinking fund that offsets an agreed percentage of initial losses, loan originators have an incentive to evaluate loan applicants more closely than they might otherwise.

If Cindy Mae equalized loan-loss levels, borrowers could pay the same interest rates as do Fannie Mae borrowers. Since income and wealth levels are lower in inner-city areas, creditworthiness criteria might be eased for a percentage of CDMA participants. For example, lower down-payments or higher mortgage payment-to-income ratios might be allowed. Whether these sorts of accommodations resulted in higher borrowing costs would depend, again, on how the enhanced risks that result were handled. If anticipated loan-loss differentials were compensated when the loans were bundled, then CDMA participants could again receive the going FNMA terms.

As for types of loans that would be eligible under CDMA, at a minimum it should accept loans for home ownership and small business; these already have been targeted under new FNMA and Small Business Administration initiatives aimed at underserved credit markets. Indeed, why not combine these two initiatives under the umbrella of a CDMA? In addition, CDMA might support the financing of human capital programs that facilitate residents' acquisition of higher education, the development of new magnet schools and training programs, and so on.

The criteria for determining which areas of a city could qualify for Cindy Mae financing could be based on guidelines now in use for existing programs such as enterprise zones or the Block Grant Program. Alternatively, a hurdle for participation could be established as follows: any census-tract area that has a minority population of at least 70% and a median income that is 80% or less of the metropolitan area's median income. In Los Angeles, this rule would make 33% of census tracts eligible for CDMA participation.

If these participation criteria seem overly inclusive, one should remember that lower-income and high-minority areas have been disproportionately excluded from participation in credit markets. For example, the bottom 40% median income census tracts in Los Angeles have received only about 17% of the mortgage loans made in the city in the past decade. Furthermore, it makes sense to have sufficiently broad geographic areas eligible for CDMA so that the benefits of diversification can be captured over a variety of individuals and areas. Besides, not every home within the CDMA-eligible area will need to be subsidized by a sizable loan-loss adjustment; some may meet or be close to meeting conventional mortgage criteria.

Conclusion

Much has been written about the growing disparities in wealth and incomes between rich and poor in the United States. Recent changes in the landscape of our financial institutions may be exacerbating this trend. If access to capital remains limited and unequal, the polarization of haves and have-nots in the United States will continue to widen. In particular, the path to economic security historically followed by the middle and working class—home ownership—will be denied to millions at the same time that the social safety net is being cut away.

Government-backed mortgage and loan securities tailored to neglected income groups in the inner cities offer two strong advantages. First, they would provide access to capital for individuals and families who are just short of qualifying for conventional mortgages, or who have been denied the option to apply by virtue of the neighborhoods in which they live. Second, Cindy Maes would help to revitalize the most productive areas of our economy, the cities. In short, these instruments would offer prosperity for people and for the nation as a whole.

Note

1. As opposed to "redlining," wherein financial institutions make fewer loans, or impose stricter terms, on communities with many minority residents and/or with a perceived high risk of loss.

REFERENCES

Caskey, John P. 1994. "Bank Representation in Low-Income and Minority Urban Communities." *Urban Affairs Quarterly,* Vol. 29, No. 4, pp. 617-38.

Dymski, Gary A., Gerald Epstein, and Robert Pollin. 1993. *Transforming the U.S. Financial System: An Equitable and Efficient Structure for the 21st Century.* Armonk, N.Y.: M.E. Sharpe.

Dymski, Gary A. and John M. Veitch. 1992. "Race and the Financial Dynamics of Urban Growth: L.A. As Fay Wray." In Gerry Riposa and Caroline Dersch, eds., *City of Angels.* Dubuque, Iowa: Kendall/Hunt Press, pp. 131-58.

Dymski, Gary A. and John M. Veitch. 1996. "Financial Transformation and the Metropolis: Booms, Busts, and Banking in Los Angeles." *Environment and Planning A.* Forthcoming.

Leyshon, Andrew and Nigel Thrift. 1995. "Geographies of Financial Exclusion: Financial Abandonment in Britain and the United States." *Transactions of the Institute of British Geographies,* pp. 1-31.

Leyshon, Andrew and Nigel Thrift. 1996. "Geographies of Financial Knowledge." *Environment and Planning A.* Forthcoming.

Taub, William. 1988. *Community Capitalism.* Cambridge, Mass.: Harvard Business School.

SECTION IV

Trade and Sectoral Policy

OVERVIEW
Trade and Sectoral Policy

by Thea Lee

THE UNITED STATES CONTINUES TO LOSE GROUND IN THE INTERNATIONAL trade arena. The 1995 merchandise trade deficit is likely to reach record levels, even as the dollar falls in value against the Japanese yen and many European currencies. At the same time, our central cities are deteriorating, and communities long dependent on military spending struggle to adjust to the post-Cold War world.

International trade, urban decay, and military downsizing are all related to the disappearance of the steady, high-paying blue-collar jobs that for decades formed the core of the American middle class. In each of these cases, government policy—deliberate or not—contributed to the destruction of the industries that supported those good jobs. By the same token, a change in government policy can help sustain a new generation of good jobs, rebuild communities, and ultimately lay the foundation for a better future.

This section includes four chapters that outline the problems and challenges now facing the United States in the areas of international trade, urban policy, and military conversion. Together, the authors lay out a vision of a more coherent, integrated trade and industrial policy. They emphasize the importance of a positive government role in crafting an activist trade policy, reshaping the international rules on labor and environmental standards, ending the bias in U.S. policies that encouraged businesses and individuals to flee cities, and engineering a smooth transition from unnecessarily high military budgets to a civilian technology policy and targeted public investment.

Thea Lee is an international trade economist at the Economic Policy Institute.

Trading Away Our Future

As the U.S. trade deficit grows, more and more goods that used to be produced here are imported, and the jobs associated with those goods are either eliminated or moved abroad. Meanwhile, the perceived need to "compete" internationally—in both import-competing and export markets—puts downward pressure on wages, particularly for those workers at the bottom of the pay and education scale.

Current trade policy, which has been remarkably consistent across Republican and Democratic administrations, has focused almost exclusively on increasing the volume of trade through reducing trade barriers and increasing protection for corporations investing abroad. As Robert Scott points out in his chapter, these policies have led to a hemorrhaging of U.S. jobs and to increasing inequality in the distribution of wages. In particular, current policy has failed to address the structural problems underlying mounting U.S. trade imbalances with Japan and China, which accounted for almost two-thirds of our trade deficit in 1994. The North American Free Trade Agreement (NAFTA), widely touted as a job-creating agreement, has instead resulted in a burgeoning deficit with our two North American trading partners, Canada and Mexico.

While marketed as "free trade," current policy in fact represents a careful orchestration of trade rules to accommodate the business interests of multinational corporations. In his chapter, Jerome Levinson describes the lopsided nature of recent trade agreements, including NAFTA and the General Agreement on Tariffs and Trade (GATT). These agreements protect the intellectual property rights of corporations and limit the ability of governments to regulate foreign investment. They do little or nothing, however, to ensure that minimal internationally accepted labor and environmental standards are applied. This shortcoming both undermines the bargaining power of American workers and encourages the governments of developing countries to repress their own labor movements and deplete their environmental resources in order to compete for scarce international capital.

Scott proposes an array of long- and short-term solutions to U.S. trade problems. In the short term, he suggests invoking the "balance of payments" exception clause in the GATT, which allows countries experiencing chronic trade deficits to implement temporary import protection.

He advocates imposing quotas on a select group of industries that account for a large portion of the trade deficit. In the long run, Scott argues that the United States must work to reform GATT rules in order to allow for more effective bilateral solutions to trade disputes in areas not currently covered by the agreement. Congress should also insist that industries granted import relief use their increased incomes to expand production and increase the competitiveness of their products.

Levinson writes that the framework for a coherent American policy with respect to worker rights is already in place; all that is needed is the political will to carry it out. He proposes that the United States (1) renegotiate the labor side agreement to NAFTA, so that the violation of workers' rights to form unions could result in the application of sanctions (this would also set a more appropriate precedent for extension of NAFTA to other countries in the hemisphere); (2) make protection of worker rights a top priority in the next round of GATT negotiations; (3) consider abolishing the generalized system of preferences legislation, which has failed to promote development but has encouraged multinational corporations to move jobs overseas; (4) use the "voice and vote" of the United States in the multilateral financial institutions to ensure that observance of core worker rights is rewarded in the allocation of funds and loans; and (5) enhance the role of the International Labor Organization.

Revitalizing Our Cities

Elliott Sclar challenges the conventional wisdom that the decline of American cities is both natural and inevitable. He argues that the shrinking economic bases, poverty, homelessness, and crime that afflict central cities and, increasingly, older suburbs is not a market outcome but rather the result of largely invisible public subsidies to automobile travel and low-density housing. In order to improve the efficiency of both services and manufacturing, Sclar contends that the United States must reverse this "economically perverse policy."

The first step Sclar recommends is "leveling the playing field" between cities and suburbs to reverse the historic bias inherent in past policies. This would entail passing along more of the costs of automobile-based sprawl (i.e. highway building and maintenance) to users rather than subsidizing these costs through general public funds. In the interim period, intra-urban transit subsidies should be increased and incentives should be provided to pedestrians and bicycle riders in order to increase the relative attractiveness of urban residence.

Second, in order to lure back the middle class, the physical infrastructure and services provided by central cities must be restored. Public housing funds should be targeted on revitalizing the excellent housing stock of older buildings located in and near central cities. "These locations," Sclar writes, "near already well-developed public transportation and other infrastructure, are cost-effective places for a sustained revitalization of America's economic base." Sclar's policies lay an essential groundwork for reversing the downward spiral our cities are experiencing. The national economic revitalization this would spark will be crucial to the U.S. ability to compete successfully in global markets.

Downsizing the Military, Investing the Peace Dividend

Ann Markusen and Michael Oden argue that the end of the Cold War provides an important opportunity to reshape national science and technology policy and industrial policy and to redirect public resources to meet fundamental national needs. They contend that the nation needs to mobilize for peace conversion on the same scale that we have mobilized for war in the past. The peace mobilization should have two goals: "moving significant resources as efficiently as possible from military-dedicated missions to civilian ones; and at the same time stabilizing and improving economic opportunities for defense-dependent firms, workers, and communities."

Markusen and Oden see potential savings of at least $350 billion over the next eight years from the military budget. They propose allocating 10% of this sum to smoothing the transition of companies, communities, and workers into alternative markets (based partly on new research and development and public investments). "An investment of this magnitude," they write, "would act as a real transmission belt between the military and civilian economy." The remainder of the savings would be applied to building a new science and technology policy linked to a major public investment program.

Conclusion

The policies outlined in this section would reinforce each other in numerous ways. The public resources freed up from cutting military spending could be directed to improve infrastructure and transportation, fund education and training, and develop energy-efficient and environmentally sound production methods. Encouraging more concentrated location of production and residential communities would save resources (land, energy, and time) now spent on commuting, and would also be compatible with modern production methods that rely on quick response and proximity to markets and skilled labor. The increase in public investment (made possible by military cuts) and improvements in private efficiency (facilitated by correcting the bias in past policy) would in turn raise the productivity of American labor. In conjunction with new trade policies, these ideas are part of the solution to stemming the long-term decline in U.S. living standards.

CHAPTER 14

TRADE
A Strategy for the 21st Century

by Robert E. Scott

THE TRADE POLICIES OF THE LAST THREE ADMINISTRATIONS, BOTH DEMOcratic and Republican, have been an abject failure. Between 1980 and 1994, the U.S. current account balance, the broadest measure of income from trade in goods and services (including investment income) went from a surplus of $2.3 billion to a deficit of $151.2 billion.[1] The United States, which had a positive net investment position with the rest of the world of $106 billion in 1980, has become the world's largest debtor, owing a net $556 billion in 1993.[2] This debt is the cumulative result of past current account deficits.

Do these ledger numbers have any real effect on American economic performance? Unfortunately, the impact is strong and harmful. When the United States imports more than it exports, capital flows in from the rest of the world in the form of direct and portfolio investment. Dependence on these foreign investment flows creates pressure to keep interest rates high, ultimately reducing living standards. The rapid growth of imports and slow growth in U.S. exports have also put downward pressure on the wages of the 75% of U.S. workers who do not have a college degree. These workers have seen their real hourly wages decline by about 15% between 1973 and 1993.[3] Trade and foreign investment have contributed to this decline in at least three ways. First, cheap imports lower wages by reducing the prices of competing goods. Second, U.S. foreign direct investment undermines the bargaining power of U.S. workers. Third, unfair trade practices abroad reduce demand for labor in high-wage manufacturing industries. If we could eliminate the 1994 current

Robert E. Scott is assistant professor of business and public policy in the College of Business and Management of the University of Maryland at College Park.

account deficit, up to 2.4 million high-wage jobs could be created in the United States.[4]

The trade deficit is largely the result of a structural imbalance in trade with a few countries in Asia. Just two countries are responsible for almost two-thirds of our 1994 trade deficit: Japan (43.5%), and China (19.5%). These imbalances reflect patterns of extreme export-driven growth in those two countries that have been sustained by artificially low exchange rates (especially in China) and by structural barriers to imports (especially in Japan), as well as carefully targeted trade and industrial policies. The "miraculous" growth experience of these economies has been built largely on exports, principally to the United States, to the detriment of jobs and income growth in this country.

These trade-related job losses and wage declines are not the inevitable result of adjusting to a new "competitive" era. Rather, they are the consequence of disastrous, purposeful trade policies that pit our own people against unregulated, low-wage markets so that corporations can prosper. The United States needs a new trade policy that is geared toward the betterment of living standards for everyone, not just the profits of a few multinational corporations and a small number of college-educated professionals.

The Failure of U.S. Bipartisan Trade Policy

Trade and foreign investment have grown faster than world income during the past few decades for a variety of reasons. These include: (1) reductions in communication and transportation costs; (2) the elimination of trade barriers and restrictions on capital mobility; and (3) the rapid growth in the number of workers in low-wage countries with basic educational skills. A large pool of such workers have been incorporated into the global economy through the opening of what were once communist countries.

The growth in world trade and investment has been facilitated in this country by a bipartisan consensus on trade strategy. Changes in administrations have had less impact on trade than on other types of public policy. U.S. trade officials, supported by international economists and lawyers (especially those representing foreign clients) have implemented a national trade strategy over the past 15 years that has never been the subject of public debate. The core of this strategy is a decision to confront the hyper-competitive economies in Asia by adopting a competitive response based on the use of low-wage labor, both at home and abroad. Another element of the strategy involves an effort, through trade negotiations, to remake the rules and legal environment of the international economy to resemble practices and principles that govern market relations in the United States. The latter has now moved to the top of the trade agenda in the form of a new campaign to convince our trading partners to adopt and enforce U.S. antitrust principles and standards.[5] These strategies must be judged a complete failure on the basis of their results to date.

The Uruguay Round of the General Agreement on Tariffs and Trade (GATT) and the North American Free Trade Agreement (NAFTA) have been the centerpieces of trade policy for the past three administrations. Despite the United States' enormous leverage in negotiating these agreements, they have not reduced the U.S. current account deficit, and they are unlikely to do so in the future. In fact, this deficit has followed a steadily increasing trend for the past two decades. Some insight into why this has occurred can be obtained by critically examining the predicted benefits of trade liberalization.

Table 1 summarizes the U.S. International Trade Commission's forecast of the job impacts of the Uruguay Round GATT Agreement and contrasts that to our own estimates. The ITC forecast a decline in manufacturing employment of 30,000 jobs as a result of the Uruguay Round but saw an overall gain of 160,000 jobs thanks to increases in agriculture and services. Our alternative forecast takes into account industry concerns including forecasts of significant job displacement in sectors such as steel, textiles, and apparel. This alternative forecast projects a loss of 912,000 manufacturing jobs, and economy-wide losses of 721,000 jobs.[6] The ITC forecast emphasizes the benefits to U.S. industries from reductions in foreign trade barriers; the alternative forecast illustrates that the opening of U.S. markets and changes to our trade laws increase the risks of rapid import surges in some vulnerable industries. These downside risks are ignored by the ITC in its formal industry forecasts.[7]

Many economists argue that trade agreements are not designed to affect the *level* of employment, but rather to move labor from low-wage import industries to high-wage export industries. On the contrary, however, trade agreements should address both job creation and job quality, for at least three reasons. First, because the economy is rarely at full employment, improvements in trade balances can increase employment. Second, because our imports are growing more rapidly than our exports, it is not clear that increases in the volume of trade have improved the overall quality of U.S. jobs. The changing distribution of jobs will depress aggregate productivity growth, and thus wages. (Note that most of the job gains forecast for the Uruguay Round, shown in Table 1, are concentrated in the low-wage service industries, while job losses are concentrated in the high-wage manufacturing industries.) Finally, the U.S. approach to trade problems, which has relied on legalistic trade remedy approaches (e.g., anti-dumping cases), has proven particularly ineffectual in dealing with structural trade problems with countries such as Japan and China, whose economies are organized differently from our own.[8] As a result, NAFTA and the Uruguay Round GATT Agreement are unlikely to solve either the depressing effects of trade on production workers' wages in the United States or our related structural trade imbalances.

Recent administrations have used negotiations over trade disputes with particular countries to shore up multilateral trade policies. These negotiations have often focused on Japan, where they have followed two tracks.

TABLE 1
Uruguay Round Employment Effects, by Industry
(Thousands of Employees)

Industry	Employment in 1993	Net Employment Effects: ITC	Net Employment Effects: Our Estimate
Manufactured Products	14,134	(30)	(912)
Agricultural Products	7,704	73	73
Services	14,153	118	118
Total All Sectors	35,991	160	(721)

Source: U.S. International Trade Commission and author's calculations.

The first has emphasized economy-wide barriers to imports in the Japanese economy, including over-regulation and the appropriate levels of fiscal and monetary stimulation. The second track has concerned specific industries, such as telecommunications equipment, glass products, and motor vehicles and parts. The Clinton Administration has been involved in several acrimonious disputes with Japan over specific industries.

The auto industry illustrates the problems with this approach. U.S. parts suppliers argue that they are systematically excluded from the Japanese market by structural trade barriers, especially the *keiretsu*.[9] News reports claim that "[a]n American shock absorber set sells for $228 in Detroit; a Japanese-made shock absorber sells in Japan for $605."[10] The Bush Administration negotiated an agreement with the Japanese government and auto manufacturers in 1992 that was supposed to increase Japanese purchases of U.S. auto parts from $9 billion in 1991 to $19 billion in 1995.[11] In 1995 the Clinton Administration declared this agreement a success and sought additional commitments for Japanese purchases of U.S. autos and parts. But the Japanese government refused to endorse numerical targets that had been agreed to by Japanese auto producers in these negotiations.

The Clinton Administration has been accused of "backing down" in settling for "an agreement that did not include the central U.S. demand" for numerical targets.[12] However, even if Clinton had obtained a firm target, it would not have solved the U.S. auto trade problems with Japan. Between 1991 and 1994 the U.S. trade deficit with Japan in motor vehicles and parts increased from $29.6 billion to $34.6 billion, despite the Bush Administration's auto agreement. In the same period, U.S. exports of vehicles *and* parts to Japan increased by less than $1.5 billion, from $1.304 billion to $2.775 billion.[13] The $10 billion increase in parts purchases (covered by the Bush agreements) was met almost entirely by sales to Japanese-owned plants in the United States, with only a small increase in U.S. exports to Japan and no discernible impact on the U.S. auto trade deficit. Confrontational tactics, which are meeting increasing resistance in Japan, cannot correct the structural trade imbalances between our two countries.

The European Union has taken a completely different approach to its trade problems with the Asian economies. It has emphasized the maintenance of a high-wage environment, with high levels of unionization and much higher minimum wages than in the United States. These policies have been supported with activist trade, investment, and industrial policies that have maintained a much larger share of employment in high-wage manufacturing industries than we are experiencing in this country. In addition, the European community has emphasized building links between firms in the EU and Japan that are designed to bridge the institutional gaps between the two legal systems, without wholesale reform of the legal environment of either partner.[14] As a result of these policies, the EU has maintained global trade balance for most of the past 15 years, and it has a larger share of its workforce employed in manufacturing. Furthermore, manufacturing wages in Europe have increased two to three times faster than in the United States since 1982,[15] and Europe also has much higher wages than the United States in its service industries. (Manufacturing wages heavily influence service-sector compensation, and trade has had a larger negative effect on manufacturing wages in the United States than in Europe.)

Depressed U.S. Employment and Wages

There are at least three ways in which trade and outward foreign direct investment have depressed the wages of workers in the United States. First, increased imports of goods from countries with low wages and large supplies of semi-skilled labor have increased competitive pressures on U.S. workers making competing products. This effect has intensified as imports from low-wage developing countries have grown very rapidly in the past 20 years. Developing countries have increased their share of U.S. imports from 27.6% in 1972 to 42.3% in 1992, at the same time that imports as a whole doubled their share of U.S. gross domestic product, from 4.6% to 8.9%.[16] The share of imports from low-wage countries in U.S. manufacturing output increased from 5.1% in 1978 to 10.9% in 1990.[17]

There is a rapidly growing economic literature on the effects of trade on wages in the United States.[18] While its effect on average wages is still ambiguous, there is an emerging consensus that trade is responsible for a significant share of the increase in wage inequality.[19] Trade theory predicts that for a country like the United States, which is relatively capital- and skill-abundant, lower tariffs on imports from low-wage countries will tend to reduce wages of production workers if import prices fall when the tariff is reduced. Sachs and Shatz found that the "[r]elative prices of less skill-intensive goods declined after 1978," which is consistent with the conditions necessary for trade to depress manufacturing wages.[20] They also examined the effects of trade on the quantity of imports and found that:

> ...the increase in net imports between 1978 and 1990 is associated with a decline of 7.2 percent in production jobs in manufacturing and a decline of 2.1 percent in nonproduction jobs in manufacturing. Since production jobs, overall, are less highly skilled than nonproduction jobs, these trends may have contributed to the widening of wage inequalities between skilled and unskilled workers.[21]

These results are also supported by Adrian Wood, who concludes in his new book on north-south trade that:

> Expansion of trade has linked the labour markets of developed countries (the North) more closely with those of developing countries (the South). This greater economic intimacy has had large benefits, raising average living standards in the North, and accelerating development in the South. But it has hurt unskilled workers in the North, reducing their wages and pushing them out of jobs.[22]

The internationalization of the U.S. economy has also increased the outflow of foreign investment from the United States to low-wage countries. This is the second factor that has increased the bargaining power of U.S. firms and depressed the wages of U.S. production workers. U.S. firms are investing abroad at an accelerating pace: the net increase in U.S. private assets abroad reached a historic peak of $146 billion in 1993, or 66% of total U.S. net private domestic investment in that year.[23]

Only a minority of U.S. foreign direct investment takes place in low-wage host countries. However, countries ranging from China to Mexico have experienced rapidly growing U.S. foreign direct investment, which is often supported by policy initiatives (such as the NAFTA) and through business and trade missions such as Secretary of Commerce Ron Brown's 1994 visit to China. While foreign direct investment can depress wages if it results in expanded imports of low-priced products, it can also lower wages by reducing the bargaining power of domestic workers. In fact, this effect can occur without any actual outflow of investment to a low-wage country—the mere threat of capital flight may be sufficient to extract wage concessions. For these reasons it is conceptually difficult to measure the effects of foreign direct investment on wages using conventional economic techniques and data. The following examples illustrate this effect:

- 4,000 workers at a Xerox plant in Webster, N.Y., accepted 33% cuts in base pay to avoid a threatened plant closure. Union leaders expressed a belief that the plant would move to Mexico or Asia if wages weren't cut.[24]
- 220 workers at the London Fog plant in Baltimore agreed to take a $1 per hour pay cut to keep the plant open.[25]
- National Service Industries threatened to move 300 jobs from its lighting plant in Lithonia, Ga., unless workers took a cut of 20% in pay and 36% in benefits. The company has been investigating production in Mexico, though the jobs in question would move to another plant in Georgia with lower labor costs.[26]
- Workers at a Leviton Co. plant in Warwick, R.I., agreed in September to freeze wages and work 12 hour shifts without overtime pay because the company threatened to move production of electrical outlets to Mexico.[27]

Unfair trade practices and effective industrial policies in other countries have also taken away jobs from U.S. workers. This is the third factor that has moved U.S. workers out of high-wage manufacturing jobs and into lower-paying occupations in non-traded goods industries. Average weekly earnings in 1989 were $589 in manufacturing versus $306 in services and $189 in retail trade.[28] Exports from the U.S. aerospace industry, one of our most competitive sectors, fell by 14.5% between 1992 and 1994, while the import share of the domestic aerospace market increased by 1.5 percentage points in the same period.[29] This decline is the result of the increased competitiveness of Airbus Industrie, which has benefitted from enormous past and continuing subsidies from countries in the EU, and of offset agreements between private firms in the United States and foreign firms and governments that transfer production abroad in exchange for aircraft sales.

Trade between developed countries is often influenced by market imperfections that make it possible for countries to earn excess wages and profits (rents, in the language of economists) that could not be obtained if markets were competitively structured. Significant market failures include scale economies, learning curves, and knowledge spillovers.[30] This trade is usually characterized by substantial amounts of intra-industry activity, where countries are both exporting and importing goods in the same industries. The patterns of trade in such industries will depend on the technologies of production, and they can be influenced heavily by government subsidies and other forms of industrial policy.

Japan stands out because it engages in surprisingly small amounts of intra-industry trade. This suggests that its government and industries are uniquely able to shield themselves from the effects of market imperfections in industries where they choose to compete. The result is a protected home market, which is often used to generate revenues and production experience that give the Japanese a huge advantage in world markets for these products, such as autos and semiconductors. Many observers have argued that Japan's trade patterns are a result of its many formal and informal barriers to trade.[31] Between 1980 and March 1995 the dollar declined in value from an average value of 227 yen per dollar to less than 90, a loss of more than 60% of its value. Despite this enormous depreciation, the U.S. merchandise trade deficit with Japan has grown from $10.4 billion in 1980 to $66.5 billion in 1994.[32]

The unbalanced nature of Japan's trade with the United States can be illustrated with data for a few key industries. Of the 1994 U.S. trade deficit with Japan, 83% was concentrated in only two industries: (1) motor vehicles and parts, and (2) electrical machinery, including sound and TV equipment.[33] In motor vehicles, the United States imported $37.4 billion worth of goods and only exported $2.7 billion worth of goods to Japan, for a net trade deficit of $34.7 billion. In electrical machinery, imports were $25.1 billion and exports were $4.7 billion, yielding a deficit of $20.4 billion. These are highly unbalanced trade flows.

In summary, increased imports of goods from low-wage countries have depressed U.S. production workers' wages, U.S. foreign direct investment in these countries has further weakened the bargaining power of our workers, and unfair trade and industrial policies of key trading partners have reduced the number of high-wage jobs in this country. U.S. trade and investment policies have contributed to increasing trade deficits and foreign direct investment, and have failed to combat the effect of foreign trade and industrial policies.

ELEMENTS OF A NEW TRADE STRATEGY

It is time for the United States to develop a new trade strategy. A successful strategy must begin with measures to staunch the hemorrhaging in U.S. trade and current account deficits. Short-term policies must also address the causes of the structural trade imbalances that have shrunken the U.S. manufacturing sector. Long-run solutions to our underlying trade and competitiveness problems will require new initiatives in the areas of international labor rights, multilateral trade policy, and domestic economic policy.

Balance of payments relief. We must recognize that our trade policies have created a balance of payments crisis for the United States. Private financial markets are no longer willing to finance all of the U.S. current account deficit. As a result, the country is losing currency reserves at a significant rate, and foreign governments have been forced to finance a substantial portion of U.S. borrowing requirements. If these governments were not intervening, the value of the dollar would collapse, in much the same way as the Mexican peso collapsed in late 1994 and early 1995. The sharp drop in the dollar in March 1995 is indicative of the kinds of pressures that will continue to plague the dollar until fundamental steps are taken to correct U.S. payments imbalances.

In the short term, the United States is entitled under the terms of the GATT to impose temporary import protection in order to correct a "balance of payments crisis."[34] The United States last utilized this authority in 1971 when President Nixon imposed a 10% import surcharge to correct a trade imbalance that ultimately led us to abandon the gold standard and fixed exchange rates. It is interesting to note that this section of GATT encourages countries to use quotas (rather than tariffs or import surcharges) to correct imbalances.[35]

As a first step to correct U.S. trade imbalances, global quotas should be imposed on a few products from industries that account for a large portion of the trade deficit, such as automotive and electronic products. Rights to temporary quotas should be auctioned so as to prevent windfall profits to importers.

A balance of payments relief policy of the type proposed here would require three legislative elements. First, a trigger or threshold criterion would have to be established. This could be based either on the level of the current account deficit (perhaps using a moving average) or on measures of government efforts to support the U.S. dollar (U.S. reserve losses and foreign official currency purchases). The Administration would monitor the indicator selected.

The second element of a balance of payments relief policy would be a set of measures that would be implemented when relief is required. These should include notification of Congress, the public, and our trading partners. After the trigger or threshold is exceeded, then the U.S. Trade Representative could identify one or more industries to be subject to a quota sufficient to reduce imports so that the current account deficit would be reduced below the trigger level by some acceptable margin (e.g., 50% of the trigger). The USTR could be empowered to negotiate export expansion agreements, with firm, quantitative targets, in lieu of import quotas, within specified time limits (e.g., 60 days). The USTR should then be required to establish a system for a global auction of quota rights and to implement this system within a specified time period after the trigger is exceeded (e.g., 90 or 120 days).

The final element of a balance of payments relief policy would be a mechanism to provide for regular review of the quotas, including a process for adjusting the quota based on progress toward achieving the balance of payments objective. Quotas would be tightened if the target accounts worsened in any period or if export expansion agreement targets were not achieved; quotas would be relaxed or eliminated when the target was achieved. The USTR should also be authorized to change industries targeted for quotas over time, in order to reflect changing trade patterns and changes in the competitiveness of U.S. producers.

Labor rights. Once temporary measures are in place, the United States must develop a set of trade, labor-market, and industrial policies to restore and maintain trade balance in the future, without undermining wage growth. This will require a reexamination of our fundamental approach to trade and our goals for international trade negotiations. Greater attention must also be given to domestic institutional changes that can raise wages for U.S. workers (including an increased minimum wage and labor law reform). Such policies have been effective in the EU and can help reverse the decline in wages for workers who don't possess a college degree. Protection of labor rights in GATT, with effective enforcement mechanisms, must become a top priority in trade negotiations, and a greater balance between labor and property rights should be pursued.

The Congress has regularly instructed the President and his trade negotiators to push for the inclusion of more substantive labor rights in trade agreements. The United States has failed to achieve its negotiation objectives for international labor standards in any of the postwar GATT negotiations, and it has also refused to adopt core International Labor Organization conventions.[36] During the same period we have succeeded in obtaining expanded protection for inventors (trade-related intellectual property rights), investors (trade-related investment measures), manufacturers facing foreign competition (subsidies and trade remedies codes), and services providers (general agreement on trade in services). Labor is the only significant factor of production that did not receive special protection in the Uruguay Trade Agreements.

Expanded labor rights are the key to raising wages and purchasing power in the developing countries. If developing countries are required to adhere to internationally recognized labor standards as a condition for gaining greater access to developed country product markets, then the downward pressure on wages will be reduced, and the demand for our exports will increase.

The Clinton Administration has developed a new campaign to promote trade and investment with a group of 10 "Big Emerging Markets." However, the United States had a trade deficit with this group of countries throughout the 1980s and 1990s—it was approximately $23 billion in 1991 and grew to $40 billion in 1994.[37] Further expansion of trade and U.S. foreign direct investment in these countries, without improvements in labor rights, will only increase the downward pressure on the wages of U.S. production workers. For these reasons, the United States should give labor standards the highest priority in future bilateral and multilateral trade negotiations. (See the chapter in this volume by Jerome Levinson.)

GATT and World Trade Organization reform. The balance of payments relief plan will also increase the pressure on the World Trade Organization (WTO) to identify reforms needed to correct structural imbalances in the world trading system. This step may require abandonment or reform of fundamental GATT principles. For example, the requirement for providing "most favored nation" access to the lowest-available tariff schedules to full WTO members may have to be violated in order to resolve fundamental bilateral trade disputes with Japan and some of the developing countries that are pursuing aggressive strategies aimed at export-led growth. In addition, measures to limit the negative consequences of foreign direct investment may involve country-specific limitations on the rights of foreign investors. This restriction would violate the WTO principle of national treatment, which prohibits discrimination in the regulation of foreign direct investment on the basis of the country of origin, and may also require reform of the Trade Related Investment Measures agreement.

Complementary sectoral policies. The provision of import relief should be accompanied by measures to ensure that domestic producers use the increased income they receive to expand production and increase the competitiveness of their products. The United States has some experience with such policies. Congress required the steel industry to reinvest all of its earnings in its core business activities when the industry obtained import relief in the 1980s. As a consequence, domestic producers invested, became much more efficient, and recaptured market share from foreign suppliers, even after the quotas ceased to limit imports.[38] However, the auto industry was not required to make such commitments when it was granted trade relief by the Reagan Administration. As a consequence, the industry increased prices substantially and few additional jobs were created.[39]

In addition, the United States needs to develop a wide range of policies to enhance the competitiveness of export industries. For example, U.S. aerospace output and employment have been reduced because aircraft manufacturers have made agreements to move production and technology abroad in exchange for aircraft sales to government-controlled or government-influenced airlines in other countries, especially in Asia. In order to solve this problem, the United States should open negotiations with the European Union to obtain a new bilateral civil aircraft trade agreement that prohibits Boeing, McDonnell Douglas, and Airbus Industrie from using the export of jobs and technologies as a marketing tool.[40]

Another critical element of an aerospace industry policy would concern the domestic and international markets for aircraft. U.S. air carriers, who have global cost advantages, have been shut out of many markets through government regulations. Aggressive measures to open access for these carriers could substantially increase demand for aircraft, which is likely to benefit U.S. airframe manufacturers.

Currently, responsibilities for U.S. trade and industrial policies are spread out over dozens of agencies, and the economic interests of U.S. firms and workers are often sacrificed for foreign policy objectives. The responsibility for developing sectoral policies should be consolidated into a single Cabinet agency that recognizes the development and maintenance of the U.S. industrial base as a top national priority.

Finally, the United States and multilateral institutions must devote increased resources and attention to the problems of development. Beyond the need for increased resources, new models of development are needed. The free market/free trade/free investment model that has been forced upon the developing world in the past 15 years has resulted in lower rates of growth, falling wages, and greater immiseration for all but a small elite in both the developed and the developing worlds. In many developing countries hyper-inflation, debt crises, and chronic instability have been reduced or eliminated, but at the cost of much lower rates of growth in per capita output. These countries can grow much more rapidly through inward-focused policies to reduce income inequality and increase investments in education and infrastructure than they can by quickly and completely eliminating all trade and investment barriers.

These steps are necessary for the United States to create an economic environment in which it is possible to reverse the inequities in the U.S. wage structures that have developed since the early 1970s and to prosper as a society in the 21st century.

Notes

1. *Economic Indicators* June 1995, p. 36.

2. Council of Economic Advisors 1986, 1995.

3. Based on a weighted average; see Mishel and Bernstein 1994, p. 140.

4. Each $1 billion of exports supported approximately 15,826 jobs in the United States in 1994. (This estimate is based on 1992 export employment multipliers published by the U.S. Department of Commerce (Davis 1995, p. 7), as updated by Scott (1995, p. 6)). We assume here that reductions in imports or expansion of exports would have similar effects on employment in the United States. Therefore, a $151.2 billion

improvement in the U.S. current account balance would result in the employment increase noted here. Net employment changes in the United States could be less than this amount, if other sectors of the economy experienced contraction at the same time.

5. Scherer 1994; Watson 1994.

6. U.S. International Trade Commission 1994 and author's calculations. Details available from the author upon request.

7. Lee (1995) contrasts predictions by various economists of significant job gains from NAFTA with the job losses that have been experienced since NAFTA took effect in 1994.

8. See, for example, comments by Lester Thurow, as cited by Watson (1994, pp. 1238-9).

9. *Keiretsu* are groups of firms (e.g., auto assemblers and parts suppliers) that have long-term relationships, often involving cross-ownership, that are difficult for outsiders to penetrate. Banks often play key roles in these organizations.

10. *Washington Post,* July 30, 1995, p. C3.

11. *New York Times,* January 11, 1992.

12. *Washington Post,* July 30, 1995, p. C3.

13. U.S. Department of Commerce, 1995a.

14. John B. Richardson, "Japan and Europe: Two Tired Giants," speech to Transatlantic Futures EU Policy Forum, November 9, 1994, as reported in *Bureau of International Affairs, International Trade Daily,* November 10, 1994.

15. Council of Economic Advisors 1995.

16. Council of Economic Advisors 1995.

17. Sachs and Shatz 1994.

18. See Burtless (1995) for a review and analysis of this literature.

19. Sachs and Shatz (1994) show that the ratio of the nonproduction to production wage (which they use in place of skilled/unskilled comparisons) fell from an average of 1.56 in the 1950s to 1.53 in the late 1970s, and then increased to about 1.65 in 1989-90. They note that this is related to the pattern of imports from low-wage countries that was discussed above.

20. There is also a competing hypothesis that suggests that the wages of less-skilled workers have been depressed by technological changes that increased the relative demand for more-skilled workers. This phenomenon is associated with differences in the rate of change in the total factor productivity of skill-intensive sectors and non-skill intensive sectors. Sachs and Shatz (1994, pp. 39-40) conclude that "the evidence points more toward shifts in trade and market prices than toward shifts in TFP growth as the relevant factor in widening wage inequalities after 1978."

21. Sachs and Shatz 1994, p. 3.

22. Wood 1994, p. 1.

23. Council of Economic Advisors 1995.

24. *Washington Post*, June 9, 1994.

25. *Baltimore Sun*, October 8, 1993 and October 21, 1994.

26. *Atlanta Journal and Constitution*, May 19, 1994.

27. *Wall Street Journal*, October 28, 1994 and *USA Today*, August 18, 1994.

28. Scott 1993.

29. Barber and Scott 1995.

30. See Scott 1993 for a further discussion of the implications of trade in such imperfectly competitive industries.

31. See, for example, Prestowitz and Chimerine 1994.

32. Council of Economic Advisors 1986; U.S. Department of Commerce 1995b.

33. U.S. Department of Commerce 1995a. Analysis based on U.S. Census trade statistics using data from the harmonized tariff schedule of the United States (HS), comparing exports with the customs value of imports.

34. This section refers to the Balance of Payment Exception (under GATT articles XII, XIII and XIV).

35. Most governments have chosen to use tariff surcharges, rather than quotas, to remedy balance of payments problems, for reasons reviewed by Jackson (1992, pp. 213-216). Blecker (1992) recommends the use of a tariff, to be applied to imports from low-wage countries, that is designed to equalize unit labor costs. A quota is recommended here because the Japanese trade surplus has not proved responsive to devaluations in the dollar, which have the same effect on import prices as tariff surcharges.

36. Compa 1993, p. 189, note 111. See also Spriggs and Scott 1995.

37. McMillion 1995.

38. See Blecker, Lee, and Scott 1993; Chimerine et al. 1994.

39. Scott 1994.

40. Barber and Scott 1995.

References

Barber, Randy and Robert E. Scott. 1995. *Jobs on the Wing: Trading Away the Future of the U.S. Aerospace Industry.* Washington, D.C.: Economic Policy Institute.

Blecker, Robert. 1992. *Beyond the Twin Deficits: A Trade Strategy for the 1990s.* Economic Policy Institute Series. Armonk, N.Y.: M.E. Sharpe.

Blecker, Robert A., Thea M. Lee, and Robert E. Scott. 1993. "Trade Protection and Industrial Revitalization: American Steel in the 1980s." Working Paper No. 104. Washington, D.C.: Economic Policy Institute.

Burtless, Gary. 1995. "International Trade and the Rise in Earnings Inequality." *Journal of Economic Literature,* Vol. 33, No. 2, pp. 800-16.

Chimerine, Lawrence, Alan Tonelson, Karl von Schriltz, and Gregory Stanko, with Clyde V. Prestowitz Jr. and Lester Coffey. 1994. *Can the Phoenix Survive? The Fall and Rise of the American Steel Industry.* Washington, D.C.: Economic Strategy Institute.

Compa, Lance. 1993. "Labor Rights and Labor Standards in International Trade." *Law and Policy in International Business,* Vol. 25, No. 1, p. 165.

Council of Economic Advisors. Various years. *Economic Report of the President.* Washington, D.C.: U.S. Government Printing Office.

Davis, Lester A. 1995. "U.S. Jobs Supported by Goods and Services Exports." Research Series OMA-1-95. Washington, D.C.: U.S. Department of Commerce, Economic and Statistics Administration.

Jackson, John. 1992. *The World Trading System: Law and Policy of International Economic Relations.* Cambridge, Mass.: MIT Press.

Lee, Thea M. 1995. "False Prophets: The Selling of NAFTA." Briefing Paper. Washington, D.C.: Economic Policy Institute.

McMillion, Charles W. 1995. "New Global Realities and Old Trade Theories." Presentation to Congressional Fair Trade Caucus, February 24. Washington, D.C.: MBG Information Services.

Mishel, Lawrence and Jared Bernstein. 1994. *The State of Working America 1994-95.* Economic Policy Institute Series. Armonk, N.Y.: M.E. Sharpe.

Prestowitz, Clyde V. and Lawrence Chimerine. 1994. *Closing the Trade Gap With Japan.* Washington, D.C.: Economic Strategy Institute.

Sachs, Jeffrey and Howard J. Shatz. 1994. "Trade and Jobs in U.S. Manufacturing." *Brookings Papers on Economic Activity,* No. 1, pp. 1-84.

Scott, Robert E. 1993. "Flat Earth Economics: Is There a New International Paradigm?" *Challenge,* Vol. 36, No. 5, pp. 32-9.

Scott, Robert E. 1994. *Short-Sighted Solutions: Trade and Energy Policies for the U.S. Auto Industry.* New York: Garland Publishing.

Scott, Robert E. 1995. "1994 and 1995 U.S.-Mexico Trade Data: NAFTA Impacts." Occasional Paper No. 56. College Park, Md.: Center for International Business Education and Research, University of Maryland.

Scherer, Frederic M. 1994. *Competition Policies for an Integrated World Economy.* Washington, D.C.: Brookings Institution.

Spriggs, William E. and Robert E. Scott. 1995. "Economists' Views of Workers' Rights and U.S. Trade Policy," Occasional Paper No. 60. College Park, Md.: Center for International Business Education and Research, University of Maryland.

U.S. Department of Commerce. 1995a. *National Trade Data Bank.* CD-ROM product.

U.S. Department of Commerce. 1995b. *Commerce News: U.S. International Trade in Goods and Services, December 1994.* February 17. Report No. FT-900 (94-12). Washington, D.C.: U.S. Department of Commerce.

U.S. International Trade Commission. 1994. *Potential Impact on the U.S. Economy and Industries of the GATT Uruguay Round Agreement.* Publication 2790. Washington, D.C.: USITC.

Watson, P. 1994. "The Framework for the New Trade Agenda." *Law and Policy in International Business,* Vol. 25, No. 4, p. 1252.

Wood, Adrian. 1994. *North-South Trade, Employment and Inequality: Changing Fortunes in a Skill-Driven World.* New York: Oxford University Press.

CHAPTER 15

INTERNATIONAL LABOR STANDARDS

The Missing Clause in Trade and Investment Agreements

by Jerome Levinson

LIKE A LOCOMOTIVE HURTLING DOWN THE TRACKS, THE FREE TRADE AND investment express is gathering speed, transforming the rules of the international economy at a breathtaking pace. Within the past two years, the Clinton Administration has obtained congressional approval of the North American Free Trade Agreement (NAFTA) and the General Agreement on Tariffs and Trade (GATT). In November 1994, President Clinton and 17 other leaders of countries in the Asia Pacific Economic Cooperation (APEC) forum agreed on lifting barriers to trade and investment over a 25-year period. In December 1994 the heads of state of all the nations in the Western hemisphere (with the exception of Cuba) agreed in Miami to the creation of a "Free Trade Area of the Americas" by the year 2005. By removing barriers to trade and investment, these agreements, if fully implemented, will greatly improve the opportunities for multinational corporations and banks to deploy capital across national boundaries.

In contrast, worker rights are left at the station. The growing bitterness of the debate within the United States over the free trade and investment regime, noted at the time of the NAFTA debate, is attributable, in great part, to this growing disparity between the international rules governing capital and labor. If that disparity continues, the bitterness will only become worse.

Yet, the United States has at its disposal instruments of policy that would enable it, both on its own and in partnership with other nations, to substantially redress this imbalance. What has been lacking is the po-

---

Jerome Levinson is an adjunct professor at the American University and a former general counsel of the Inter-American Development Bank.

litical willingness of American administrations to elevate worker rights to the same plane of importance as the property rights of big business.

The New Focus on Worker Rights

Why has the issue of linking worker rights to trade and investment agreements, as well as to the lending by multilateral financial institutions like the World Bank, the International Monetary Fund, and the Inter-American Development Bank, arisen now with such intensity? Four factors are at work: the stagnation of U.S. wages over a 20-year period, the debt crisis of the 1980s, the end of the Cold War, and NAFTA and the conclusion of the Uruguay Round of the GATT.

Stagnation of real wages. Average real wages in the United States have stagnated for the past 20 years, with younger and non-college-educated workers experiencing significant reductions in earnings.[1] Academic studies disagree as to the relative importance of foreign competition as a cause of this stagnation,[2] but 10 years ago the Morgan Guaranty Trust Company summed up the relationship it had observed between foreign competition and the stagnation of real wages in the United States: "[A]verage real wage gains have been negligible, maintaining their stagnation of the last ten years or more." Foreign competition, it noted, "has been the key factor."[3] U.S.-based multinational corporations, said Morgan, were well positioned to take advantage of these tendencies: "The long run shift of comparative advantage in manufacturing to the NICs [newly industrializing countries] helped them penetrate the U.S. domestic market even before the dollar's rise. U.S. manufacturers are keenly aware of the cost savings attainable through contracting for production in low wage areas abroad." This same trend has accelerated recently, particularly with respect to Mexico.

American workers know this story. They perceive that companies are more willing to use foreign competition and the threat of moving production to low-wage areas to achieve concessions in collective bargaining. This perception of the link between the relocation of production abroad and wage stagnation has fueled a deep disenchantment with the free trade and investment regime.

The debt crisis. The debt crisis began in August 1982 when Mexico defaulted on its international loans from commercial banks. In doing so, it brought an end to the direct access to international credit markets that the newly industrialized countries had enjoyed in the preceding decade. Throughout the rest of the 1980s, these countries then became primarily concerned with attracting more foreign direct investment rather than loans. Developing country governments dismantled many restrictions on foreign investment, such as limitations on ownership and local content requirements.

Exports from these countries were increasingly targeted on the United States, the market relatively most open to Third World imports. In contrast, other industrial countries' imports from these regions were flat.[4] The multinational financial institutions increasingly emphasized export-led growth and the removal of barriers to foreign capital as conditions for granting loans. Countries such as Mexico and Indonesia were reluctant to modify repressive labor relations regimes, since a cheap supply of labor constituted an important selling point in attracting foreign investment.

The end of the Cold War. During the Cold War, the U.S. government's tendency to tolerate abusive labor relations practices in Third World countries was offset by the fear of communism. The 1917 Bolshevik revolution in Russia created competition, worldwide, for the allegiance of workers. Fear of communist domination of international labor movements led to U.S. support for the establishment of the International Labor Organization (ILO) and a list of worker rights known as "Labor's Magna Charta": the right of association, a wage "adequate to maintain a reasonable standard of living," an eight-hour work day, and the principle that "men and women should receive equal remuneration for work of equal value."[5]

The Cold War intensified U.S. fears that workers in poor countries would be seduced by the allure of communist propaganda. The United States aligned itself with trade union movements that were independent of the communists. Sometimes, as in Chile in the 1980s, these movements joined popular coalitions in opposition to military governments. Multinational corporations could not count on an unambiguous anti-labor, anti-union climate supported by the U.S. government.

This situation changed with the end of the Cold War. Instead, U.S. enthusiasm for fostering free trade unions lapsed. U.S. government policy concentrated on establishing the conditions necessary for attracting foreign investment. These conditions did not include encouraging respect for basic worker rights.

The end of the Cold War had a further consequence. Eastern Europe and the former Soviet Union abandoned the socialist economic model; they entered the competition for the same pool of investment capital as the newly industrializing countries and other developing countries. China, nominally still committed to socialist norms, began to compete aggressively for foreign investment; India, one of the most closed economies in the world, with a traditional deep suspicion of foreign investment, changed direction and dismantled many of the obstacles to direct investment by foreigners.

The cumulative effect of these changes in the international economic environment—the increased ability of U.S.-based multinational corporations to relocate production abroad, the debt crisis, the embrace of export-led economic growth by the newly industrialized countries, the end of the Cold War, and the heightened global competition for foreign investment—strengthened the position of capital relative to workers, not only in the United States but around the world.

NAFTA and GATT. The proposal for NAFTA crystallized these tendencies in a way that nothing before it had done. Mexico was unlike other low-wage countries: in addition to cheap labor (one-seventh the cost of American factory labor), Mexico was endowed with a sophisticated entrepreneurial and middle class, attuned to U.S. tastes and values; a high-productivity export sector close to the United States; reasonable infrastructure and communications facilities; and a labor sector tightly controlled by a government anxious to attract foreign investment.

Mexico agreed in NAFTA to an intellectual property regime in keeping with U.S. desires and to provisions that barred it from imposing restrictions on foreign investment. These provisions institutionalized President Carlos Salinas's unilateral initiatives. The way thus seemed clear for a surge in foreign investment, primarily from the United States but also from Japan and other advanced countries, that would make Mexico a major export platform for goods and services destined for the U.S. market. That possibility became a reality in the aftermath of the devaluation of the Mexican peso in December 1994; with the relative price of Mexican goods falling, Mexico quickly converted a trade deficit with the United

States into a surplus. This turnabout undermined the original rationale for NAFTA, that is, that a rising U.S. trade surplus with Mexico would result in the creation of substantial net new jobs in the United States.

And when the Uruguay Round of the GATT was concluded in December 1994, largely meeting U.S. demands for stricter protection of property rights of U.S. corporations, an international trade and investment regime now seemed in place that would facilitate not only trade in goods and services but also the mobility of investment capital.

The Case for International Labor Standards

President Clinton has said:

> While we continue to tear down anti-competitive practices and other barriers to trade, we simply have to ensure that our economic policies also protect the environment and the well-being of workers. And as we bring into the orbit of global trade people who can benefit from the investment and trading opportunities we offer, we must ensure that their policies benefit the interests of their workers.[6]

Clinton's affirmation of worker rights as an essential ingredient of the newly emerging international trade and investment regime reflected the intense opposition that had arisen among workers within the United States to NAFTA and GATT. That opposition was based in large part on the growing perception that, in the absence of such linkage, there would be a great temptation for countries to compete for the limited pool of investment capital by racing to the bottom with labor (and environmental) conditions.

This tendency was given its most candid expression by the Prime Minister of Malaysia in an interview with the *Wall Street Journal:*

> "The likelihood is that to resolve your immigration problem from Mexico, you will move your production there but prevent others from doing so," he said. As a result, he fears, U.S. producers could take advantage of cheap labor in Mexico to produce products now imported from Asia....The prime minister said he doesn't want Malaysian workers to follow those in South Korea where strikes have brought higher wages but slower productivity growth, contributing to an economic slowdown.[7]

In other words, in order for Malaysia to compete with low-wage

Mexico and its repressive labor relations regime, Malaysia must maintain a similar regime.

Certainly it is true that, in countries like Mexico, there is a continuous general downward pressure on wages. This is a function of underdevelopment: migration from depressed rural areas to urban centers constantly replenishes a pool of workers willing to work for subsistence wages. But it is quite another thing when governments deliberately prevent workers from organizing independent trade unions that would have the capacity to negotiate aggressively for a fair share of productivity gains.

In Brazil, where truly independent trade unions are allowed to function, and where rural migration from the impoverished northeast to the industrialized south and center of the country has been endemic, an independent union movement is able to influence national economic policy and, at the plant level, effectively represent worker interests. That influence has been compatible with an industrial plant that has been increasingly competitive internationally and has helped to channel worker energies into electoral politics and pressure for progressive social policies. Thus, it is not necessarily true that repressive labor practices are essential to maintenance of an international competition policy.

American workers and others in advanced industrial societies are doubly disadvantaged. They are asked to compete with workers in Mexico, Indonesia, and Malaysia, for example, where the governments, in order to gain competitive advantage, do not permit free trade unions to function. Wages, benefits, and working conditions in these countries are often deliberately repressed, with the active collusion of the government. At the same time, workers in the United States are assured that the free trade and investment regime is in their interest because it will open markets for American exports. But a policy of labor repression stunts the growth of a domestic market for such exports among U.S. trading partners.

Not surprisingly, then, American workers and their counterparts in other advanced industrialized societies increasingly see an international trade and investment regime that appears indifferent, and frequently downright hostile, to worker rights. And they are right to see it in that light.

Congressional Initiatives

The U.S. Congress has in the past explicitly recognized the anomaly of aggressively pursuing an open international trade and investment system without a simultaneous commitment to respect for basic worker rights. In the 1980s, it gave the executive branch the authority to deny the advantages of preferential trade agreements to countries that failed to respect internationally recognized worker rights. For example, the Caribbean Basin Initiative, which allowed duty-free entry into the United States of products from beneficiary countries in Central America and the Caribbean, gave the President discretion to deny such status to a country that failed to afford workers "reasonable workplace conditions" and the right "to organize and bargain collectively."[8]

The Generalized System of Preferences legislation, like the Caribbean Basin Initiative, permits duty-free entry of selected products from designated beneficiary countries. In 1984, the Congress adopted an amendment to the legislation that excluded any country that "has not taken or is not taking steps to afford internationally recognized worker rights to workers." The amendment defined such rights to include freedom of association; the right to organize and bargain collectively; prohibitions on forced labor; a minimum age for the employment of children; and acceptable conditions of work with respect to minimum wages, hours of work, and occupational safety and health.[9]

Another worker rights provision was adopted in 1985 relating to the Overseas Private Investment Corporation, a federally chartered and operated corporation that provides insurance and financing for American-owned private investment in developing countries. The 1985 amendments required that insurance and financing be denied to U.S. companies investing in countries that are not "taking steps to adopt and implement laws that extend internationally recognized worker rights as defined in [the Generalized System of Preferences Renewal Act]."[10] Congress instructed the U.S. trade representative to consider whether a country is "taking steps" to promote worker rights by determining whether it is a signatory to the ILO Charter, has laws that parallel the Generalized System of Preferences list of internationally recognized worker rights, and continues to make progress implementing these rights. Three years later, in the 1988 Omnibus Trade and Competitiveness Act, Congress added a worker rights amendment that defines unfair trade practices subject to retaliatory countermeasures. It thus elevated abuse of worker rights to the same status of unfair trade practices as threats to the property rights of American corporations, "dumping," "targeting," and abuse of intellectual property rights.[11] The Act defines "unreasonable" labor practices as any act, policy, or practice, or any combination of acts, policies, or practices, that denies workers the same basic rights as set forth in the Generalized System of Preferences legislation, with the additional requirement that it constitute "a persistent pattern of conduct."

More recently, in 1994, the Congress extended the same principle of respect for internationally recognized worker rights to legislation governing U.S. participation in the Bretton Woods institutions and the regional development banks. The secretary of the treasury is directed to "instruct" the U.S. executive director of each international financial institution governed by the legislation to use the "voice and vote" of the United States in each such institution to encourage borrowing countries to "guarantee internationally recognized worker rights," as defined in the Omnibus Trade and Competition Act.[12]

The cumulative effect of these worker rights amendments over the past decade ought to elevate protection of worker rights to the same plane as protection of the property rights of American corporations.

The Executive Branch Drops the Ball

The executive branch has not shared the congressional determination to link effective enforcement of worker rights to the newly emerging international trade and investment regime. The North American Agreement on Labor Cooperation (NAALC), negotiated by the Clinton Administration as a parallel agreement to NAFTA, excluded industrial relations—the right to freely associate, organize, and strike—from dispute settlement procedures that could end in fines or sanctions. And even where sanctions were contemplated, for example, when there has been a "persistent pattern" of failing to enforce laws relating to health and safety, child labor, or minimum wages, the procedures were so convoluted that the chief Mexican negotiator felt safe in assuring Mexican entrepreneurs that it was highly improbable that the stage of sanctions would ever be reached.[13] The NAALC thus failed to confront the central problem of Mexican labor relations: the failure of Mexican authorities to enforce their own laws, constitution, and international commitments to assure internationally recognized worker rights.[14]

This failure of the NAALC to protect worker rights is in striking contrast to NAFTA's protection of corporate property rights. The chapters on intellectual property and investment are tightly drafted and contain clear sanctions for violations and a detailed mechanism for settlement of disputes. Furthermore, they are incorporated into the main body of the agreement.[15]

In concluding the Uruguay Round of negotiations of GATT, the Clinton Administration succeeded only in obtaining an agreement to put the issue of worker rights on the agenda for discussion by a working group. At the same time, it untied labor and human rights considerations from trade and investment negotiations with China. It was willing, however, to risk a major confrontation with China over that country's failure to protect the intellectual property rights of American corporations, continuing the double standard evident in the NAFTA negotiation. And despite egregious abuse of worker rights in Indonesia, it has failed to revoke trade preferences for that country. Indeed, since 1984 the revocation of preferences has been used more to punish politically offending regimes than as an instrument for affirming American commitment to worker rights.[16]

A Coherent Policy to Protect Worker Rights

The architecture for a coherent American policy with respect to worker rights related to trade, investment, and development policy is in place. What is needed is political will.

First, the North American Agreement of Labor Cooperation should be renegotiated to incorporate industrial relations issues as a grievance that could result in trade sanctions. The grievance procedure itself should be streamlined and simplified so that its use becomes a real possibility. A number of actions have been brought before the U.S. National Administrative Office, which was established under the NAALC, alleging that Mexico has failed to assure the right of free association nominally guaranteed to Mexican workers by Mexican labor law and Mexico's constitution.

A recent decision by the National Administrative Office involving the Mexican operations of Sony graphically illustrates how the requirement that unions be registered with Mexican authorities is used by those authorities to obstruct the formation of unions independent of government control.[17] This is a part of the larger problem of Mexican development policy, in which independent unions are deliberately suppressed and wages kept down for the purpose of attracting foreign investment.

Second, the Administration should set forth a clear and consistent position that core worker rights are to be an integral element of any future GATT negotiation. That position should be closely coordinated with like-minded European governments and other participants. Undoubtedly, such a position will encounter opposition from the governments of a number of major developing countries, particularly in Asia, that see repressive labor relations regimes as part of their competitive advantage and the demand for worker rights as cover for protectionist tendencies in the advanced industrial countries.

But internationally recognized worker rights are a necessary corollary to an international free trade and investment regime. Without such rights, the system is unbalanced and is not deserving of the support of the American worker. It is worth noting that unions (and workers) in a number of developing countries (Malaysia, Indonesia, Chile) often seek support from U.S. sympathizers to achieve the rights that are not accorded them by their own governments. When these governments oppose making internationally recognized worker rights a part of trade and investment negotiations, they are not always speaking on behalf of their own workers.

Third, the Generalized System of Preferences legislation, which increasingly appears to be a vehicle for multinational corporations to take advantage of repressive labor relations regimes and increase exports to the United States, should be reconsidered. If extended at all, such extension should be limited to a selected number of African countries, where the rationale for such preferential status is clear.

It is difficult to conceive any basis, for example, for continued preferential status for Malaysia other than the fact that important U.S. electronic companies have established manufacturing plants there. And the failure by the USTR to recommend denying such status to Indonesia, a notorious abuser of worker rights, makes a mockery of the worker rights provisions in the Generalized System of Preferences. It is no answer to say that denial of such preferences would prejudice American companies that might lose out on important contracts to, say, Japan. A country like Indonesia needs the United States as much if not more than the United States needs it. Japan is no more likely to open its market to Indonesian manufactured goods than it has been to U.S. products. And, for geopolitical reasons, Indonesia needs the United States to offset the influence in Asia of Japan and, increasingly, China.

Fourth, the Administration should aggressively assert the "voice and vote" of the United States in the multilateral financial institutions to persuade them to incorporate effective implementation of worker rights in the country performance criteria they use in allocating resources among their borrower-member countries. These institutions undermine core worker rights by their single-minded insistence upon promoting labor market flexibility, which in practice often translates into enabling companies to arbitrarily fire workers.[18]

Finally, the Administration should seek an enhanced role for the International Labor Organization. Determinations of worker rights abuse by that organization could be utilized as a part of the multilateral financial institutions' evaluation of worker rights in its country performance assessments, and as one of the grounds for determination under U.S. legislation of individual country compliance with worker rights mandates.

The ILO has the advantage of being both a multilateral organization and one that includes labor and management representatives. It is also a United Nations affiliated organization, like the Bretton Woods institutions, although it is distrusted as an "interested party" by these institutions. An enhanced role for the ILO would not only take the sharp edge off U.S. promotion of international worker rights, it would also introduce a needed element of balance into the considerations of the multilateral financial institutions. Above all, it would end the current incoherence of a U.S. policy that nominally promotes respect for worker rights but funds institutions that undermine respect for such rights.

The dismantling of barriers to trade in goods and services is, in conjunction with other factors such as technology, corporate downsizing, and changes in the workplace, eroding the social compact in the United States that facilitated the right of labor to organize free trade unions, bargain collectively, and strike. That legislation represented a political consensus that an unbridled market for labor was not in the interest of American society. But the philosophy underlying that body of legislation is being supplanted by the internationalization of production and the increasingly free movement of capital and goods and services.

The question for the future is whether American political leadership adapts to this new international economic environment, as it did to the integration of the American continental market, by trying to assure an equitable balance between capital and labor that permits the gains from advances in productivity to be broadly shared. And, in practical terms, that goal means an aggressive assertion, unilaterally and in the international arena, of the proposition that internationally recognized worker rights are as important to an international trade and investment regime as is the protection of corporate property rights.

Notes

1. Mishel and Bernstein 1994, chapter 3.
2. See Belman and Lee 1995 for a survey of this literature.
3. Morgan Guaranty 1985.
4. IMF 1985.
5. Charnovitz 1987.
6. Clinton 1994.
7. *Wall Street Journal,* March 3, 1993.
8. U.S. Congress 1983.
9. U.S. Congress 1984.
10. U.S. Congress 1985.
11. U.S. Congress 1988.
12. U.S. Congress 1994.
13. Negrete 1993.
14. Levinson 1993.
15. Levinson 1993.
16. Amato 1990.
17. U.S. National Administrative Office 1995.
18. Levinson 1994.

REFERENCES

Amato, Theresa A. 1990. "Labor Rights Conditionality: United States Trade Legislation and the International Trade Order." *New York University Law Review*, Vol. 65, April, pp. 79, 115.

Belman, Dale and Thea Lee. 1995. "International Trade and the Performance of U.S. Labor Markets." In Robert Blecker, ed., *U.S. Trade Policy and Global Growth*. Economic Policy Institute Series. Armonk, N.Y.: M.E. Sharpe.

Charnovitz, Steve. 1987. "International Trade and Worker Rights." *SAIS Review*, Vol. 7, No. 1, pp. 185-89.

Clinton, William. 1992. "Expanding Trade and Creating American Jobs." Speech Delivered at North Carolina State University. Raleigh, N.C., October 4.

Clinton, William. 1994. "President Clinton on Trade and Labor Standards." Remarks by the President in Statement with European Union Leaders, January 11.

International Monetary Fund. 1985. *Annual Report*. Washington D.C.: IMF.

Levinson, Jerome I. 1993. *The Labor Side Accord to the North American Free Trade Agreement: An Endorsement of Abuse of Worker Rights in Mexico*. Briefing Paper Series. Washington, D.C.: Economic Policy Institute.

Levinson, Jerome I. 1994. *New Priorities in Financing Latin American Development: Balancing Worker Rights, Democracy, and Financial Reform*. Washington, D.C.: Economic Policy Institute.

Mishel, Lawrence and Jared Bernstein. 1994. *The State of Working America 1994-95*. Economic Policy Institute Series. Armonk, N.Y.: M.E. Sharpe.

Morgan Guaranty Trust Company. 1985. "Countering World Deflation." *World Financial Markets* (Newsletter), December.

Negrete, Ingrid. 1993. "Mexico Official Defends Nafta Dispute Process." *Journal of Commerce*, August 20.

U.S. Congress. 1983. *Interest and Dividend Tax Compliance Act of 1983*. 19 U.S.C.@@ 2701-2706 (1988).

U.S. Congress. 1984. *The Generalized System of Preferences Renewal Act of 1984*. 19 U.S.C. @@ 2461-2465 (1988).

U.S. Congress. 1985. *Overseas Private Investment Corporation Amendments Act of 1985*. Codified in scattered sections of 22 U.S.C. (Supp. III 1985) and 31 U.S.C. (Supp. III 1985).

U.S. Congress. 1988. *The Omnibus Trade and Competitiveness Act of 1988*. 19 U.S.C. @ 2411 (1988).

U.S. Congress. 1994. *Foreign Relations, Export Financing and Related Programs 1995, Appropriations and 1994 Supplemental Appropriations.* 22 U.S.C. 1621, Encouragement of Fair Labor Practices (1994).

U.S. National Administrative Office, North American Agreement on Labor Cooperation. 1995. *Public Report of Review, NAO Submission 94003.* Washington, D.C.: Bureau of International Labor Affairs, U.S. Department of Labor.

CHAPTER 16

DEFENSE CONVERSION

Investing the Peace Dividend

by Michael Oden & Ann Markusen

POLICY MAKERS ARE ONLY BEGINNING TO REALIZE THE EXTENT TO WHICH the Cold War provided an over-arching rationale for national government activities, both small and large. The need for a modern national highway system was met through the passage of the National Defense Highways Act, secondary and higher education gained impetus from Sputnik, and even the National Endowment for the Arts was established to meet a 1960s Soviet cultural offensive head-on. The sputtering out of the Cold War provided an opportunity to establish a much-needed offensive on the home front—a new national mission to generate sustainable economic growth and tangibly improve the quality of life for citizens and workers. The conversion of the Cold War economy provides a framework within which science and technology policy, industrial policy, and public investment choices can be redesigned to meet fundamental national needs.

Yet today, in the absence of a large external threat, the basic legitimacy of federal government functions is under fire and a new ethos of budget austerity has taken hold. Ironically, only the military budget, a bloated artifact of the Cold War, remains sacrosanct.

A clear opportunity still exists to change direction and enjoy the fruits of a post-Cold War world. Even though military budgets (currently at over $260 billion in budget authority) stubbornly remain what economists term "sticky downward," there is strong public opinion favoring other spending priorities. To achieve defense savings and allocate them

Michael Oden is coordinator of the military conversion and economic adjustment research program at the Project on Regional and Industrial Economics (PRIE) at Rutgers University. Ann Markusen is director of PRIE.

to sounder public investments elsewhere requires a coherent and well-funded but temporary conversion strategy tied to new public investment projects meeting popular public needs. Comparable to impressive efforts in the past to mobilize for war, the nation needs a mobilization for peace, targeted at two goals: moving significant resources as efficiently as possible from military-dedicated missions to civilian ones; and at the same time stabilizing and improving economic opportunities for defense-dependent firms, workers, and communities.

We briefly review the status of military spending and defense needs and the results of our research on recent progress in reorienting the nation's workplaces, military bases, technology, human resources, research labs, and local economies. While crediting new conversion initiatives with surprisingly good results, given their low level of funding and less than participatory structure, we suggest a much bolder five-year conversion program that would make a major contribution toward the nation's economic revitalization. A robust conversion program, we argue, must tie conversion assistance to new job creation in sectors and activities that demonstrate a clear public interest and national need.

The "Sticky Downwards" Defense Budget

Currently, Pentagon planners and military contractors bemoan the fall in military spending from the unprecedented levels of the mid-1980s. Weapons procurement has indeed dropped by 65% in real terms since 1985. However, comparing current spending to that of the 1980s to argue against further cuts is not compelling: military procurement in the mid-1980s substantially exceeded (in real terms) procurement in every post-World War II year except 1952, the peak of Korean/Cold War mobilization.[1] Defense spending remains at or above Cold War levels in real terms. The Clinton FY 1996 request would give the Pentagon 2% more in inflation-adjusted dollars than it had in 1975 at the dead-center of the Cold War.[2] Military budget authority in the latest defense plan remains slightly higher than levels in the mid-1970s. Astonishingly, spending in the 1990s is projected to be at about 85% of average real spending in the previous four decades of the Cold War even though our current most lethal adversary, North Korea, spends about $5 billion-$10 billion on its military, or 2-4% of what we do.[3]

Further military cuts to bring spending into line with realistic security needs is a very attractive source of badly needed public investment for three reasons. First, we do not need current levels to be secure. Independent scholarly assessments of defense requirements suggest we could get by on one-third to two-thirds of what we now spend yet still retain the world's biggest military, capable of meeting all feasible security challenges.[4] Savings would be greater to the extent we developed serious cooperative security and nonoffensive defense strategies.[5] But what about the unexpected: the re-emergence of a dangerous dictatorship out of the tumult of the former Soviet Union, or aggression by North Korea, Iraq, Iran? Given the nearly complete unraveling of the Russian military establishment, the United States and its rich allies would have roughly five years to ratchet up their defense capabilities to meet any re-emerging threat. Regional threats by small, relatively poor countries could be managed with much less military force structure and greater dedication to fashioning strong multilateral responses.

Second, military expenditure is a poor foundation for innovation and technical dynamism for the nation. In the first two decades after World War II, computers, semiconductors, communications satellites, and commercial aircraft were nurtured by both government research and development and procurement markets.[6] Military R&D and procurement support was hardly an efficient way to bring forth new technologies and industries, but it was the main large-scale public mechanism to support the national innovation effort. In more recent years, university and private R&D efforts are yielding more important innovations, and increasingly the Pentagon itself must turn to the commercial market, even to foreign firms, for the leading-edge technologies it needs. Yet well over half of public sector R&D is still committed to increasingly esoteric military weapons work.

Finally, public opinion unambiguously favors reducing, not increasing, military spending. Americans continue to want a strong defense, but they do not endorse the global Lone Ranger prerogatives embodied in the Clinton Administration's bottom-up review (which recommended a defense plan premised on fighting two wars simultaneously) and the expense entailed. A recent survey shows that, while only 12% of people polled think we spend too little on defense or space, nearly 80% think we do not spend enough to improve education or health care.[7]

But reducing military spending and freeing up funds for productive public investment has proven exceedingly difficult. For obvious reasons, the Pentagon (and other agencies like the Department of Energy and NASA, which have major defense programs) is resistant to efforts to efficiently realign them with a more realistic security posture. First, there is the relatively monolithic power of the Pentagon and related insider security experts to assess security needs and justify its budgets. No other major public agency is so insulated from public scrutiny, and none elicits fewer challenges from independent scholars, despite its size and spotty record with regard to weapons system performance, cost overruns, and repeated instances of bribery and fraud. Advisory boards setting agendas for future military strategy and weapons procurement programs are typically packed with representatives of defense contractors and Cold War institutes and are devoid of input from ordinary citizens or public interest groups.[8] By contrast, welfare and labor programs are heavily scrutinized by independent evaluators, often at public expense.

Even when the Pentagon is willing to end weapons programs or close bases, the geographical concentration of prime contracts and isolation of many military facilities create serious political counter-pressures.[9] Absent real alternatives like major public investment markets, military dependent companies and communities marshall all available resources to keep defense dollars flowing, even when it is demonstrably clear that continued funding is simply an exorbitant public works program. The 1980s buildup, by stimulating job growth and migration to these types of communities, compounded the problem by shifting political power toward "gunbelt" locales in the 1990 redistricting of Congress. Politicians from these communities have often been in the forefront of advocating a meaningful national conversion program, but, rebuffed to date, they are often forced to fall back on maneuvering for more military spending.

Finally, the relatively weak performance of the economy, especially in terms of job and wage growth, means that fewer opportunities exist for firms, workers, and communities to find alternative livelihoods when defense cuts loom. While deindustrialization in the 1980s was partly obscured by the debt-financed military buildup, in the 1990s the two are occurring in tandem, as defense cuts and broader fiscal policy austerity reinforce new "lean and mean" corporate strategies to throw workers out of work. This trend is markedly different from past periods of defense cuts, after World War II, Korea, and even Vietnam. Thus, even though the cuts are relatively more gradual today than in the past, the resulting displacement calls for more concerted efforts at short-term structural adjustment.

The Record: Five Years of Defense Conversion 1989-94

Defense outlays have been falling since 1989, following reductions in budget authority that began in 1986 to reverse the Reagan buildup. Since 1989, defense budget authority has declined by roughly $90 billion in real terms, and defense outlays by over $80 billion. In the spring of 1993 the newly elected Clinton Administration launched the Defense Reinvestment and Conversion initiative. When unveiled, it appeared to be a rather bold $19 billion, five-year effort to offset the effects of post-Cold War cutbacks on companies, workers, and communities. It included projects directly related to conversion and adjustment and a group of new civilian R&D initiatives that offered some opportunities for defense-serving companies and institutions. However, funding for the proposed program was concentrated in later years, and the support needed to fully finance the initiative has proved elusive, given ambitious deficit-reduction targets. Actual appropriations for the conversion and reinvestment initiative for 1993 and 1994 fell below the levels proposed in the initial five-year plan. Moreover, some of what was counted as conversion and technology reinvestment included ongoing defense programs that were repackaged and downsizing costs such as early retirement and compensation for uprooted Department of Defense (DoD) personnel.

The lion's share of new conversion funding went to dual-use technology initiatives, including both the Technology Reinvestment Project (TRP) and ongoing projects of the Advanced Research Projects Agency (ARPA) in the DoD that had, according to program proponents, a dual-use focus. Accepting most administration classifications, the TRP and other dual-use initiatives received more than $2.3 billion in funding over 1993-94 fiscal years. The second-largest share of overall spending went to pay transitioning costs for DoD uniformed and nonuniformed employees—nearly 27% of the total. Another 20% went to assist firms in more direct conversion efforts and for defense industry worker and community assistance.[10]

In addition, new money was provided to an array of civilian R&D projects that may provide some opportunities for defense-oriented companies. Activities such as the Intelligent Vehicle Highway System, the NASA Aeronautics Initiative, and the Advance Technologies Program of the Commerce Department provide some new R&D and product development opportunities to defense firms. These and other initiatives were funded at roughly $930 million in 1994. Total funding for conversion-related initiatives was in the neighborhood of $4.4 billion over 1991-94; adding in the money for all the other federal technology projects brings the total to about $5.3 billion.

However, the total package, broadly defined, represents only about 5% offset to defense cuts.[11] In curious contrast, the cost cap on two Seawolf submarines currently being built solely to "preserve the submarine industrial base" equals $4.75 billion, close to the total spent on all conversion and new civil R&D in the administration package.[12] Most of this entire program is now being targeted by Republican budget cutters.

Yet our research suggests that certain well-targeted federal conversion programs have been surprisingly successful despite the limited scale and scope of the overall program. This finding has been most true of programs to aid community economic development planning and providing technical assistance and loans to small- and medium-sized firms. It is less true of R&D support and worker-adjustment programs. Furthermore, even where federal dollars are not forthcoming, state and local efforts and "best practice" initiatives by defense companies themselves have created successful models for conversion, showing that the naysayers are wrong. In what follows, we briefly review the record of transition in the defense economy over the past five years.

Services for Affected Workers

DoD personnel. Roughly 500,000 uniformed personnel left the services between 1989 and 1994, and close to 300,000 nonuniformed DoD personnel have also been released over this period.[13] Early retirement and severance payments for DoD employees are decent, but actual training and transition assistance is weak.[14] The most substantial training and education benefits are actually available to uniformed personnel through the Montgomery GI Bill.

More importantly, the downsizing of the armed forces has not been accompanied by a comparable "job start" strategy for job growth for the communities and occupational groups who have increasingly relied upon the armed services as a path for upward and interregional mobility over the decades. Inner-city and rural youth are disproportionately represented among young recruits since the military became the main employment and training avenue open to individuals from disadvantaged groups. As involuntary separations have increased and the number of slots diminished, few new opportunities have opened up. The Clinton Administration's National Service Program was designed as a partial substitute for career-launching military service, substituting two-year civilian service jobs for military ones. But it has been funded at a woefully inadequate level, providing only 30,000 summer jobs and many fewer year-round positions, many of which go to middle-class, educated students. Budget rescissions currently proposed by Republicans to the FY 1995 authorization would gut the program. Without a shift of defense dollars to this complementary civilian job creation program, the on-the-job training, skills enhancement, and employment available to urban and rural youth will shrink dramatically.

Defense industry workers. Adjustment programs for defense industry workers form the most disappointing front in the conversion effort. In community after community where defense facilities have closed, the record resembles that of auto and steel regions in the 1980s. Two years after layoffs, 20-40% of the workforce is still unemployed, a large number of those who have found work have taken substantial pay cuts, and many have had to involuntarily retire early or migrate to other regions. Defense workers have been on the front lines of deindustrialization in the 1990s.

For the most part, the failure of defense-worker-adjustment programs to effectively deal with displacement can be attributed to the virtual absence of meaningful federal and state policies to deal with structural unemployment. Defense-worker adjustment was tacked onto an existing federal job retraining architecture designed to deal with cyclical unemployment. The current approach lacks the tools to improve labor-market flexibility in the case of a structural change such as a major fall in defense activity.

Examples of the system's specific failures abound. If a company uses attrition or downsizes slowly, those involuntarily laid off aren't served. Even in cases of mass layoffs, defense companies have often shirked Worker Assistance and Retraining Notification (WARN) provisions. Workers are often kept in the dark about benefits and programs for which they qualify. There is little customized counseling and almost no worker involvement in the design of programs. Most training institutions offer programs tailored to a different labor segment—first time, entry-level job seekers. There is little information about the quality of training or post-training experience, and almost no accountability on the part of the institutions themselves. Defense workers tend to be concentrated in occupations where growth is slow or negative, and hence a significant subset need long-term retraining in entirely new occupations and skills. Yet current programs offer only short-term retraining and placement services. Income support for workers in training is often of inadequate duration to cover one's family and housing expenses while pursuing a quality program.[15]

One new approach pioneered by the United Auto Workers at their Warren, Mich., tank plant involves setting up a Workers Center off site, but close to the plant, where laid-off workers can spend time receiving individualized counseling, retraining, job search services, and adjustment assistance while networking with other workers in similar straits. Although more expensive than the low-level one- or two-day résumé-writing workshops the week before layoffs, such centers will ensure more rapid reemployment at better jobs.[16]

To cover all workers, offer effective counseling, and provide income support would cost the federal government about $5 billion to $6 billion a year. Under Secretary Robert Reich, the Department of Labor's ambitious new program for a comprehensive worker-adjustment and retraining overhaul is currently limping along at levels far below this. However, this amount could be raised easily by canceling a few Pentagon Cold War white elephants, like the Seawolf submarine, the new nuclear-powered aircraft carrier, and the irrepressible Star Wars research program.

But even if worker-adjustment programs were fully funded and improved substantially, defense workers across the nation would still be asking, "retraining for what?" Currently, job programs are assigned to the fiefdom of the Department of Labor, cordoned off from the agencies like Treasury, Commerce, and Defense where the big decisions on the economy are made. As long as economic policy continues to be fashioned without regard to worker displacement, and programs for workers are designed without linkages to job creation, workers will be justifiably skeptical. Although unions like the Machinists and the United Auto Workers and the union-supported Work and Technology Institute, with its WE*CAN coalition, have been in the forefront of the conversion-design effort, union locals often feel compelled to support more defense spending and arms exports in the absence of concrete alternative job opportunities offering livable wages.

Services for Defense-Oriented Firms

Federal aid to help defense firms shift gears from military to non-DoD markets has been on the rise, but it remains a tiny percentage of procurement contract cuts. Defense companies, skilled at strategic planning for long-term weapons systems, are not required or even encouraged to do alternative use planning. They are apt to fight for a larger share of the smaller defense pie, to lobby for higher military budgets, and to push for increased arms sales abroad, thereby increasing our long-term security problems.

What defense companies are offered from Washington to diversify is generally confined to two types of programs: dual-use technology matching grants from the Pentagon's Advanced Research Projects Agency (the TRP program), funded at about $500 million in 1994 but, with budget rescissions, likely to be cut to about $120 million in FY 1995; and modest technical and management assistance through locally run business assistance or manufacturing extension services supported by various small programs in the Departments of Defense, Labor, and Commerce. The TRP's technology-development programs, the biggest element of TRP, construes the conversion challenge as a technology problem. As a result, these programs have met with mixed reviews by the companies and institutions that could utilize them. By contrast, the "softer" assistance and extension programs are establishing a good record of promoting diversification and job retention.

The biggest impediment to conversion is the encouragement and outright federal subsidy of wholesale consolidation and downsizing by the large defense firms. The risks and opportunities available determine whether companies choose conservative strategies centered on shedding labor and capacity to serve a smaller defense market, or more innovative efforts to develop new products for alternative markets. Current federal procurement, arms export, and defense industry policies have combined to make downsizing highly profitable for the largest prime contractors in the short term.[17] The big contractors have been able to slash labor and other expenses at a faster rate than sales have declined. In light of the weak incentives offered for diversification, it is unsurprising that large companies have tended to downsize into familiar defense niches.

Research on defense-dependent firms, both large and small, suggests that three major challenges confront them in this era of defense downsizing: management and organizational restructuring, market reorientation, and finance.[18] Because of the deep divergence between DoD and non-DoD markets, attempts to move into new commercial areas typically require fundamental organizational changes. Successfully converting companies have all undergone radical organizational restructuring to reposition them in commercial markets, where cost, rapid product introduction, quality, and timeliness are essential to success. Achieving the necessary improvements has often meant striking new accords with their workforces, including expanded cooperation and stakeholding. They must also build up new marketing expertise, shifting from sales efforts targeted at the Pentagon and foreign military attachés to large and diverse civilian customer bases. Also, to make the shift to new products and new markets for existing technologies, they must find new sources of finance to tide them over the six-month to two-year gap between defense cuts and successful realignment.

For the most part, federal programs do not adequately address these interrelated demobilization needs of defense companies. Technology does not rank at the top of defense companies' problems, but federal conversion programs nevertheless tend to stress technology development and deployment. Extension services perform better on this score than TRP-type technology development programs, but even here, research suggests that more modestly funded full-service programs aimed at assessing and addressing firms' financial, management, and marketing needs are more successful than pricier teaching factories and other technology-intensive approaches.[19]

Despite the inadequacy of federal interim assistance to defense companies, a surprising number are successfully converting and stemming some job loss.[20] The record is better at smaller companies, but even giants like Hughes, TRW, and Rockwell are aggressively diversifying, staking their future on high-growth civilian markets. By laying a foundation for future growth, in the long term they will likely outperform those firms, like General Dynamics, Northrop/Grumman, and McDonnell Douglas, that are simply milking their mature defense businesses. As limited as public conversion assistance has been, our research suggests that it has been crucial in helping small- and medium-sized firms survive and diversify. However, lack of demand-side opportunities from new public investment or high rates of general economic growth has meant that even successful diversifiers generally have to reduce employment significantly.

Converting the National Research and Development System

Since World War II, 30-50% of the total national R&D effort, both public and private, has been supported by defense-related missions.[21] Defense R&D also stimulated significant private R&D among prime contractors competing to win new weapons development and production contracts.[22] Since the end of the Cold War, overall public and private R&D investment has been stagnant. National R&D expenditures have grown by less than 1% annually over the 1989-93 period in real terms. As a share of GDP, national R&D fell from nearly 2.7% in 1989 to 2.5% by 1993.[23]

A substantial body of scholarship suggests that investments in military R&D are yielding fewer and fewer spillovers in the form of new technologies and revolutionary new products compared to the early postwar period, while crowding out more promising commercial R&D.[24] To effectively refortify innovation, we need to radically reorient our national R&D efforts to clear and well-understood civil and commercial goals. This is a national challenge that has substantial repercussions for the longer-term future of our economy.

In an effort to begin this transformation, the Departments of Defense, Energy, and Commerce have fashioned technology transfer and development programs to encourage the adoption of defense-financed innovations and the creation of new dual-use technologies. To date these programs, despite winning a big share of new conversion funding, have to be accorded mixed marks, for several reasons. For one, they have been heavily criticized by various groups within the business community for violating "level playing field" rules. Many smaller companies contend that giving taxpayer money to research efforts whose result is the private property of select companies and not available to others results in unfair competition. For another, much of the research, especially on the development side, would probably have been done by the companies anyway. In general it is difficult to evaluate the results of these programs, both because they are relatively new and because of the absence of good metrics, or measures for evaluation. But it is an inherent problem that improving the competitiveness of companies, often big multinationals and sometimes even foreign firms, has been conflated with improving citizen well being. Certain new technology or product developments may indeed eliminate more domestic jobs than they create. Some citizens and labor groups are increasingly critical of the absence of demonstrable payoffs in terms of jobs and community stability.

These drawbacks bolstered Republican attempts to eliminate the Department of Defense's Technology Reinvestment Program as well as Commerce's Advanced Technology Program (ATP). They have also surfaced in debates over the future of the national weapons laboratories—Los Alamos, Livermore, and Sandia—now funded at $4 billion a year and overdue for major cuts. Technology-transfer programs of large magnitudes have been mounted at the labs, each with hundreds of separate Cooperative Research and Development Agreements (CRADAs), worth hundreds of millions of dollars, mostly with large American multinational corporations. While the labs defend their industrial partnership programs as contributing to American competitiveness, critics view them as revenue-raising devices or, worse, as attempts to court big-business support in defense of their swollen budgets in Washington. Many small businesses, especially within the lab regions, are intensely critical of CRADAs as leapfrogging the region and unfairly subsidizing their larger competitors. In contrast, efforts to encourage new business formation through spinoffs of employees, ideas, and technologies receive very low levels of funding.

The labs seem reluctant to eliminate the barriers to this route for conversion, preferring to horde labor and budget resources.[25]

The big issue posed by the end of the Cold War is, what stimuli will replace the sources of research and procurement funding once provided by the military mission? Proponents of market-led growth argue for an overall curtailment of federal spending and a return of tax dollars to the private sector, but there are few reasons to believe that private-sector dynamics will really be sufficient to replace the role defense played in the economy. Global competition, corporate takeovers, and consolidations have all taken their toll on the level and growth of company-funded R&D. Without an explicit and well-funded civilian technology policy tied to an equally bold public investment and procurement program, the U.S. innovation system, untethered from its former Cold War moorings, is in severe danger of a long-term decline.

Services for Affected Communities

Military base closures. Bases are hard to close because many communities are so dependent upon them, including rural towns that host air force bases and inner cities with shipyards. To insulate the process of base closing from obstructionist politics, the Congress in the late 1980s designed a new institution, the Base Realignment and Closure Commission (BRACC), to expedite the process. The commission has succeeded in managing three rounds of base closing, in 1989, 1991, and 1993, minimizing the political distortion of the process.

However, mechanisms to effectively transform military bases into reusable land and structures for alternative uses have not kept pace. Although the Pentagon's Office of Economic Adjustment (OEA) offers modestly sized planning grants to communities requesting them, no requirement exists for advance planning by the services for future base closures. Nor is there any serious evaluation of joint use possibilities for bases while military activity continues. Encouragingly, the FY 1995 defense authorization bill at least required that communities that engage in advanced planning not be penalized as being "more prepared" for closure as their cases are considered by BRACC.[26] But base re-use is hampered by severe environmental damage at many sites, the legacy of the immunity of military bases from environmental regulation. Current Pentagon/congressional plans would lower the commitment of funds for base cleanup.

Furthermore, although the law provides for devolution of surplus military facilities to state and local government, in practice this transfer has been encumbered by military preferences for mothballing rather than closing facilities and by legal and administrative delays. DoD agencies have first claim on facilities at closed or realigned bases, and reserve forces in particular have been aggressive about acquiring base property—19 of the 26 bases slated for closure in the 1990s now house National Guard or reserve units. Their occupation of base facilities adds little to the economies of surrounding communities and may preclude alternative redevelopment of attractive facilities.[27] Moreover, funds for base redevelopment from the Economic Development Administration have been severely constrained, and are nowhere near the level needed. The resulting uncertainty for communities hosting bases has strongly skewed local economic development efforts toward keeping bases open rather than planning for closing.

Nevertheless, the historical record shows that many military bases can, over the long term, provide a foundation for successful economic development. OEA studies of 98 facilities shuttered in the 1960s and 1970s suggest that re-use resulted in a net increase in the number of civilian jobs. Although we do not yet have good data on the types of jobs created on former bases or who holds them, more recent in-depth case studies of base closing show that state and local government redevelopment has often created new jobs, expanded the tax base, and provided housing and recreational facilities for the community on former military properties.[28]

Once again, however, the successful downsizing of the domestic base structure is being hampered by a paucity of federal resources. Over the past 20 years the federal government has spent over $500 million to assist communities where bases have closed, far more than in the current program.[29] The Economic Development Administration, which sponsored and funded actual re-use projects, is still a shadow of its former self and has been retargeted for elimination by the Republican Congress. A parallel attack on DoD environmental cleanup money will only further hinder the closure process. The lack of a coherent adjustment program of adequate scale threatens to derail the base closure process entirely, a step that will fritter away federal resources maintaining totally unnecessary military facilities.

Defense industry restructuring. Of all the conversion efforts we have studied, those mounted by state and local governments to deal with defense industry restructuring receive the highest marks for effectiveness at a modest price. While many of these programs rely on federal funds, the design and delivery of services is generally managed by local economic development groups, often with substantial input from affected parties, including firms, military base commanders, trade unions, and community groups. Perhaps the greatest benefit of OEA planning grants has been the impetus they have provided for groups to coalesce around a new style of economic development planning.

In St. Louis we found that an OEA-funded effort had helped to build a region-wide economic development process that tackled the area's manufacturing restructuring problem, centered especially on downsizing at McDonnell Douglas and challenging the traditional emphasis on building downtown convention centers and casinos as the only legitimate province of economic development planning.[30] Similarly, on Long Island, active involvement by a wide range of parties, including bankers, high tech businesses, state and local development agencies, and Brookhaven and Cold Spring Harbor Labs, has helped to assemble a sophisticated menu of economic development services, from a revolving loan fund to intensive technical assistance to small- and mid-sized firms and startups. Close to 50 small- and medium-sized firms are participating, and we found clear evidence that these programs had stimulated diversification and employment retention.[31] In Massachusetts, the state's Industrial Services Program has mounted an impressive set of services for defense-dependent communities and firms, while in Washington, the state has worked on developing a cooperative network of manufacturers trying to shift gears.

Management of local economic development initiatives at the state or local level ensures that the results are closely tailored to the setting. In many cases, impending shutdowns or layoffs have precipitated a wholesale effort, aided by conversion-planning assistance, to think strategically about regional industrial policy—including an assessment of existing assets, workforce skills, and comparative advantages for alternative ways of earning a livelihood. Proposed new initiatives are then matched to this vision of the region's economic future.

These inspiring development efforts continue to be constrained by inadequate funding. Once a plan is fashioned, there is usually not enough funding from either federal or state/local sources to create the revolving loan funds, incubators, technical assistance projects, or workers' centers and networks at a scale that will change the trajectory of regional economic performance.

A Conversion Strategy With Teeth

Much of the post-Cold War conversion effort has been crafted and sold as a "competitiveness" strategy, rather than as a program for national economic recovery and innovation. Overly general and relying on new, more subtle external threats, "competitiveness" has been used to justify public support for corporate agendas, encourage wholesale downsizing, and legitimize stripping away even more regulatory and workplace protections. In practice, this strategy has turned out to be flawed, for several reasons. First, "American" companies, especially those positioned to benefit from the new-tech transfer, are increasingly multinational. They have successfully gutted the U.S. Preference Clause and other mechanisms designed to insure that domestic rather than foreign jobs result from taxpayer-financed R&D. Second, the dual-use and dual-benefit criteria governing many technology-transfer programs unduly narrow the field for real conversion by emphasizing military applications and then subsidizing a great deal of research that would have been undertaken anyway. Third, widespread criticism about picking winners and losers in public programs where the results are fully privatized may result in formidable legal challenges. Finally, "low road" competitiveness strategies based on more deregulation, wage and workplace concessions, and business tax cuts are more appealing to many in the business community.

In our view, there is no defensible substance to the competitiveness rubric as recently applied in federal policy making. But there is a crucial role for government to play in providing for infrastructure, basic innovation, and public goods. National defense can now be purchased at a much lower price, freeing up significant resources for higher priority national missions. Among the latter are environmental quality and remediation;

the development of alternative and clean energy sources; improvements in transportation systems; rebuilding of the urban infrastructure; and the provisions of better public education, training, and health care for those excluded from the current system. Each of these involves efforts that will not be forthcoming from the private sector without government leadership, and each represents a pressing public interest.

In place of competitiveness, the nation should have a new national needs strategy that embraces missions such as energy, environment, transportation, and education as new frontiers, similar to defense and space in the earlier postwar period. As in those arenas, a combination of research and procurement should be used to achieve these goals. New missions should not arise from a supply-side, technology-push approach, but from a hard-nosed assessment of national priorities. The appropriate institutions to serve those needs should be identified through a process of competition and evaluation, and resources within them reallocated to the tasks at hand. To help bridge the structural gap between currently defense-dependent firms, facilities, and communities and what will be needed in the future, a strong program of interim conversion assistance is needed.

We provide below a simple and straightforward scheme to finance a real public research and investment agenda and a conversion program with powerful incentives for resource redeployment. The following tables provide a general demonstration of how substantial defense savings could fund significant public investments in new missions. The specific priorities, programs, and implementation mechanisms would need to be debated and specified.

On the defense side, we assume that the compelling alternative defense plan offered by William Kaufmann in his book, *Assessing the Base Force: How Much Is Too Much?*, was implemented in 1993. Even with the large reductions portrayed in the table, this carefully thought-out alternative defense plan would still leave the United States with the world's dominant military force.

Instead of funding the overblown and wasteful military posture embodied in the Clinton administration's bottom-up review, we could capture resources for more vital national security needs. By expressing Kaufmann's cost estimate of an alternative force structure in real terms and subtracting it from the latest long-term defense budget plan, we could

TABLE 1
Potential Savings in Budget Authority, Administration Versus Kaufmann Alternative Security and Weapons Complex Restructuring
(Millions of 1995 Dollars)

Year	Budget Authority 1995 Defense Plan	Budget Authority Kaufmann Alternative	Net Savings From Alternative Security	Savings From Reduced Nuclear Weapons R&D	Total Net Savings
1992	$304,278	$304,278			
1993	278,966	271,455	$7,511	$522	$8,033
1994	256,887	245,250	11,638	1,022	12,660
1995	252,608	221,654	30,954	1,500	32,454
1996	239,761	200,251	39,511	1,949	41,460
1997	230,193	180,935	49,258	1,896	51,154
1998	230,211	172,165	58,046	1,844	59,890
1999	229,803	163,708	66,094	1,793	67,887
2000	232,179	155,774	76,406	1,745	78,150
Cumulative Total	1,950,609	1,611,192	339,417	12,271	351,688

Sources: Department of Defense (1994), Table 6.8; *Budget of the United States Government*, Fiscal Year 1996 (Washington, D.C.: GPO 1995), Table 5.1; Kaufmann (1992), pp. 87-93.

save over $339 billion (in real 1995 dollars) over an eight-year period. Add to this the significant savings from cutting most nuclear weapons research, and total savings climb to nearly $352 billion. Other, more radical alternative security proposals would generate even more savings.

Constraining overwrought military allocations frees up substantial resources for high-priority domestic missions:

- We propose allocating 10% of the savings to fund a serious short-term conversion drive. We would bias spending toward the middle years to help move companies, communities, and workers into the alternative markets created by the new alternative R&D and public investments as well as growing commercial markets. Based on the lessons learned

TABLE 2
Spending Available for Alternative Priorities
(Millions of 1995 Dollars)

Year	Total Alternative Security Savings	Spending on Direct Conversion Projects	Spending on Alternative Science and Technology Initiatives	Spending on Alternative Public Investment	Spending on Urban Revitalization
1993	$8,033	$3,517	$1,054	$1,957	$1,505
1994	12,660	7,034	1,313	2,438	1,875
1995	32,454	7,034	5,931	11,016	8,473
1996	41,460	7,034	8,033	14,918	11,475
1997	51,154	5,275	10,705	19,881	15,293
1998	59,890	3,517	13,154	24,428	18,791
1999	67,887	1,758	15,430	28,656	22,043
2000	78,150	0	18,235	33,865	26,050
Cumulative Total	351,688	35,169	73,854	137,158	105,506
Percent of Total	100%	10%	20%	40%	30%

Sources: Department of Defense (1994), Table 6.8; *Budget of the United States Government*, Fiscal Year 1996 (Washington, D.C.: GPO 1995), Table 5.1; Kaufmann (1992), pp. 87-93.

over the last few years, the program should emphasize large-scale alternative-use planning, financial and technical assistance to firms, community and base redevelopment funding, and a major fund for long-term training patterned on the GI Bill for workers displaced from defense who could not be supported by alternative demand. Specifics can and should be debated, but an investment of this magnitude would act as a real transmission belt between the military and civilian economy.

- We also propose substantial investment to build a new science and technology policy focused on meeting public needs in the environmental, energy, infrastructure, and transportation areas. There would be ample funding to provide for major applied research shaped by these public needs as well as more basic science research, which is currently under severe pressure without the Cold War impetus. Funding new science and technology objectives at this level would increase the national R&D effort significantly, in contrast to the current trend in which modest new civilian R&D fails to make up for military R&D cutbacks.

- These science and technology initiatives would be linked to a major public investment program broadly defined to include infrastructure, new transport, environmental improvements, and education and training. In addition, a serious effort to rebuild the nation's cities and create new life and opportunities for their citizens would also be advanced. The investment in the production of public goods would tie into refocused R&D support to provide launch markets for new industries.

These proposals can, of course, be dismissed as just another wish list. Yet such an agenda properly sold, with bold leadership, is not farfetched. It would meet all the criteria that have traditionally captured public support for large-scale national projects: it would create net employment; it would deliver substantial public benefits; it would lead to pioneering innovations in science and technology; and it would provide private companies and their workers with major new launch markets in environmental, energy, and other sectors with massive growth potential.

Conclusion

The U.S. economy needs considerable new investment if income levels and the quality of life are to be sustained.[32] Much of that investment must be initiated in the public sector for infrastructure, education, and research and development, which in turn will stimulate private-sector investment. But in the 1990s, sources for public-sector investment funding appear to have dried up. The single largest discretionary budget category that offers potential for significant reallocation of funds is the military budget, which remains stuck at Cold War levels and is absorbing billions for unnecessary weapons and equipment.

We have shown that a major obstacle to shifting funds from the military side of the ledger to domestic public investment is the absence of mechanisms for ensuring rapid and efficient reallocation of workers, technology, equipment, facilities, and structures from military-dedicated missions to the civilian economy. Programs begun in the 1990s show some promise, but are woefully underfunded and encumbered by their subordination to bloated defense budgets and the competitiveness agenda. Nevertheless, experiments and progress achieved with and without conversion assistance demonstrate that conversion can and is occurring, albeit not rapidly enough to sustain employment and diffuse political pressure to reverse military spending cuts.

We suggest that presidential and congressional candidates in 1996 be pressed both on their support for military expenditures versus domestic investment and on their programs for mobilizing for peace. Since public-opinion polls strongly support the shift toward domestic investments, it should not be difficult to make this issue a serious litmus test. At the same time, we cannot achieve this goal without taking care of those communities and workers in jeopardy.

The gap between estimates of defense needs in the Republican Contract With America, which would increase defense spending from 1994 levels, and those of moderates like Kaufmann is enormous, as we have shown. This represents the single largest pot of funding available for a viable invest-in-America program. Failure to mobilize these funds for a robust investment program will only compound the slippage of the American economy, prolonging income erosion and increasing job insecurity. As we see it, the nation confronts a lopsided choice, with only post-Cold War realism offering an acceptable alternative.

NOTES

1. Department of Defense 1994.
2. Bischak 1995.
3. Korb 1995.
4. Kaufmann and Steinbruner 1991; Forsberg 1992.
5. Forsberg 1993; Fischer 1993; Vogele 1993; Sharp 1993.
6. Markusen and Yudken 1992; Stowsky 1986a, 1986b.

7. Miller 1995.
8. Adams 1982.
9. Markusen, Hall, Campbell, and Deitrick 1991.
10. Defense Budget Project 1994.
11. Department of Defense 1994.
12. Holzer 1995.
13. Department of Defense 1994.
14. Pemberton 1994.
15. Mueller et al. 1993; Oden et al. 1993; Mueller and Gray 1994.
16. Baldwin 1995.
17. Velocci 1994, 1995.
18. Oden et al. 1994; Feldman 1995; Kelley and Watkins 1994.
19. Oden et al. 1993.
20. Oden et al. 1994; Oden et al. 1993.
21. National Science Foundation 1993.
22. Lichtenberg 1988.
23. National Science Foundation 1994.
24. Stowsky 1986a; Alic et al. 1992; Lichtenberg 1987; Dumas 1986; Melman 1983.
25. Markusen et al. 1995.
26. Defense Authorization Act for FY 1995, 1994.
27. Hill 1993; Pages/BENS 1994.
28. Hill 1995.
29. Mayer 1990.
30. Oden et al. 1993.
31. Oden et al. 1994.
32. Baker and Schafer 1995.

REFERENCES

Adams, Gordon. 1981. *The Iron Triangle: The Politics of Defense Contracting.* New York: Council on Economic Priorities.

Alic, John, Lewis Branscomb, Harvey Brooks, Ashton Carter, and Gerald Epstein. 1992. *Beyond Spinoff: Military and Commercial Technologies in a Changing World.* Cambridge, Mass.: Harvard Business School Press.

Baker, Dean and Todd Schafer. 1995. *The Case for Public Investment.* Washington, D.C.: Economic Policy Institute.

Baldwin, Marc. 1995. "Workers Centers as an Institutional Response to Military-Related Job Loss." U.S. Department of Labor. Mimeo.

Bischak, Greg. 1995. "The Battle Over the Defense Budget: FY 1996 and Beyond." Working Paper. Washington, D.C.: National Commission for Economic Conversion and Disarmament.

Defense Budget Project. 1993. *Final FY 1994 Defense Authorization and Appropriations: Defense Reinvestment and Transition Programs.* Washington, D.C.: Defense Budget Project.

Defense Budget Project. 1993. *Technology Reinvestment Project: Potential Military Bargain.* Washington, D.C.: Defense Budget Project.

Department of Defense. 1994. *National Defense Budget Estimates for FY 1995.* Washington, D.C.: Office of the Comptroller.

Dumas, Lloyd. 1986. *The Overburdened Economy.* Berkeley, Calif.: University of California Press.

Feldman, Jonathan. 1995. *The Successful Conversion of Defense-Serving Firms to Commercial Activity.* Ph.D. Dissertation, Rutgers University, forthcoming.

Fischer, Deitrich. 1993. "Non-Offensive Defense as Component of a Comprehensive Strategy for Peace and Security." Paper presented at the 89th Annual Convention of the American Political Science Association, Washington, D.C.

Forsberg, Randall. 1993. "Cooperative Security: Reconciling the Competing Paradigms of Non-offensive Defense and Collective Security in a Global Approach to Post-Cold War Security Needs." Paper presented at the 89th Annual Convention of the American Political Science Association, Washington, D.C.

Hill, Catherine and Jim Raffel. 1993. "Military Base Closures in the 1990s: Lessons for Redevelopment." Briefing Paper 15. Washington, D.C.: National Commission for Economic Conversion and Disarmament.

Hill, Catherine. 1995. "The Role of Local Control in the Success of Base Redevelopment." Ph.D. Dissertation, Rutgers University, forthcoming.

Holzer, Robert. 1995. "U.S. Navy Fears Costs of Seawolf Near Ceiling." *Defense News,* January 16-22.

Kaufmann, William. 1992. *Assessing the Base Force: How Much Is Too Much?* Washington, D.C.: Brookings Institution.

Kaufmann, William and John Steinbruner. 1991. *Decisions for Defense: Prospects for a New Order.* Washington, D. C.: Brookings Institution.

Kelley, Maryellen and Todd Watkins. 1994. "In From the Cold: Prospects for Conversion of the Defense Industrial Base." Working Paper, Department of Political Science, MIT, December 1994.

Korb, Lawrence. 1995. "The Readiness Gap: What Gap?" *New York Times Magazine,* February 26.

Lichtenberg, Frank. 1987. "The Effect of Government Funding on Private Industrial Research and Development: A Re-assessment." *The Journal of Industrial Economics,* Vol. 36, pp. 97-104.

Markusen, Ann et al. 1991. *The Rise of the Gunbelt.* New York: Oxford University Press.

Markusen, Ann and Joel Yudken. 1992. *Dismantling the Cold War Economy.* New York: Basic Books.

Markusen, Ann, James Raffel, Michael Oden, and Marlen Llanes. 1995. "Coming in From the Cold: The Future of Los Alamos and Sandia National Laboratories." New Brunswick, N.J.: Project on Regional and Industrial Economics.

Mayer, Andrew. 1990. "Military Base Closings." Washington, D.C.: U.S. Congressional Research Service.

Melman, Seymour. 1983. *Profits Without Production.* New York: Alfred A. Knopf.

Miller, Jon D. 1995. "Public Attitudes Toward Spending for Scientific Research." Chicago Academy of Sciences paper presented at the 1995 Conference of the American Association for the Advancement of Science, Atlanta.

Mueller, Elizabeth et al. 1993. "Retraining for What? Displaced Defense Workers Come Up Against EDWAA." Working Paper 57, Center for Urban Policy Research, Rutgers University, New Brunswick, N.J.

Mueller, Elizabeth and Mia Gray. 1994. "Displaced and Mismatched: The Inadequacy of Federal Retraining Programs for Defense Workers." Working Paper 75, Center for Urban Policy Research, Rutgers University, New Brunswick, N.J.

National Science Foundation. 1993. *Science and Engineering Indicators.* Washington, D.C.: NSF.

National Science Foundation. 1994. *National Patterns of R&D Resources.* Washington, D.C.: NSF.

Oden, Michael, Catherine Hill, Elizabeth Mueller, Jonathan Feldman, and Ann Markusen. 1993. "Changing the Future: Converting the St. Louis Economy." Working Paper 59, Center for Urban Policy Research, Rutgers University, New Brunswick, N.J.

Oden, Michael, Elizabeth Mueller, and Judy Goldberg. 1994. "Life After Defense: Conversion and Economic Adjustment on Long Island." Working Paper 82, Center for Urban Policy Research, Rutgers University, New Brunswick, N.J.

Pages, Eric. 1994. *Military Base Closings.* Washington, D.C.: Business Executives for National Security.

Sharp, Jane M. O. 1993. "How to Adapt International Security Institutions After the Cold War." Paper presented at the 89th Annual Convention of the American Political Science Association, Washington, D.C.

Stowsky, Jay. 1986a. "Beating Our Plowshares Into Double-Edged Swords: Assessing the Impact of Pentagon Policies on the Commercialization of Advanced Technologies." Working Paper No. 17, Berkeley Roundtable on the International Economy, University of California at Berkeley.

Stowsky, Jay. 1986b. "Competing With the Pentagon." *World Policy Journal,* Vol. 3, No. 4, pp. 697-721.

U.S. Congress, House of Representatives. 1994. *National Defense Authorization Act for Fiscal Year 1995.* Washington, D.C.: U.S. Congress.

Velocci, Anthony. 1994. "Defense Firms Show Financial Prowess." *Aviation Week,* May 30.

Velocci, Anthony. 1995. "Profit Wave Uncovers Nagging Paradoxes." *Aviation Week,* May 29.

Vogele, William. 1993. "Security Policies and Cooperative Security After People Power® Revolutions." Paper presented at the 89th Annual Convention of the American Political Science Association, Washington, D.C.

CHAPTER 17

URBAN REVITALIZATION
The Short Road to Long-Term Growth

by Elliott Sclar

ALL ECONOMICALLY ADVANCED NATIONS HAVE URBAN-BASED ECONOMIES, and the United States is no exception. Approximately three-fourths of the American population lives in metropolitan areas. One-quarter lives in central cities and the remaining half in the suburbs. Not only do we live in urban-based metropolitan regions, but we are highly concentrated within a few of them. Over half of the entire American population lives in just 34 metropolitan areas.

Despite this economic dependency on urbanization, it is common knowledge that America's central cities are in severe trouble. Their economic bases are shrinking as their rates of poverty, homelessness, and crime are rising. An ominous recent development is that these center-city trends are becoming increasingly typical in some of the older suburbs. Despite the geographic centrality of these cities to their metropolitan areas, the notion of any public intervention to redress these problems is viewed by virtually all of our political leaders as a luxury we can ill afford at present.

According to the current political conventional wisdom, cities are no longer economically essential. In a service-based economy, sustained by an abundance of relatively inexpensive and widely dispersed transportation and telecommunications infrastructure, decentralization is more efficient and desirable than the older forms of urban concentration, derived from 19th-century needs. Life in the 21st century will be lived on a spatially flat playing field. Cities, suburbs, and rural areas are all equally advantageous. Only places that learn to keep their taxes and public spending low can hope to attract the footloose service enterprises that will create the next century's prosperity. Consequently, any public action to ad-

---

Elliott Sclar is professor of urban planning at Columbia University.

dress the problems of center cities is a luxury and not a necessity, and can only be done from the vantage point of a prosperity that is yet beyond our reach. Accordingly, spending on cities is no longer an investment that enhances national productivity but a drain on scarce resources.

The politics and experiences that shape this reasoning are not hard to decode. The suburban populace, now the national majority, is, on average, more affluent and has a higher voter turnout than does the smaller group living in central cities. The suburban-based state and national political leaders who have emerged from this demographic realignment reflect the anti-urban values of their constituents. Many suburban residents proudly proclaim that they have not set foot in "downtown" or "the city" in years. Their daily experiences convince them that the older center cities and, increasingly, the inner ring of older suburbs are little more than holding pens for intractable social problems. Their everyday experience tells them that both the metropolitan future and the American future are found in the shopping malls, office parks, and wired home offices at suburbia's outer reaches.

The principal difference among these newly dominant suburban political actors is the degree of sympathy they have for the plight of the residents of central cities. The liberals, who admit that there may be a structural as well as a moral component to the problem, are more willing than the conservatives to provide sympathy and social programs. Urban woes, the liberals argue, have in part been brought about by technological change that has made both low-wage labor and high-density living obsolete. The liberal solution is to defend social welfare programs and anti-discrimination laws that might facilitate the removal of the more able urban residents from their high-density, low-opportunity traps to the low-density hinterlands where opportunity abounds. Conservatives have little patience for the notion that there is a structural element to the plight of the urban poor. In the individualistic intellectual constructs through which they view life, conservatives see the problems of city residents as the self-inflicted wounds of moral turpitude. These urban residents, conservatives believe, must learn to heal themselves of the public profligacy that feeds off the welfare state and the personal promiscuity that leads to out-of-wedlock births and the use of illegal drugs. Public intervention is too easily transformed from a temporary helping hand into a permanent incentive to persistent moral flabbiness.

What's Wrong With This Picture?

This popular view of central cities is wrong. It is based upon both an incomplete understanding of how the contemporary global economy actually functions and of how American public policy has drained the cities of resources. Along the way it has distorted the relative costs associated with cities, suburbs, and rural areas to the disadvantage of both its central cities and the nation as a whole.

In both the service sector and the manufacturing sector, the efficient, centralized density of cities is increasingly critical to international competitiveness and hence national prosperity. However, given the current state of political affairs, it is difficult to break the stranglehold of our economically perverse anti-city policies or our strong commitment to subsidizing the costs of metropolitan sprawl. Can we develop the political ability to reverse this situation? This chapter lays out the case for the economic importance of central cities and suggests some policy approaches that may be viable even in the present political context.

The New Economic Reality

There is widespread agreement that the economy of the 21st century will be intensely information-based,[1] centered on producer services industries. These range from high-end activities such as legal services, advertising, finance, insurance, real estate, data processing, and telecommunications to such less-prestigious activities as security and custodial services and messenger and package delivery services. Despite the notion that high-end producer services and information-intensive industries can locate anywhere that is reachable by phone lines, satellites, or package delivery services, the reality is otherwise. It is one thing for ad agencies, banks, and law firms to e-mail their messages back and forth; it is quite another for these diverse experts to have easy face-to-face contact. Investment bankers want to meet the people to whom they make the big loans. Retailers want personal presentations from their ad designers and media buyers. It is no accident that biotechnology firms cluster in just a few locations even as important basic biological and medical research takes place almost everywhere. This need for face-to-face contact favors urban locations. In addition, it is no accident that most innovative telecommunication advances occur in urban areas. Only cities can sustain sufficient telecommunications intensity to justify the high fixed costs of having the most state-of-the-art technology.

Hence, despite high rents, high taxes, and a host of urban problems, many firms, especially in the expansive producer services sector, still opt to cluster in center cities. While national job growth between 1980 and 1985 was about 8%, jobs in producer services, which are by-and-large urban, grew by 20%.[2] Surely such phenomena are indicative of the enduring economic importance of central location.

While manufacturing in general and urban manufacturing in particular have fallen dramatically as a share of total employment and gross domestic product, it would be a fatal mistake to dismiss the significance of these sectors. The future location of producer service jobs is closely linked to the future location of manufacturing.[3] In other words, national competitiveness in services is critical to competitiveness in manufacturing, and vice versa.

Urban locations are becoming favored production sites for manufacturing as well. The key here is the shift away from standardized mass-produced goods to more varied or customized products. The former were most efficiently churned out on large sites located on cheap land far from the urban core. Information technology has made small batch production more competitive with long runs of standardized products. As a result, operations located in the center of a rich network of transportation and communications infrastructure have become cost effective. More flexible firms have proven to be more competitive because they are able to adjust output quickly even as demand is changing. New work systems enable these firms to maintain a much smaller inventory of inputs, minimizing the amount of costly capital tied up in unnecessary parts and storage space.

"Just-in-time" (JIT) delivery is one element of these new forms of work organization. Developed in Japan, where space always commands a premium, JIT requires an extremely reliable freight distribution system and a well-developed telecommunications infrastructure linking retail outlets to factories, warehouses, and suppliers. In the most advanced production systems, a product can be designed specifically to fit an individual customer's unique needs. As the products are produced, electronic data interchange notifies a host of component suppliers of their need for additional parts. As new, more flexible manufacturing methods continue to evolve and mass production fades, the increasing importance of transportation and telecommunications linkages between producers and retailers, and the reduced need for production space, will make urban industrial areas, once abandoned as inappropriate for mass production, increasingly valuable as efficient sites for the specialized flexible industrial production required in the new information age. For example, the borough of Queens in New York City experienced a 30% drop in its available manufacturing space between 1993 and 1995 as many small manufacturers, eager for close-in locations, scooped up available sites.[4] The proximity between factory and market and the cost structure of providing telecommunications and transportation infrastructure will continue to favor more central locations. Further, because cities are the repository of an enormous existing national investment in physical infrastructure, rehabilitating our investment there will be significantly less costly than adding new higher cost and inherently less efficient capacity at the metropolitan fringe.

The more competitive international markets become, the more crucial efficient location will be to the success of American enterprise. Therefore, the more valuable locations will be the old abandoned industrial sites on the edges of major cities. While much is made of the fact that all the new auto assembly plants being built in this country by foreign manufacturers have been located in rural areas of the Southeast, that trend is more a reflection of the huge locational subsidies accorded these manufacturers than of the inherent efficiency of these out-of-the-way locations. It is noteworthy that the best-selling American-built car, the Ford Taurus, is constructed without artificial subsidy by unionized workers in a plant in South Chicago. It is certainly more than competitive with the highly subsidized foreign plants. There is no longer any inherent manufacturing advantage to exurban sites. Rather, it is all a question of relative public subsidy.

Fiscal Realities

The current apparent efficiency of living and working in low-density areas is a fiscal illusion. It is created through large but mainly invisible public subsidies to both automobile travel and low-density housing. Absent these subsidies, it would be difficult to explain, from an economic point of view, why the fastest-growing portions of metropolitan regions continue to be the distant peripheries while decay continues to spread from the more centrally located cores. The simple, popular answer is that residents and businesses made choices to move, and the efficient market merely accommodated them. But individual choices are made from available options. If, as a matter of public policy, relatively more heavily subsidized suburban options compete with relatively less-favored urban ones, it is difficult to see how the outcome could be otherwise. A more powerful economic policy analysis must delve into the dynamics that create these options.

The mainstays of this policy are federal housing and transportation subsidies as well as the exemption of homeowner capital gains from taxation. The costs of mortgage interest and local property taxes are both deductible from federal income tax, so there is a clear advantage to suburban homeownership over urban renting. Although the recent emergence of condominium multiple dwellings has to some extent mitigated the suburban bias of America's premier housing subsidy, it is still preponderantly a benefit to the free-standing single-family suburban home.

The federal government, through its highway legislation, embarked on a massive campaign to underwrite both the capital and operating costs of highways, the main route of automobile travel. Cars operate most efficiently where density is lowest. This subsidy too was somewhat mitigated by more modest subsidy programs for urban transit and by taxes on the free parking typically provided by suburban employers. However, the meager transit subsidies are now under attack by both the Clinton Administration and Congress. Subsidies to automobiles outstrip subsidies to mass transit by a ratio of 7 to 1. The net impact of these skewed transport subsidies ensures that the only individual travel costs associated with sprawl continue to be the relatively small out-of-pocket ones for gas and, occasionally, parking.

Finally, homeowners enjoy a tax-free imputed rent when their property goes up in value. They also receive a deferral of capital gains taxation when the property is sold to buy another house, and a one-time tax-free gain on most of the value if they give up homeownership after they reach age 55. As a result of this three-part federal subsidy package, the preference for owning over renting—and, in a relative sense, suburbs over cities—is underscored.

At the same time, the standard method of providing local services through local property taxes and local zoning serves to make life in the newest and most peripheral communities seem even better, at least in the beginning. When a rural community first begins to become suburban, it has neither the historic costs of past infrastructure investment nor the service costs of congestion embedded in its municipal tax rate. Its entire fiscal effort, financed off of rising property values, is devoted entirely to new infrastructure for the use of the new residents. More importantly, thanks to subsidized highways, this rural area inherits its initial access as a more or less free public good. But, as the evidence of the past half-century shows, these advantages last only until the next wave of even more peripheral development begins.

Infrastructure Reality: The Case of Transportation

Infrastructure is the invisible but tangible physical underpinning that holds up society. It consists of the highways, mass transit facilities, water and sewer lines, utility lines, airports, and railroad terminals that make it possible for large numbers of people to enjoy a high standard of living in both cities and suburbs. Cities, because of their ability to co-locate large numbers of people in small spaces, economize greatly on these costly elements. If low transport and telecommunications costs, agglomeration economies (the benefits from close proximity to others in the same industry), and superior access to markets were no longer important to the economy, we would be witnessing as rapid a dispersal of urban centers in other nations as in our own. But we aren't. Indeed, as the noted urban historian Kenneth Jackson observed, "the United States is not only the world's first suburban nation, but it will also be its last."[5]

Supporting the same level of economic activity in low-density suburban locations requires that physical infrastructure be extended and maintained over longer distances. The Housing and Urban Development Department-sponsored study, *The Costs of Sprawl* (1974), indicated that the cost of providing housing in low-density unplanned suburban areas was 60% higher than providing the same number of units in planned, high-density urban areas. More than half of these costs in suburban areas are subsidized.[6] Sprawled development requires that ever-increasing numbers of workers commute in increasingly diverse patterns over ever-increasing distances. This mode of transportation in turn undermines the viability of alternative, less-expensive, less-polluting, and more efficient mass transit modes.

The traffic congestion associated with this development pattern is imposing severe costs on the economy. According to a recent study,[7] every time a firm relocates from an urban to a suburban location, the number of automobile trips made by the firm's employees during the day increases 12 times. Thus, a large part of our growth in vehicle-miles and in traffic congestion is being driven by the relocation of firms from urban to suburban areas.

Our heavy dependence on automobile transportation and the infrastructure costs required to support it are reflected in the amount of money we spend on transportation relative to other countries. The United States devotes between 15% and 18% of GDP to transportation, while Japan spends only 9%. In large part because of high commuting costs, American families spend between 15.2% and 22.5% of their annual income on transportation-related expenses, while a Japanese family only spends 9.4%.[8] These differences in costs are reflected both in the costs that firms pay directly for transportation and also indirectly for the costs that firms pay out in wages.

The cost of building more highways to overcome increasing traffic congestion will pose an onerous fiscal burden. According to the Federal Highway Administration, our current annual expenditures on highways of $14.6 billion would have to be increased by 35% just to bring the existing physical infrastructure back up to its 1983 condition. In order to maintain average user costs (which include the costs of congestion) at current levels ($400 billion per year), current expenditures would have to be increased by 113%. Encouraging the use of mass transit and higher-density living and working patterns provides a more cost-effective solution.

Refurbishing the quality of life in older urban and close-in suburban neighborhoods would prove to be a highly cost-effective investment. These slowly decaying areas are an important undervalued asset for providing efficient high-quality housing to the diverse workforce that the next century's economy will demand. Cities and older suburbs contain a broad range of housing types for people in all walks of life in close proximity to one another and to the efficient locations of 21st-century work. And they are already connected by urban mass-transit systems. If urban areas were able to receive a significantly higher percentage of new housing investment, the need for massive increases in highway expenditures could be avoided, as traffic could be shifted from single-occupancy vehicles to more efficient modes such as public transportation, walking, and bicycling.

The alternative to investing in cities and older close-in suburbs will be to continue to invest in the deconcentration of existing metropolitan areas. Such a trend is disadvantageous not only to the center city, existing suburban areas, and the national economy as a whole, but also to the environment. Currently 29% of energy consumption and a quarter of the toxic emissions causing global warming derive from the transportation sector. While more fuel-efficient vehicles and alternative fuels may offer some hope, the current explosion of vehicle-miles traveled is undermining the progress on air and water pollution that these innovations could make. As for land use, many cities have to dedicate over half of their available land to road infrastructure, compared to less than 25% in Japanese cities.

The Political Reality of a City-Friendly Fiscal Policy

The realities of the consequences of suburban sprawl make a strong and rational economic case for reinvesting in our central cities. Everyone—urbanite, suburbanite, and exurbanite—would benefit from the stable land use and efficient economy that would result. Instead of a constant battle against spreading decay, we would have urban and suburban communities in which people could work and raise families. We would have rural areas close at hand that preserve their environment and provide open space for all to enjoy. We would be better able to pay wages that were both internationally competitive and, thanks to more efficient land use patterns, capable of sustaining a pleasant lifestyle.

Unfortunately, a rational economic case is not the same thing as a viable political one. One result of our present city-suburb fiscal arrangements is that change represents risk. People can always be concretely clear about what they will lose, while the gains are always abstract. Yet not to change is to leave a political and economic dynamic in place that can only get worse for everyone. Present federal policies that subsidize suburbanization increasingly do so at the cost of further eroding urban tax bases even as the number of lower-income residents dependent upon government support increases. Higher-income urban residents, not wishing to pay taxes for services such as public hospitals and public housing, can avoid them by moving to suburban municipalities beyond the central city's taxing authority. This exodus further undermines urban public services and the quality of urban life. Consequently, even more residents head to suburban townships, where they receive more direct service value for each federally deductible property tax dollar they pay.

Center cities have few resources to work with to stave off disaster. The typical urban economic development policy these days involves setting up a business retention strategy. The goal is to stabilize the tax base by convincing businesses that are threatening to leave to stay. This is invariably done by offering tax concessions, on the theory that, while the city will incur short-term revenue losses, it will more than recoup them by the long-term vitality in the economic base. While the tax concession strategy occasionally helps keep business in the city, it is not clear that it has the hoped-for long-term effects when the extraordinary ends up as the routine. For example, when CBS recently sought, and received, major tax concessions from New York City, it had no plans to leave—it merely sought the same breaks its potentially departing competitors had received. Hence, instead of a targeted tax break, the city ends up with a de facto general reduction in business taxes. Yet firms still keep leaving, following their middle-class employees and customers who are seizing upon the federally subsidized opportunity to get better public schools and better services. The net effect is that we have an effective federal policy to continually extend the urban fringe ever further into the hinterlands.

When firms leave cities like New York, a frequently cited cause is the poor quality of the public services provided. The fact that poor quality correlates with lowered revenues, made worse by tax concessions, is not the firms' problem. More important, this tax concession strategy amounts to nothing more than a negative-sum game as more localities join in. It is not uncommon for a large employer to set up two locales in a tax concession bidding war, with one locality or another to retain a facility. Not only does success in one place invariably mean failure someplace else, but the winner receives far less in tax revenues than would otherwise have been the case. Although the data is incomplete, some expert observers now believe that the tax competition has become so intense that, increasingly, municipalities do not even receive sufficient tax revenues to offset the services these businesses use, let alone defray other pressing urban service costs.

As national economic stagnation continues, this accelerating negative-sum game of competitive tax cuts has helped to foster a uniquely vicious cycle of spending cuts that have been disproportionately hard on cities. The decrease in the tax base that this competition causes has led cities to underinvest in both their capital and labor. As a result, crucial investments in the maintenance of the health, safety, education, housing, and retraining of their workforces and the modernization of their transport, telecommunications, water, sewer, and power infrastructures have been badly lagging. In effect, the areas in which public action is most crucial to private-sector productivity have been most neglected. For example, office buildings in the Wall Street area are rapidly losing their tenants, and everyone recognizes that the only way to revitalize the area is to make it as accessible to suburban commuters as is the midtown area. But improved access requires a major investment in infrastructure of funds that the city does not have. The mayor has proposed instead massive tax cuts and relaxation of zoning regulations in the hope that these will give the private sector incentives to upgrade buildings and build new ones. Given that increasing numbers of people are already shunning the area as inconvenient, why assume that making more modernized space available will make a difference? Why would landlords throw good money after bad, even with public incentives? The only rationale for this approach is that it does not involve new city expenditures.

Throughout the 1960s and 1970s such urban deterioration was partially mitigated by a flow of federal funds to urban areas, largely for social programs. This support has now all but disappeared. In 1991, 61% of city governments were facing fiscal difficulties, and 26.5% were in serious fiscal distress. Federal support for cities has fallen from a high of 25% of total municipal revenues in 1979 to 12% by the end of the Reagan presidency. The recent moves by the Administration and Congress to further cut aid to cities will only make matters worse.

Recent studies by David Aschauer (1989) and Alicia Munnell (1990) provide evidence that a large part of the declining growth of U.S. productivity can be linked to the decline in the level of public investment. It is precisely the growing inability of local, and particularly urban, governments to invest in America's urbanized people and their infrastructure that explains much of this observed decline in public investment and hence in national productivity.

Back-Door Regional Planning: A Potential Way Out

The answer to the nation's urban problems is the same as it has been for most of this century: regional planning. Regional planning has had great success in cities as diverse as Indianapolis, Minneapolis, and Portland, Oregon. However, outside of a small coterie of academics, planning professionals, and officials in smaller metropolitan areas, this notion has no popular political appeal. Because it requires a realignment of local political power, it almost invariably meets stiff resistance from local elites. Consequently, a politically viable broad-based approach to something so comprehensively rational must be advanced in a somewhat roundabout manner.

The overarching theme for this new approach to urban policy must be national economic revitalization. It must stress that the policy is not about cities per se but about stabilizing and enhancing the lives of everyone in metropolitan America. While the direct focus must be on public reinvestment in center cities and older suburbs, the indirect focus must be on the benefits for everyone. The policy that emerges must be one that encourages higher-density development. For that to happen, the structure of public subsidies that have in the past encouraged sprawl have to be reversed by policies that encourage the modernization of older public transportation infrastructure and the building of newer infrastructure, plus neighborhood revitalization and housing rehabilitation programs that make older center-city neighborhoods viable alternatives to suburban and exurban living. The three following goals should guide the agenda:

- *The playing field between city and suburb must be leveled.* The implicit subsidies to sprawling forever outward must either be equalized with subsidies to urban areas or eliminated. Unless the true costs of sprawl are borne by those who engage in the process, it will not stop.

- *The physical (i.e., water, sewerage, power, transportation, communications, and housing) infrastructure and the service levels in education, public safety, and transit in central cities must be restored.* It is not enough to level the playing field; it is also necessary to make up for past disinvestment. Unless the urban public realm works well, it will be difficult to effectively create the level playing field of the first objective or to entice an expanded middle class back into the city. Without an expanded middle class, social and physical urban polarization will continue.

- *The industrial land and abandoned neighborhoods of center cities must be primary targets for revitalization.* The vast expanses of under- or unutilized land that lies within 10 miles of center cities must be given high priority as efficient locations for production in the new era of transportation and telecommunications-intensive just-in-time manufacturing. Similarly, the residential neighborhoods with their excellent stock of older buildings must be thought of once more as locations for housing all classes of citizens. These locations, near already well-developed public transportation and other infrastructure, are cost-effective places for a sustained revitalization of America's economic base. In this regard, more than anything else, transportation policy will be the most politically viable means of redressing the inefficient pattern of regional metropolitan development. Metropolitan transportation policy must have two objectives: to minimize the costs of providing convenient mobility, and to reduce the need to travel at all. While the first goal is obvious, the second requires some explanation. Mobility is not an end in itself; rather it is a means to gain access to locations where valued activities occur. Consequently, to the extent that access can be enhanced by improving the co-location of activities, or by the creation of mixed land uses, the same end can be achieved at far lower cost. Thus, land-use planning interventions that diminish the need to build an extra lane on a suburban highway or that make it possible for families with two or more working adults to get by with only one car fulfill the mission of transportation policy as well as enhancements in the provision of services.

As noted above, recent studies indicate that the relocation of firms from urban to exurban areas is a principal cause of the rapid increase in vehicle-miles traveled and has led in turn to traffic congestion, the need for expanded suburban road infrastructure, and the desire to move even further out from the core. These extra infrastructure costs could be avoided if firms were no longer compelled by poor public policy to relocate further out of central urban areas. First, the subsidies to transportation modes that encourage sprawling development must be ended. The first step, from the point of view of economic efficiency, is to increase user charges to cover the full costs of automobile-based sprawl. The easiest way to do this administratively would be through increases in gasoline taxes to the point where the receipts entirely cover the costs of maintaining the road network. Gasoline in the United States costs about $1.25 per gallon, lower in real terms than what it cost before the first oil crisis in 1973. In Japan and Germany gasoline costs about $4.00 per gallon, and in both cases most of the difference is taxes. A gasoline tax increase of around $1.00 per gallon would not be economically unreasonable, but it would be politically impossible. A more hopeful avenue toward shifting the cost of driving onto users may be found in the American enthusiasm for Intelligent Vehicle Highway Systems (IVHS), the term used to describe the range of computerized methods for better controlling traffic flow on highways. Among the notions it includes are map systems to help motorists get where they are going more efficiently and guidance systems to divert highway congestion as it occurs. As IVHS technology is implemented around the country, it can be used to shift gradually from gasoline taxation to road user fees. From an economic point of view, such fees offer the best way to discourage the overuse of increasingly scarce and expensive road infrastructure. The taxation of employer-provided parking and the granting of tax deductions to employees who commute by transit is a good first step. Larger tax credits should also be considered for firms that provide transit allowances or bicycle facilities.

Instead of lowering transit subsidies, as is now the trend, federal and local governments should increase them. Lowering fare costs and increasing the quality of service will, over time, lower the average operating costs of mass transit by boosting ridership. In the short run, ridership increases will be small and price driven, but in the long run they will engender a more powerful and lasting shift as they begin to make less dense land uses an unattractive alternative. Such a shift of subsidy priorities will also lead to a net saving of public resources. A recent study for the Conservation Law Foundation (1994) found that in Boston the publicly subsidized costs of a typical commuter trip by single-occupant auto is $10.60, by commuter rail $6.13, and by car pool $5.15. Thus, if sizeable numbers of auto commuters could be induced to switch to one of these other modes of transport, the expected decrease in public costs is considerable—between 42% and 51%.[9] For nonmotorized modes such as bicycling and walking, the economic and environmental savings are even larger.

Cities need to be encouraged to undertake both mixed-use zoning and bicycle- and pedestrian-network planning. Subsidies should be given to parking garages that provide bicycle parking facilities and to buildings that provide bike parking and showers. Local commuter rail and transit authorities need to be encouraged to provide bicycle parking facilities or to make provisions for commuters to bring their bicycles onto trains.

More generally, the era of public policy in which the provision and maintenance of roads and highways has been a virtual free public good from the user's perspective must, once and for all, be ended. Failing in that, subsidies to nonauto modes should be equalized. Providing one mode of transportation free of charge or at heavily subsidized prices while competing modes are maintained as either private enterprises or as public ones with high "copayments" has led to a serious misallocation of resources.

The notion of more fully charging users of transportation for the services they enjoy has appeal across the political spectrum. Thus, it is more likely to pick up support if a sustained campaign to make the general public aware of the costs and benefits is launched. More than anything else, then, one of the most politically viable approaches to urban revitalization might be something as simple as a call for reasonable transportation pricing.

Conclusion

A recent *New York Times* article describing life in the latest northern New Jersey subdivisions refers to the new residents as "settlers."[10] The subtitle of Joel Garreau's *Edge City* (1991) was *Life on the New Frontier.* References to settlers and frontiers inadvertently reflect an anachronistic flaw in American thinking. The standard American model of changing one's surroundings substitutes personal movement for community improvement. If things aren't going well where you live now, start fresh somewhere else. At the dawn of a new century, if we care about our future, such personal churning is no longer a viable substitute for determined collective action. We have just about run out of "theres" with which to replace distasteful "heres." We can no longer afford to maintain the illusion of imaginary new frontiers for imaginary settlers. We have to begin conserving the massive and substantial investments made by the real settlers who built our cities in the first place. We have to know that our need for efficiency and our desire for comfortable lives are not antithetical. Mending our metropolitan cores is the pathway to both. To continue degrading our built environment in the name of enhancing our quality of life is a guaranteed road to self-destruction.

Notes

1. See, for example, Reich 1992, Sassen 1991, and Castells 1989.

2. Castells 1989.

3. Cohen and Zysman 1987.

4. Trager 1995.

5. Jackson 1985, 304.

6. A more recent (1984) study of suburban density came to about the same conclusion. It found that the per capita costs for public infrastructure rose by almost 60% as development proceeded from a relatively high density of 4.5 units per acre to the urban/rural periphery, where density is typically about 1 unit per every five acres. The data were drawn from a study of Loudon County, Va. The study is cited in an unpublished paper by Todd Litman, "Transportation Cost Survey," February 1992.

7. Douglass 1990.

8. Sclar and Hook 1993.

9. While the specific costs here are unique to metropolitan Boston, the order of magnitude in the differentials is about the same in every major American metropolis.

10. *New York Times,* July 3, 1995.

REFERENCES

Aschauer, David. 1989. "Public Investment and Productivity Growth in the Group of Seven." *Economic Perspectives* (Federal Reserve Bank of Chicago), September-October.

Cohen, Stephen S. and John Zysman. 1987. *Manufacturing Matters: The Myth of the Post-Industrial Economy.* New York: Basic Books.

Conservation Law Foundation. 1994. "Road Kill: How Solo Driving Runs Down the Economy." Boston: Conservation Law Foundation.

Castells, Manuel. 1989. *The Informational City.* London: Blackwell.

Douglass, G. Bruce. 1990. "Suburban Trip Generation and Some Notions About Changing Traffic Patterns." *Travel Characteristics at Large Scale Suburban Activity Centers.* Transportation Research Circular No. 323. Washington, D.C.: Transportation Research Board.

Garreau, Joel. 1991. *Edge City: Life on the New Frontier.* New York: Doubleday.

Jackson, Kenneth T. 1985. *Crabgrass Frontier: The Suburbanization of the United States.* New York: Oxford University Press.

Munnell, Alicia. 1990. "Why Has Productivity Growth Declined?" *New England Economic Review,* January/February.

Real Estate Research Corporation. 1974. *The Costs of Sprawl: Environmental and Economic Costs of the Fringe.* Prepared for the Council on Environmental Quality, Office of Policy Development and Research, Department of Housing and Urban Development, and Office of Planning and Management, Environmental Protection Agency. Washington D.C.: U.S. Government Printing Office.

Reich, Robert B. 1992. *The Work of Nations: Preparing Ourselves for 21st Century Capitalism.* New York: Vintage Books.

Sassen, Saskia. 1991. *The Global City: New York, London, Tokyo.* Princeton, N.J.: Princeton University Press.

Sclar, Elliott and Walter Hook. 1993. "The Importance of Cities to the National Economy." In Henry G. Cisneros, ed., *Interwoven Destinies: Cities and the Nation.* New York: W.W. Norton.

Trager, Cara S. 1995. "Manufacturing Emigrates to Queens." *Crains New York Business,* June 26-July 2.

AFTERWORD
Political Reality

by Ruy Teixeira

THE CHAPTERS IN THIS VOLUME HAVE OUTLINED A SERIES OF ACTIVIST policies that adapt the liberal tradition of concern for working Americans to the problems of today's economy. The overriding purpose of these policies is to reverse the ongoing erosion in American living standards and restore the economic base for middle-class prosperity. As such, these policies would be of considerable help to the overwhelming majority of Americans—help that is surely needed.

But are such progressive economic policies politically feasible? That is, do they have the kind of public support needed to translate policy ideas into reality? As things stand now, the answer is—with some exceptions like raising the minimum wage and getting tough on trade—"probably not," because the very people who would benefit the most from the policies outlined here are precisely the ones deserting liberals and the Democratic Party in droves. What's more, these potential supporters are not leaving for some left-wing alternative, but rather for a Republican Party for which such activist policies are anathema.

In the longer run, however, these policies may not only be politically feasible, but they may provide the only reasonable hope for reviving the political fortunes of both liberals and the political party (the Democrats) to which they are intimately linked. This is because the long-term political success of both liberals and Democrats will be determined by which story voters believe about eroding living standards. If voters continue to believe that the government is either responsible for declining living standards or could only make things worse, Democrats start every election

Ruy Teixeira is director of the politics and public opinion program at the Economic Policy Institute.

with two strikes against them and will achieve limited success. But consistent advocacy of the policies outlined in this volume *and the political story to which they are intimately linked* could shift the blame away from government toward where it properly lies—with irresponsible corporations and politicians who have lost interest in the living standards of the average American. This shifting of the political terrain would then provide liberals and Democrats with the electoral advantage they currently lack and a solid political base for the implementation of progressive economic policies.

To understand this point—why policies that are not popular in the short run provide virtually the only way out in the longer run—it is necessary to understand first what happened in the last election and what this says about the current political context.

WHO DESERTED THE DEMOCRATS IN 1994?

In 1994, Democratic support declined 10 percentage points from 1992 among high school dropouts, 11 points among high school graduates, and 12 points among those with some college, all groups hit by serious long-term wage decline. In contrast, among those with a college degree, who have fared the best economically, Democratic support was firm (see **Figure A**).

The same basic pattern applies if we compare 1994 and 1990, the last off-year election. The decline in Democratic support is again concentrated among the non-college-educated: down nine points for high school graduates and 11 points for those with some college (see **Figure B**). The chief difference is that the 1990-94 comparison shows very little change among high school dropouts. This underscores the curvilinear nature of Democratic support: they are doing better at the ends of the education distribution while collapsing in the middle.

Among whites, where the decline in Democratic support between 1992 and 1994 was concentrated (black Democratic support actually went up slightly), the shift away from the Democrats among the non-college educated was especially pronounced. And among non-college-educated whites, the anti-Democratic shift was sharpest among men (see **Table 1**). Democratic support declined 20 percentage points (to 37%) among white

FIGURE A
Change in Democratic Support by Education Group, 1992-94

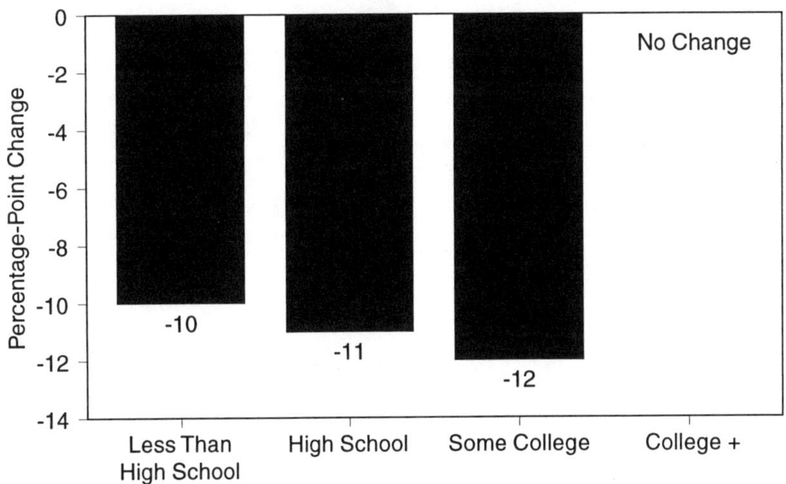

Sources: 1994 VNS exit poll; 1992 VRS exit poll.

FIGURE B
Change in Democratic Support by Education Group, 1990-94

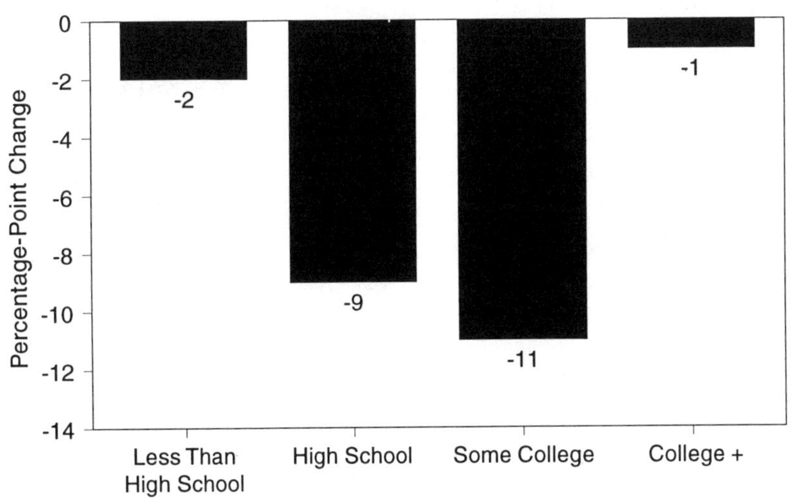

Sources: 1994 VNS exit poll; 1990 VRS exit poll.

TABLE 1
Erosion of Democratic Congressional Support Among Whites

	Percent Vote Democratic			Percent Change in Real Hourly Wage, 1979-93
	1992	1994	Change 1992-94	
White Men				
High School Dropout	64	53	-11	-26
High School Graduate	57	37	-20	-17
Some College	46	31	-15	-11
College Graduate	43	37	-6	+2

	Percent Vote Democratic			Percent Change in Real Hourly Wage, 1979-93
	1992	1994	Change 1992-94	
White Women				
High School Dropout	58	53	-5	-12
High School Graduate	54	44	-10	-2
Some College	50	40	-10	+7
College Graduate	50	52	+2	+14

Sources: 1994 VNS exit poll; 1992 VRS exit poll; 1979 and 1993 Current Population Survey earnings files.

men with a high school education and 15 points (to 31%) among white men with some college. It is non-college-educated men who have suffered the largest wage declines over the last two decades, as suggested by the data in the table.[1]

It is important to note, however, that Democratic losses among white non-college-educated voters extended to women as well. For example, Democratic support declined 10 points among both white women with a high school diploma and those with some college (see bottom panel of table), a substantial loss among a large group of the electorate. Thus, to ascribe the fall-off in Democratic support to "angry white males" is to miss the point. A lot of non-college-educated white men *and* women were the true culprits.

Some argue that at least the Democrats maintained their base among the college-educated, and aren't they the largest single education group in the electorate (43% of voters, according to the Voter News Service exit poll)? Unfortunately for this argument, exit polls significantly overstate the numbers of college-graduate voters.[2] More reliable voting data available from the Census Bureau[3] indicate that voters with a college education amounted to about 29% of the electorate in 1994, actually less than the number of voters with just a high school diploma (about 31%) and far outweighed by the overall number of non-college-educated voters (about 71%). This breakdown means the political implications of the severe dropoff in Democratic support among the non-college-educated are even worse than they initially appear: not only are non-college-educated voters deserting the Democrats in droves, they constitute the overwhelming proportion of the electorate.

What is true of the electorate as a whole is also true of Perot voters, the key swing group in the electorate. Indeed, once adjusted to reflect voting patterns in the Census data, Perot voters are even more dominated by the non-college educated (see **Table 2**). And, consistent with what we have seen among other groups, they moved massively away from the Democrats, dropping 17 percentage points to 32%, an astonishingly low level of support—in fact, even lower than the Democrats' poor showing among white non-college-educated voters in general (see **Figure C**). This level of support from swing voters will effectively cripple the Democrats if repeated in the future.

TABLE 2
Education Distribution Among 1992 Voters: All Voters vs. Perot Voters

	All Voters	Perot Voters
Education Level		
High School Dropout	12	12
High School Graduate	33	35
Some College	28	30
College Graduate	27	23

Source: Teixeira, Ruy A. 1994. "The Politics of the High-Wage Path: The Challenge Facing Democrats." Washington, D.C.: Economic Policy Institute.

FIGURE C
Democratic Support of Key Voter Groups, 1994

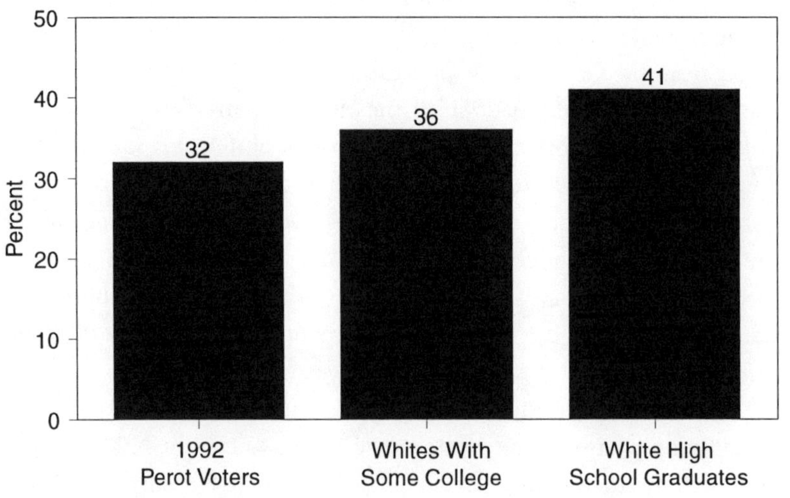

Source: 1994 VNS exit poll.

Moreover, analysis of wage data linked to the VNS data indicates that the Perot voters who voted Republican in 1994 were precisely the ones under the most economic stress: their estimated wage losses since 1979 were more than double the losses suffered by Perot voters who voted Democratic. In other words, among the Perot voters, an economically stressed group[4] in general due to the heavy dominance of the non-college-educated, the most economically stressed tended to break Republican in 1994.

Thus, the connection between declining living standards and activist policy initiatives to address this decline appears exactly the opposite of what one might expect. Those suffering the most—with some exceptions (chiefly blacks)—are moving *away* from the Democratic Party, the historic vehicle for such policy initiatives, rather than toward it. And the current destination of these defectors is a Republican Party whose views on even mild government activism—much less the progressive economic policies described in this volume—are actively hostile.[5]

Why Declining Living Standards Hurt the Democrats

These results raise an immediate question: why would those whose living standards are declining be propelled toward the Republicans? Why would voters direct anger over declining living standards toward the relatively liberal party, the Democrats—supposedly the "party of the common man"—rather than the conservative party, the GOP, with its historic commitment to the interests of the well-off?

The reason for this is that the target of political blame for long-term changes in the economy and society depends on which story the average person believes about these changes. In this respect, long-term changes (like declining living standards) differ from short-term changes in the business cycle (booms and recessions) that simply benefit (or hurt) the incumbent party—the party on whose watch the growth (or decline) takes place. Thus, even if there's good news in the business cycle, liberals and the Democrats keep getting hurt by declining living standards because the story the public believes about these long-term changes casts them as the villain.

More precisely, the dominant story among the general public is that the long-term decline in living standards has to do with wasteful government spending[6] (especially on the poor, minorities, and immigrants, who are themselves seen as a cause of declining living standards), high taxes, inefficient and obtrusive public administration, selfish behavior by interest groups, and excessive social tolerance and valuelessness. Since these problems are identifiable with the Democrats—the party of activist government, poor people, minorities, liberal interest groups, and social tolerance—it is the Democrats who get the blame.

Accepting this blame means that liberals and the Democrats start every election with two strikes against them. They might still win under the right circumstances—Bush was unpopular enough and the overall economy bad enough for them to triumph in 1992[7]—but unless the circumstances are extraordinary, they are likely to lose badly. Hence, their trouncing in 1994 despite our having reached a relatively favorable point in the business cycle.

The voters' assignment of blame helps explain why the conventional election forecasting models got it so wrong in 1994, predicting only minor Democratic losses.[8] The models captured only the pro-incumbent, short-term effects of decent economic growth, completely ignoring the very strong anti-Democratic effect of declining living standards. Clearly, we are in a new political era in which aggregate economic statistics—and the models driven by them—will be of little use in predicting electoral fortunes.

Why the Democrats Get the Blame

This analysis of why declining living standards hurt liberals and the Democrats raises a further question: why does the public believe this anti-government, anti-liberal, anti-Democratic story about living standards, instead of some other story?

There are essentially three reasons. First, the American public is inclined to be skeptical of government to begin with. Therefore, it is not so difficult to steer people in an anti-government direction when appropriate conditions arise.

Second, those appropriate conditions have been provided by the declining living standards of the last several decades. In a situation where middle-class incomes stagnate and economic prospects deteriorate, people blame the government for failing to do anything about it and conclude that their tax dollars—dollars they could use to support their families—are doing little good. Indeed, the general perception among the middle class is that taxes go out of their pockets and into someone else's (less deserving) pockets. This perception corrodes middle-class beliefs in government fairness.

Finally—and perhaps most critically—there has been an aggressive push by Republicans and allied political forces to promote this anti-government story. This is hardly surprising, given the public's receptiveness to the story and the political benefits to be derived from selling it. What is somewhat more surprising is the weakness of the Democratic counter-story about the erosion of middle-class living standards.

This weakness is apparent on several levels. To begin with, the Democratic story is rarely advanced forcefully and, when it is mentioned, tends to focus on "neutral" forces like technological change and globalization rather than clear targets like footloose multinationals, uncaring corporations, Wall Street bond traders, foreign economic competitors, politicians who serve the rich, and so on. Moreover, the story lacks the coherence provided by the anti-government story, which is able to link problems with values and communities to problems with crime and schools to problems with getting by economically. In other words, the anti-government story is able to speak, coherently and forcefully, to all the different aspects of declining living standards[9] that worry the average American voter. The Democratic counter-story, in contrast, does not even begin to provide this breadth and power.

Implications for the Future of Progressive Economic Policies

The direct implication of this analysis is that most progressive economic policies are not feasible until the dominance of this anti-government story is broken. Until then, the public is highly unlikely to support the extensive government activism and spending that such policies entail.

Indeed, to the extent the public believes the anti-government story, supporting those policies would simply be throwing good money after bad. From the public's standpoint, it makes much more sense to cut government and taxes and reduce the deficit, up to and including balancing the budget. At least that way—so the story goes—less money gets wasted and perhaps people even get a refund (tax cuts) on the defective product (government).

Liberal and Democratic electoral fortunes are unlikely to revive while the anti-government story is dominant. No matter how the Democrats try to reposition themselves, they cannot avoid being identified as the party of activist government. Therefore, they will continue to be cast as the villain of the story and continue to be held responsible for declining living standards.

This is not a good situation, obviously, either for progressive economic policies, for liberals, or for the Democrats. But it does suggest a certain confluence of interests that could potentially lead to a happier ending. It may be the case that the very thing that motivates liberals' embrace of progressive economic policies—the need to raise American living standards—is central to breaking the "hegemony" of the anti-government story and, therefore, to improving electoral fortunes.

Given the cross-class nature of Democratic Party elites, perhaps only the threat of electoral meltdown can succeed in altering the party's reticence about policies that challenge business prerogatives and priorities. In other words, if the party had a choice, it probably wouldn't challenge these prerogatives and priorities. But, from an electoral standpoint, there may not be any choice left.

MAKING PROGRESSIVE ECONOMIC POLICIES POLITICALLY FEASIBLE

This analysis raises a critical question. It may be the case that discrediting the Republican, anti-government story about declining living standards is central to both reviving Democratic electoral fortunes and advancing progressive economic policies—and, indeed, that the two goals are closely interlinked. But how is this to be done in the current hostile political climate?

A first step in loosening the hold of the anti-government story would be to push a few progressive economic policies that have some short-term political viability. These include raising the minimum wage, getting tough on trade, taxing the foreign profits of U.S. companies, cutting corporate subsidies, and defending, if not extending, education and training programs. All these policies and programs enjoy consistently high support in public opinion polls, would have some positive, if limited, impact, and would potentially allow liberals and Democrats to launch a serious critique of Republican priorities.

The latter is the most important aspect of pushing this limited set of politically viable programs, since it facilitates the telling of an alternative story, which is the key to shifting the political terrain and developing the political base for more extensive activist policies. In this alternative story, the government and the poor do not take the blame for declining living standards; therefore, dismantling the government isn't the main policy recommendation. Indeed, instead of the government taking the blame, the villains of this story are targets clearly identifiable with the Republicans and their wealthy allies.

The story includes the following elements. Declining living standards are unambiguously laid at the door of irresponsible corporations and politicians who have lost interest in the living standards of the average American, and who think the national interest lies in maximum freedom to pursue their own profits and power, both here and abroad. This may not be entirely fair, but there is little evidence the average voter wants a story with multiple qualifications and sub-villains. They want a basic, clear story and, if they do not get it from liberals and Democrats, they will simply get it somewhere else.

A second element to this story is the contention that these corporations and politicians have "chosen" a path for the country that does not inexorably follow from economic progress (globalization, technological change, the "new economy"), but does inexorably drive down living standards by eroding the material basis for family and community life. It is therefore possible and necessary to choose another path.[10]

Finally, it is important that the breadth of the anti-government story—its coverage of both the social and economic aspects of declining living standards—be matched in our alternative story. After all, voters are not just concerned about declining wages and incomes, but also about the deterioration of other aspects of their daily lives, from shattered communities and values to unsafe streets to ineffective schools. Therefore, the link between the eroding material base for family and community institutions and the decline in the quality of these institutions must be made explicit.

For example, when economic pressures force both spouses to work and work longer hours, the time available for "investment" in their children and their communities is reduced. Also, job insecurity and downsizing have taken a toll, from uprooting individuals and entire communities to increasing the level of everyday stress. Indeed, a host of material changes—aided and abetted by the irresponsible corporations and politicians of our story—now deny ordinary Americans the resources (jobs, incomes, time, stability) to develop the good schools, safe streets, and pleasant communities currently enjoyed by the well-off.

All this suggests a simple three-sentence summary of the story that can be effectively contrasted with the Republican's three-sentence story (which everyone now knows by heart). The anti-government forces say: the *deficit* is the *crisis*, the *cause* is *big government,* and the *solution* is *cutting gov-*

ernment. Liberals and Democrats can and should insist that: *declining living standards* are the *crisis*, the *cause* is *corporations and politicians who don't care about living standards,* and the *solution* is *using government for your purposes, not theirs.* There is no reason why everyone in America can't learn this story by heart as well.

The nature of this story also clarifies the limits of the "New Democrat" strategy, still viewed in elite political circles as the best strategic approach for the Democrats. By its very nature—focused obsessively on the (valid) insight that Democrats need to improve the image of big government—the New Democrat approach implicitly accepts the notion that big government is the problem. But this only amounts to a softer version of the Republican anti-government story that currently dominates the political landscape. As a result, the New Democrat strategy leaves the Democrats with the same two strikes against them at election time—witness the 1994 election results—despite some real improvements in their party's image.

Another implication of this analysis is the centrality of challenging the notion that the budget deficit is the real crisis in this country. Conservatives and Republicans love this claim, since the causal connection between crisis and big government is so clear. Indeed, so long as this claim is accepted, their basic story stands and the argument focuses only on the best method of reining in government. Only if liberals and Democrats insist that the real crisis is not the deficit but declining living standards can our story lead to its desired conclusion.

All this suggests that the policy arguments advanced in this book, even those whose short-run political feasibility is low, have an important role to play in the current political debate. For example, the arguments about the true salience of the deficit, its relationship to health care costs, and its lack of relationship to declining living standards can play a key role in debunking the assertion that the deficit is the real crisis. In addition, virtually all the policies advanced in this volume, whatever their short-run political feasibility, have the advantage of specifically addressing how it is possible to "use government for your own purposes" and actually raise living standards. Thus, many of these policies can and should be incorporated into the alternative story that liberals and Democrats need to advance.

NOTES

1. See Lawrence Mishel and Jared Bernstein, *The State of Working America 1994-95* (Armonk, N.Y.: M.E. Sharpe, 1994), Table 3.19, for supportive data on non-college-educated men of all races.

2. See Ruy A. Teixeira, *The Politics of the High-Wage Path: The Challenge Facing Democrats* (Washington, D.C.: Economic Policy Institute, 1994).

3. November 1994 Current Population Survey.

4. For evidence that Perot voters as a group have suffered relatively high long-term wage losses, see Teixeira, op. cit.

5. Note, however, that this shift against the Democrats cannot be equated with an ideological realignment toward the Republicans, as some have suggested, because a significant segment of Republican support came from an unusually high rate of support among people who considered themselves conservatives (F. Steeper, *This Swing Is Different: Analysis of 1994 Election Exit Polls* (Southfield, Mich.: Market Strategies, 1994)). Multivariate analysis shows no difference in the relationship between conservatism and the House vote in 1992 and 1994, once partisanship is controlled for. Indeed, the big change was an increased tendency for independents to vote Republican in 1994, hardly an indicator of an ideologically driven realignment (R.A. Teixeira and J. Rogers, "Who Deserted the Democrats?" *The American Prospect*, Fall 1995).

6. See, for example, a *Business Week* poll reported in the March 13, 1995, issue.

7. They may also have had some success shifting the blame for declining living standards away from government and the Democrats toward the Republicans and their wealthy allies, using an earlier version of the alternative story recommended later in this chapter.

8. M.S. Lewis-Beck and J.M. Wrighton ("A Republican Congress? Forecasts for 1994," *Public Opinions*, Fall 1994) predicted a loss of only five Democratic House seats, less than one-tenth of the actual Democratic 52-seat loss.

9. For further discussion of a broad definition of "living standards" that goes beyond the narrowly economic, see the exchange between John Judis and Jeff Faux in the Summer 1995 issue of *The American Prospect.*

10. For more detailed versions of this alternative story, see J. Cohen and J. Rogers, "After Liberalism," *Boston Review*, April/May, 1995; R.A. Teixeira and G. Molyneux, *Economic Nationalism and the Future of American Politics* (Washington, D.C.: Economic Policy Institute, 1993); and J. Judis and M. Lind, "The New Nationalism," *The New Republic*, March 27, 1995.

INDEX

EPI PUBLICATIONS

EPI BOOK SERIES

The State of Working America 1994-95
by Lawrence Mishel & Jared Bernstein
1-56324-533-7 (paper) $24.95
1-56324-532-9 (cloth) $55.00

Trade Policy and Global Growth: New Directions in the International Economy
edited by Robert A. Blecker
1-56324-531-1 (paper) $22.95
1-56324-530-2 (cloth) $52.50

Beyond the Twin Deficits: A Trade Strategy for the 1990s
by Robert Blecker
1-56324-091-2 (paper) $22.95
1-56324-090-4 (cloth) $51.95

School Choice: Examining the Evidence**
edited by Edith Rasell & Richard Rothstein
0-944826-57-1 (paper) $17.95

Beware the U.S. Model: Jobs & Income in a Global Economy**
edited by Lawrence Mishel & John Schmitt
0-944826-58-X (paper) $24.95

The New American Workplace: Transforming Work Systems in the United States*
by Eileen Appelbaum & Rosemary Batt
0-87332-828-0 (paper) $19.95
0-87332-827-2 (cloth) $45.00

Transforming the U.S. Financial System: Equity and Efficiency for the 21st Century
edited by Gary Dymski, Gerald Epstein, & Robert Pollin
1-56324-269-9 (paper) $25.95
1-56324-268-0 (cloth) $62.95

New Policies for the Part-Time and Contingent Workforce
edited by Virginia L. duRivage
1-56324-165-X (paper) $22.95
1-56324-164-1 (cloth) $51.95

Unions and Economic Competitiveness
edited by Lawrence Mishel & Paula B. Voos
0-87332-828-0 (paper) $20.95
0-87332-827-2 (cloth) $46.95

Except where noted, books can be ordered from M.E. Sharpe, 80 Business Park Drive, Armonk, N.Y. 10504, or call toll free **(800) 541-6563.**

* From ILR Press **(607) 255-2264**   ** From EPI **(800) EPI-4844**

All orders for Economic Policy Institute studies, working papers, seminars, and briefing papers should be addressed to: EPI Publications, 1660 L Street, NW, Suite 1200, Washington, D.C. 20036, or call (800) EPI-4844. Orders can be faxed to (202) 775-0819. EPI will send a complete catalog of all publications. Discounts are available to libraries and bookstores and for quantity sales.

STUDIES, BRIEFING PAPERS, & WORKING PAPERS

Living Standards & Labor Markets

Where's the Payoff?
The Gap Between Black Academic Progress and Economic Gains
by Jared Bernstein
April '95 (55 pages, $12)

Time Is Still Money: Americans Prefer Overtime Pay to Comp Time
by Edith Rasell
May '95 (6 pages, $5)

The Role of Labor Market Institutions in Employee Training: Comparing the U.S. and Germany
by Kirsten Wever, Peter Berg, & Thomas Kochan
December '94 (44 pages, $10)

The Impact of Safety and Health Committee Mandates on OSHA Enforcement: Lessons from Oregon
by David Weil
November '94 (60 pages, $10)

Who Wins With a Higher Minimum Wage
by Lawrence Mishel, Jared Bernstein, & Edith Rasell
February '95 (14 pages, $5)

The Impact of Employer Opposition on Union Certification Win Rates:
A Private/Public Sector Comparison
by Kate Bronfenbrenner & Tom Juravich
October '94 (28 pages, $10)

Raising the Floor:
The Effects of the Minimum Wage on Low-Wage Workers
by William Spriggs & Bruce Klein
May '94 (92 pages, $12)

Profits Up, Wages Down: Worker Losses Yield Big Gains for Business
by Dean Baker & Lawrence Mishel
September '95 (14 pages, $5)

Government & the Economy

Cost and Quality Matters:
Workplace Innovations in the Health Care Industry
by Ann Greiner
July '95 (86 pages, $12)

Robbing the Cradle?
A Critical Assessment of Generational Accounting
by Dean Baker
September '95 (54 pages, $12)

Up From Deficit Reduction
by Max Sawicky
November '94 (80 pages, $12)

Jobs on the Wing:
Trading Away the Future of the U.S. Aerospace Industry
by Randy Barber & Robert E. Scott
August '95 (96 pages, $12)

Revising the Consumer Price Index: Correcting Bias, or Biased Corrections?
by Dean Baker
April '95 (8 pages, $5)

The Case for Public Investment
by Dean Baker & Todd Schafer
January '95 (19 pages, $12)

The Bottom Line on the Balanced Budget Amendment: The Cost to Each State, Congressional District, and Individual
by Jeff Faux, Jared Bernstein, & Todd Schafer
January '95 (15 pages, $5)

America's Inheritance:
More Than Just Debt
by Todd Schafer
June '94 (8 pages, $5)

Back to Investment: A Proposal to Create a Capital Investment Fund
by Jeff Faux, Dean Baker, & Todd Schafer
February '94 (9 pages, $5)

Jobs and the Environment:
The Myth of a National Trade-Off
by Eban Goodstein
January '95 (44 pages, $12)

Paying the Toll: Economic Deregulation of the Trucking Industry
by Michael Belzer
April '94 (84 pages, $12)

Lost in Findings:
A Critique of the Interim Report of the Bipartisan Commission on Entitlements and Tax Reform
by Max Sawicky
November '94 (13 pages, $5)

Paying For Health Care:
Affordability and Equity in Health Care Reform
by Edith Rasell & Kainan Tang
February '95 (54 pages, $10)

Lead-Based Paint Abatement in Private Homes: A Study of Policies and Costs
by Meg Koppel & Ross Koppel
August '94 (38 pages, $5)

Trade & Competitiveness

New Priorities in Financing Latin American Development:
Balancing Worker Rights, Democracy, and Financial Reform
by Jerome Levinson
June '94 (64 pages, $12)

False Prophets:
The Selling of NAFTA
by Thea Lee
July '95 (20 pages, $5)

Politics & Public Opinion

The Politics of the High-Wage Path: The Challenge Facing Democrats
by Ruy Teixeira
November '94 (25 pages, $10)

Economic Nationalism and the Future of American Politics
by Ruy Teixeira & Guy Molyneux
October '93(40 pages, $12)

About EPI

The Economic Policy Institute was founded in 1986 to widen the debate about policies to achieve healthy economic growth, prosperity, and opportunity in the difficult new era America has entered.

Today, America's economy is threatened by stagnant growth and increasing inequality. Expanding global competition, changes in the nature of work, and rapid technological advances are altering economic reality. Yet many of our policies, attitudes, and institutions are based on assumptions that no longer reflect real world conditions.

Central to the Economic Policy Institute's search for solutions is the exploration of policies that encourage every segment of the American economy (business, labor, government, universities, voluntary organizations, etc.) to work cooperatively to raise productivity and living standards for all Americans. Such an undertaking involves a challenge to conventional views of market behavior and a revival of a cooperative relationship between the public and private sectors.

With the support of leaders from labor, business, and the foundation world, the Institute has sponsored research and public discussion of a wide variety of topics: trade and fiscal policies; trends in wages, incomes, and prices; the causes of the productivity slowdown; labor-market problems; rural and urban policies; inflation; state-level economic development strategies; comparative international economic performance; and studies of the overall health of the U.S. manufacturing sector and of specific key industries.

The Institute works with a growing network of innovative economists and other social science researchers in universities and research centers all over the country who are willing to go beyond the conventional wisdom in considering strategies for public policy.

Founding scholars of the Institute include Jeff Faux, EPI president; Lester Thurow, Sloan School of Management, MIT; Ray Marshall, former U.S. secretary of labor, professor at the LBJ School of Public Affairs, University of Texas; Barry Bluestone, University of Massachusetts-Boston; Robert Reich, U.S. secretary of labor; and Robert Kuttner, author, editor of *The American Prospect,* and columnist for *Business Week* and the Washington Post Writers Group.

For additional information about the Institute, contact EPI at 1660 L Street, NW, Suite 1200, Washington, DC 20036, (202) 775-8810.